POCKET
OF
PAIN

a memoir by
LADYWARFIELD

Copyright© 2023 Lady Warfield

All rights reserved

No part of this publication may be reproduced, distributed, or transmitted in any form or by any means, including photocopying, recording, or other electronic or mechanical methods, without the prior written permission of the publisher, except as permitted by U.S. copyright law. For permission requests, contact the author.

For privacy reasons, some names, locations, and dates may have been changed.

Book design by Lady Warfield for Punk Goddess Studios
Front cover image courtesy of Thurston Howes

Second Edition, Hardback: October 2025
1 2 3 4 5 6 7 8 9

ISBN 979-8-9885393-4-6

Punk Goddess Press
www.punkgoddesspress.com

Printed in the United States of America

POCKET

OF

PAIN

IN PRAISE OF

"Lady Warfield's candid storytelling offers readers relentless optimism in the face of harrowing times. Her narrative exudes strength."
—Jen Knox, award-winning writer and Author.

"Lady Warfield has taken 80s nostalgia and woven it into a timeless tale of young transformation. She proves to readers that we all have the strength to persevere when it feels like the world is closing in."
—Stephanie Elizabeth Long, Writer & Reviewer for Reader Views.

"Beautifully written and heartfelt, this is a story of triumph, endurance, self-worth, insight, and survival; and you cannot beat the music and GenX time period!" —Christine Macdonald Author of Face Value

"Lady Warfield has created a poignant and memorable tale that will resonate with readers long after they turn the final page."
— Barbara Clark, Executive Coach

"Truly so good with such heart. I highly recommend this book! It reads like fiction in the best possible way! Love Love Love!"
— Brandy Knight, Author of Divinity Speaks

"For anyone growing up in the 70's and 80's *Pocket of Pain* will have you re-living your own teenage love stories and sexu-al awakening!"
—Nadine Schwartz, Producer/Director Kamafilms

"What I loved most is how the author captures that feeling of pushing through—finding strength where you didn't know you had it. It's raw and honest." —Amazon Anonymous

"This memoir is simultaneously hard to read and a page-turner, evoking empathy from any audience — male, female, young or old, *Pocket of Pain* will strike a chord. For all the GenXers out there, Lady Warfield's myriad references to life in the '80s will make you smile throughout"
— Amazon Anonymous

A NOTE FROM THE AUTHOR

The characters and events portrayed in this book are taken from memories long stored, separated, and compartmentalized. Their written form on the page are aligned to the truth that this author experienced. When in doubt, I interviewed people I knew during this period and consulted journals and records to stay as true to the timeline as I could. Sometimes scenes, landscapes, dress, and mannerisms have been created or altered to fill the voids of lost memories. Sometimes the order of events have changed to maintain a narrative flow. But the facts are there, only dressed up to enhance pace, language, and narrative. Some characters have been completely changed; some are not included; some names have changed and some have not. Any similarity to a real person, living or dead, is coincidental and not intended by the author. Mostly.

Those minor adjustments aside, this is the actual story of my life between the ages of sixteen and nineteen. This could have been written as fiction, and if you prefer to think of it as such, that's okay. But telling my story was important to me, and if it helps anyone who feels alone, scared, or lost to find their voice, then it was worth the risk of being vulnerable.

"And the day came when the risk
to remain tight in a bud
was more painful than
the risk it took to blossom."
– Anaïs Nin

CONTENTS

POCKET OF PAIN	xx
1 | SWEET SIXTEEN	1
2 | THE CHAPERONE	10
3 | PLAYING FRENCH	16
4 | MY KNIGHT	23
5 | TRANSITIONS	29
6 | CAT AND MOUSE	36
7 | CHERRY PICKING	45
8 | DOUBLE TROUBLE	51
9 | CHURCH GIRL	55
10 | PLANS	61
11 | PROMISES	68
12 | AFTER SHOCKS	77
13 | FATHER'S LITTLE GIRL	81
14 | LOST LITTLE GIRL	85
15 | THE BIG BAD WOLF	88
16 | WHO PROTECTS US	93
17 | DARK, UNCERTAIN MOMENTS	99
18 | THAT'S SO PUNK	105
19 | THE LAST DANCE	108
20 | ON THE COVER OF A MAGAZINE	112
21 | SUMMER DREAMS	116
22 | BETRAYAL	122
23 | SENIOR BENEFITS	125
24 | DIAMONDS AND DANGER	133
25 | LEGAL WARS	140
26 | DANGEROUS GAMES	147
27 | PLANS TAKE HOLD	158
28 | TESTING THE BOUNDARIES	164
29 | WHAT'S REAL ANYHOW?	171
30 | AT LAST	176
31 | FRESH ON A DREAM	183
32 | GIRL ON CAMPUS	187
33 | SHADOWS	190
34 | NUMBER ONE FAN	196
35 | HOLIDAY OBLIGATION	203
36 | DID I DREAM LAST NIGHT?	207
37 | IT'S MY TURN	214
38 | SICK GIRL	223
39 | IT'S A NEW WORLD	231
40 | TAKING THE LEAD	238
41 | MICKY MOUSE EYES	247
42 | ENDINGS . . .	251
43 | THE SUMMER OF '85	255
44 | NOT YOURS ANYMORE	262
45 | MOVING IN	267
46 | SHAME	270
47 | WINTER'S GLOOM	277
EPILOGUE | SOME TIME LATER	284
ACKNOWLEDGEMENTS	289
ABOUT THE AUTHOR	290
THE PLAYLIST	291

POCKET OF PAIN

When I was a little girl, I dreamed of being an actress in one of those classic western movies. Actually, I wanted to live in a western film, like *The Train Robbers*. The one with Ann-Margret and John Wayne.

At the age of nine, I stood in front of the mirror stuffing tissues into my shirt to see if I could look as voluptuous and sexy as Ann-Margret. Then I'd pull on my beloved blue-suede cowboy boots over my corduroys—or, if it was hot out, I'd pair them with bare legs and shorts. I'd carefully place my cowboy hat over my tangled shoulder-length blond hair, cock my head to the side, and imagine just how fierce I would be, like Jane Fonda from *Cat Ballou*.

I rode the canyons in Palos Verdes, California, on my tired, old horse, Kaleb, while the hot summer sun beat down on both of us. His name was inherited; we certainly didn't have any religious upbringing inspired by such biblical names. Although my dad told me it meant Dog, I preferred the definition of Brave.

The dust formed a cloud around us from the path left by Kaleb's hooves. The smell of eucalyptus trees lulled me into a hypnotic fairy tale where I envisioned an adventure looking for lost gold alongside my partner—usually starring John Wayne or another actor from my long list of future husbands, which included Steve McQueen, Robert Redford, and Paul Newman ... oh, and Tom Burg from down the street.

I wanted to be beautiful, sexy, and tough. And yet, I still wanted a strong, handsome man to sweep me off my feet, throw me over his shoulder, and take me home with him.

My mom would say, "Careful what you wish for."

1 | SWEET SIXTEEN

"Wild Horses," The Rolling Stones

My father sat in his dark study surrounded by his sailboat racing trophies and flags. The black West Point marching hat with the plume in front sat up high on the top shelf along with the other items he'd picked up from the military academy, the Air Force, and his adventures sailing around the South Seas when he was a young man. He was something of a systematic pack rat.

Rays of light streamed through the slits in the blinds, making little bits of dust particles dance in front of me, while the rest of the room was dark and off-limits.

Sitting behind his desk, obscured by a violent cloud, he seemed angry. But this was how he always looked. If he wasn't screaming and yelling at someone, stomping through the house, muttering swear words, and slamming doors, he was sitting behind his desk frowning. You would never know what his mood would be like when you knocked and entered. It was rare to see his silly side. But when he laughed, he took you on a ride with him—his eyes twinkled, and his laughter was warm. He was authentic. Whatever the emotion was, he didn't hide it.

"Vermont is a long way from Virginia for a teenager to travel without her parents," my father growled.

He didn't look up when I came in, just listened to my long and rushed speech, or so I hoped, while he continued to read through his papers. But by his comment I knew I was in for a battle. It was a long shot, but I really wanted to go on the ski trip, so I argued and defended it with everything I could think of. Chaperones were going, I told him; what could go wrong? Besides, my older brother, who was a senior, was going too.

I stomped my foot with impatience and ran my hand through my hair for the fifth time. "Come on, Dad, Joe will be there, and all his friends."

Plus, my friend Marybeth was going, but I didn't mention that my other two friends, Moe and Bambie, weren't going because their moms wouldn't allow it. They were strict, just like my dad.

"That's what I'm afraid of. You're only a sophomore and they're seniors." Lowering his newspaper, he peered up at me over his reading glasses. Those thick glasses he wore increased the size of his eyes. It really creeped me out. "Why do you want to hang out with them?" he said, suspicion framing his voice.

"It's not about hanging out with them," I said with every bit of effort I could to make it look like this was the most ridiculous idea ever. "It's about skiing, Dad! Come on. You never let me do anything. What's the big deal?"

By bedtime, he'd caved. I knew it was a tough decision for him; he still didn't want to let his little girl grow up. I'd only just turned sixteen, after all. He'd just recently allowed me to go out with boys. But so far, the two dates I'd gone on with my brother's friends were boring disasters. Yawn-fests. He was extremely relieved when I came home from my first date and said, "Ugh, he was so boring."

But to be fair, it was Virginia that was "so boring." We moved when I was twelve and I still dreamt of going back to California where we once lived in a neighborhood filled with kids my age. We could ride our bikes on the street and play ball till dark, walk or skateboard to school together. We danced to the Bay City Rollers's "Saturday Night" on warm summer night sleepovers. I'd lie on the hot patio that surrounded our pool in the sun, listening to the soft voice of Olivia Newton-John singing "Have You Never Been Mellow" as it drifted out from the patio screen door.

And then a sudden "job transfer"—the third one, by the way: California to Massachusetts, back to California, and now Virginia. He packed us up with promises of ranches, horses, and open fields.

Instead, we lived high up on the top of a hill in the middle of the woods. Below us was a perilous winding road where you never saw an adult on a bike, let alone a kid. My nearest friend, Julie, lived almost a mile away through the woods. But she was already planning her escape to boarding school in the fall. She would be over an hour away, across the river in Maryland.

I hated Virginia. I hated that we'd moved here. Everything had gone all wrong. The house was stifling and the fights between my mom and dad were getting worse. I hated how dark it felt in the winter, and I missed looking out and seeing mountains, canyons, ocean, and city, instead of a blanket of trees. The never-ending forest only had one use: a place to escape. I missed the smell of eucalyptus trees, the dusty warmth from those bridal paths and all my friends that were left behind.

"It takes eight hours to drive to Killington!" Marybeth slumped lower in the seat, with a frown deeply drawn on her face. "Maybe even longer on this slow-ass bus."

We sat in the back of the bus as far from the driver and the chaperones as we could. They were cute, but they were chaperones. The muscular one, who looked like a bodybuilder, was the older brother of a girl I went to church with. They looked old enough to be in college. I didn't recognize the other guy. Under his bulky turtleneck sweater, he also appeared big and probably worked out with the muscular one. He looked a little like the actor Glen Scott from Urban Cowboy. The bigger chaperone had this soft, sweet baby face, but this guy had a kind of dangerous look. Maybe it was the scars on his face.

"Look what I have," I said as I reached into my bag and pulled out a plastic bag filled with weed.

"Shit! Where did you get that?" Marybeth's long brunette hair was pulled back at her temples with little rubber bands instead of barrettes. She was wearing the dark blue cowl-neck sweater I loved. Marybeth reminded me a little bit of Mindy from the TV show Mork and Mindy, but much prettier.

"I know it's crazy!" I said, my voice dropping to a whisper. "I've never bought it before. Moe told her boyfriend that I wanted some to bring on the trip. Did you know he sells drugs? I mean, just pot. I think. But god, if only her mother knew!" I pushed my hair out of my eyes and leaned in close to her. "I just thought we would meet more people if we had some pot. You know?"

We both looked up over the seat in front of us, peering through the cloud of pot smoke that already lingered over the heads of our fellow conspirators. The sounds of laughter and voices singing to the Rolling Stones's "Wild Horses" washed over us while we witnessed a bong being passed around as if floating through the air, guided by ghostly hands. We turned and looked at each other.

"Cool!" I said, and giggles spilled out of us, which mingled with the sounds in the bus. "I guess the bus driver and chaperones don't care if we smoke pot! But let's just stay clear of my brother."

We had big plans: skiing every day, partying with our friends, and all with little or no adult supervision.

Our first day at what I liked to call Camp Musky, because our room smelled like a combination of body odor and skunk, was spent unpacking and running around the giant lodge trying to find ways to entertain ourselves. We climbed aboard the big bus that morning to go skiing but soon abandoned it because a storm was coming in, the clouds so low over the mountains that it was too dangerous to attempt to ski. Only the best stayed on the slopes, like my brother and his friends.

Most of the day we spent playing practical jokes on each other. I couldn't get the bitter taste of perfumed lotion out of my mouth thanks to some ingenious switch of the toothpaste.

Marybeth and I shared a room with four other girls, which was furnished with three bunk beds. We soon found it crowded, but an endless source of entertainment.

"Tonight, we're getting beer and having a party in the room," called Gabriella, who was in the adjoining bathroom curling her hair with her hand-painted pink curling iron. "So don't forget to give money to Drew before he goes to buy some."

"I don't want to just hang out in our room. Hey, what the—?" Nancy, who was sitting on the top bunk, quickly moved off to the side and uncovered something wedged down under her blanket. She pulled out a huge black rubber dildo and held it up high. "Who put this in my bed?" she yelled, indignant. Her scorched red cheeks gave away her embarrassment.

The room filled with shrieks of laughter from all the girls. I was bent over, holding my stomach—it hurt so bad from laughing—when the door swung open, and in stormed Charles, Tony, and Peter. All friends of my brother.

Charles, super tall and lanky, was Marybeth's recent crush. And Tony, well, Tony was Gabriella's brother. Both looked alike with their dark hair and classical roman noses. You could say she was super slutty—but you could say he was too, a male version, just not quite so obvious. They both liked to show cleavage.

I used to have a crush on Tony when I was in eighth grade. He would have been a sophomore. He actually asked my dad if he could take me out. But, nope, my dad said I was too young. I was furious. All the screaming and tears did nothing. In the end, I didn't go. And then the next year, when I was old enough to date him, I'd completely lost interest. His gold chain and open-shirt Travolta thing just seemed gross.

"What's going on in here, young ladies?" Peter announced in mock surprise, but not very good at holding back his grin.

This just made me laugh even more. Peter was super funny and adorable, and a good friend from church. He had a massive crush on my best friend Moe—the one dating the drug dealer. I used to have a massive crush on Peter the year before. Maybe all of my brother's friends, at one time or another, either asked me out or I had a crush on them. Peter had lovely thick, shiny dark brown, almost black hair with fair skin and huge dimples. But he was so silly most of the time it was hard to take him seriously. This is probably why we became good friends. In fact, Moe, Peter, and I were like the three amigos. A very mischievous trio.

It was obvious that he, Charles, and Tony were responsible for the hidden dildo.

Nancy tossed the dildo at him and yelled, "Get out of here!"

"Yeah, get out!" we all yelled along with her.

"Fine, don't have a cow," Charles said in a faux hurt voice. "We know when we're not wanted."

As the door shut behind them, Gabriella came out of the bathroom, rolling her eyes. "Could these boys be any less mature?" She tossed her long black hair. "It's going to be a challenge to find anyone worthy of my red lipstick."

Marybeth and I looked at each other and rolled our eyes. Gabriella was like a predator when it came to boys. I was sure she wouldn't have any trouble finding somebody "suitable."

"Suzanne, your brother Joe is hot." Gabriella looked at me with her heavily made-up eyes, while her long diva-red nails pointed towards the empty spot where the boys had exited out the door. "Maybe he's not such a loser as the rest of those boys."

"Err … yeah. I guess?" I glanced at Marybeth, and she gave me a look that warned me not to say anything I would regret.

"All I know," Cindy interrupted, "is that tomorrow better be some awesome skiing weather." She was curled up in her bed, reading a book. "That's why I came on this trip."

"What? Skiing?" Gabriella looked at her like she was some troll that had crawled out of a hole. "Girl, skiing is just a quarter of this journey. Get with the program!"

A bell sounded from somewhere, and Marybeth jumped off the bed and headed to the door. "Come on, everyone, dinner's being served. Let's go."

The next day, after breakfast in the big hall, Marybeth and I got our ski stuff together and joined the rest of the group on the bus. We weren't the only ones with fuzzy-head hangovers. The night before was pretty much a group effort of "how much beer can you consume in one night." The end of the evening was spent with me holding Marybeth's head propped over a toilet bowl.

Thankfully, the chaperones didn't make an appearance. They were probably off having their own party.

It started out a very nasty, blustery day at the top of the mountain, but by early afternoon the sun was high, and the wind had calmed down.

"Lex—you know, my brother's friend—he's such an asshole," I told Marybeth as we sat swaying on the chairlift. It had stopped for the fourth time. "I thought he was super cute, but last night, when we were all hanging out, he fucking pinched my boob!"

"What? Oh my god! Why didn't you say anything to me before?" She looked shocked.

"Well, you were off with Charles. I didn't want to interrupt." I sighed. "Besides, it was just humiliating. I mean, what the fuck? I don't know, maybe he was just really drunk or something." But he'd done it with this superior attitude like he was giving me some reward. All I knew was that it really hurt, and it was embarrassing. Humiliating. Another piece of proof that guys in high school sucked. I was really hoping '82 was going to be the year for me. So far, it was just as shitty. But it was only February, so there was still hope.

"What a fucking hoser!" Marybeth said and turned to me, and we both buckled over laughing. Quoting from Strange Brew was one of our favorite things.

"Yeah! Take off, you hoser," I yelled at the passing skiers underneath us. "I'm gettin' whiplash from my burp."

"Yikes! Did you see that?" I could feel my face turning scarlet as I hid behind my scarf.

"What?" Marybeth craned her head to look over the lift, trying to see what had just freaked me out.

"Ugh. Doug!" I moaned behind my scarf. "You know Doug. He's a senior, a friend of Peter's. I didn't know he was on the ski trip! I didn't see him last night. Oh my god, he's so hot. He's got a girlfriend. You know that really pretty girl with red hair? Oh, but he's soooo hot." I looked at her in desperation. Doug was my all-time crush, but an off-limits-he-never-notices-you kind of crush. "Oh my god, Marybeth, he heard me yelling 'hoser' and looked up at me and grinned!"

"What? No way, are you serious?" She pulled my scarf down and peered at my face to see if I was serious.

"Yes. I'm serious." I nodded manically. "Man, I don't get him. He is so nice to me, and sometimes I think he likes me, but he's got a girlfriend. And unlike my brother's other friends, he's never asked me out. I think he just teases 'cause I'm his friend's kid sister and because Moe and I dressed him up as a girl for the Buy a Senior for a Day Fund." I groaned. "Shit. Now he knows I'm a dork!"

The chair started up again, and our frozen legs swung back in motion with the lift. Suddenly I felt depressed. The thought of finding a strong and handsome man to sweep me off my feet would remain a childish fantasy forever.

At the top of the hill, it was cold and windy, and I could barely see which way to go. We checked our straps and adjusted our goggles, then took off. Early in the day, when we first got to the mountain, I took it really slow. It took most of the day to build up my confidence and eventually I felt great. I looked pretty damn cute too, I thought; my tangerine-colored ski suit with the white racing stripe down the side made me look like a professional racer. Or so I hoped.

I lost sight of Marybeth soon, but it didn't matter, I'd catch up with her at the bottom of the hill. As I came down the hill, I left the cold gray clouds behind, and entered a sunny, bright winter wonderland. Warming up and releasing any last bit of anxiety or fear I held, I decided to take the trail where the moguls were. There's nothing like it: speeding down the hill, gaining control, jumping mogul after mogul. I was in heaven.

And then it happened. My ski detached as I was in the air about to land from a jump, and instead I landed right on my face. I didn't cry, but my face throbbed, cold and hot at the same time. I stood up and looked around. I had completely lost track of Marybeth. Finally, I spotted her on the lift coming back up. I could see her mouth moving with the soundless words, "Oh my god …" If I didn't feel like shit, I would have laughed.

I stood there by myself with streaks of blood all over my jacket, skiers just zooming by. It wasn't that severe, but superficial cuts can really bleed.

Finally, to my relief, a guy stopped. He reached into his coat and handed me a Kleenex. As he adjusted his pole straps and turned to leave, he said over his shoulder, "You should get that looked at." Then left.

"Asshole," I muttered, and leaned down, unbuckling my other ski. Picking them both up, I started the long walk down the mountain, on my own.

2 | THE CHAPERONE
"Crimson and Clover," Joan Jett & the Blackhearts

The smell of burnt cedar mixed with hot chocolate and French fries engulfed me as I walked into the old ski lodge at the bottom of the mountain. The enormous fireplace gave me a welcoming hug as I took in the huge beams and rafters, which were made from real logs. The cavernous room was filled with the laughter and bodies of tired, excited, and content skiers sitting at tables and benches, all under the watchful gaze of the surrounding deer heads, which were suspended from their lookout points along the walls.

Around the fireplace sat several kids from our trip. They were all enjoying hot chocolate and filling the room with their laughter. Making out in the corner, I saw Susan and her perfect blond feathered hair with James from track. Matt and Diane snuggled by the fireplace, and in the middle of the room amid a larger group of seniors, Peter stood laughing and slapped Doug on the back. That awful boy, Lex, the one I thought was so cute until he pinched me, was hanging out with a group of guys, telling jokes. What did I ever see in him? That pinch hurt so much—physically, yeah, but it was humiliating. It was so mean. *How could he do that to me?*

Marybeth, who somehow had made it back before me, was sitting by the fire with Charles, deep in conversation. She would be glued to him for the rest of the trip, while I hung out in the room reading or playing crappy tunes on the old piano down in the lounge area of the lodge.

Now I felt ridiculous and depressingly sorry for myself. Scanning the room, feeling out of place and on the verge of tears, I turned around and walked right into the chest of the chaperone, the one we didn't know.

Even though he wore a thick, woolen turtleneck sweater, I could tell he was fit. I nearly bounced off his muscles. As I looked up from the wall that was his chest, my gaze met dark, curious eyes. I blinked and looked down, but I ended up focusing on his mouth. His mouth was just as captivating as his eyes; they held mysterious answers to questions not yet asked.

There should be a warning signal here, but—dangerous and sexy older guy ... this was new to me. And I immediately blew off any of those words of warning floating through my head.

"What happened to you?"

I froze in place as he reached over with his hand to trace the cut that ran down my cheek: from my eye to my lip. "You look as though you were in a cat fight," he said, teasing me. *Is he making fun of me?*

He loomed over me, standing really close, his height compatible with my six-foot frame.

Speech seemed impossible at that moment. I started to talk but had to swallow to get my mouth going again. *Very dry*, I thought. Finally, I stammered clumsily, "I wiped out on the slope."

"Let me get something to clean your cuts."

It was like the whole room behind us receded. Nobody else existed. Like in a movie, where the spotlight shines down on you, and everything else is in darkness. He turned and walked away, and for a moment I wondered if the whole thing was a dream. Would he come back? I shook my head. But that kind of hurt.

There was something about him. Even in that brief moment, I felt a zing of electricity between us. But maybe that was static electricity from his sweater and the heat in the room.

I stood there feeling awkward. Slowly, the noise of the room returned while I waited—my hands fidgeting at my side—to see if it was real.

But he did come back! He gently took my hand and led me over to a bench in the back and sat me down. It was as if we glided over. Sound disappeared around me again. I don't know how I got there. One moment I was standing, the next I was sitting as he gently wiped the blood off my face with some cotton and hydrogen peroxide, being extra careful around my nose. *Where did he get it?* I wondered.

"Hmm, you have a beautiful nose," he said softly, leaning back, tilting his head, and looking at me with a nice curl to his lips. "There, that's better. I think you'll be fine, no serious scarring or anything, but you should take it easy, you could have a concussion."

"Um, thanks," I replied lamely, suddenly embarrassed by his intense gaze. I looked down at my hands, and quickly shoved them between my legs to keep them from uselessly fluttering about.

"Would you like some hot chocolate?" He smiled and stood up.

I started to stand, but he put his hand on my leg and said, "I'll get it. Just wait here."

I stared at my thigh where just a second ago his hand rested, and again I was left to wonder what the heck was going on. *This is crazy: sexy older guy, paying a heap of attention to me? He must be really bored with all of us stupid high school kids and this is some kind of practical joke.*

"My name's Steve." He sat back down next to me, handing me a mug of hot steaming cocoa. "I noticed you on the ride up, sitting in the back with your friend. What's your name?" he asked as he sipped his own hot chocolate.

His brown turtleneck sweater hugged his body, which seemed like a style Steve McQueen would wear. The corduroy jeans were pretty snug too, tucked neatly into his ski boots. Now that I had an up-close-and-personal look at him, I could tell that he definitely lifted weights. His arms were way bigger than average, but the other chaperone's arms were bigger. That guy was freakish. Steve was ... well, he just looked strong. Like he could lift me up and throw me over his shoulder. Most of the guys I knew didn't look like that. I wondered how old he was.

His hair was sandy brown and layered. Almost shoulder length, but not. He sat there and stared at me with a grin on his face, and I realized I still hadn't answered his question.

"Uh, my name is Suzanne." God, what an idiot I sounded like. All squeaky voiced.

"So, why are you on your own, Suzanne? What happened to your friend?"

Automatically I glanced around the room and I located Marybeth over by the fire with Charles, deep in conversation. Steve caught my gaze and nodded with a look of understanding in his eyes.

"Looks like she'll be tied up for a while." He grinned at me and I could feel my face turn crimson.

He reminded me of one of those chivalrous characters from the romance novels my dad forbade me to read in junior high. Of course, I read them anyway. "That stuff is trash, it will warp your mind," he'd say in a fit of fury when he'd catch me reading them. I wasn't sure what he meant. Was it the highly sexual content, or the idea of women being rescued and treated like objects of desire? Either way, it seemed better than sitting around and reading Nancy Drew books every night.

We sat there and talked for what felt like hours. He seemed honestly interested in every word I said. He wanted to know about my brother, and who his friends on this trip were. He asked me how old I was when I learned how to ski—five, by the way—and told me he had barely skied before. He wanted to know what my favorite things were to do: dancing and painting. He talked a little bit about himself, but it was like he wanted to know all about me. Everything about me. It was exhilarating.

"You're twenty-one?" I said, a bit shocked, and sad. I knew as soon as he realized I was only sixteen he would find some way to excuse himself and disappear. He probably thought I was a senior; being tall, most guys assumed I was older. Not a sophomore.

"Yes, I am. Is that a problem?" He tilted his head to the side, a funny smile on his face. "I would guess you're somewhere between fifteen and seventeen. Am I right?"

"Yes, I mean, I'm sixteen." I shook my head. "I don't have a problem with you being twenty-one. Do you ... I mean, do you mind that I'm only sixteen?" I realized what I was saying and looked down, my ears and cheeks feeling hot again. *Damn.* I didn't mean to assume anything was really happening more than just talking to some nice guy. We just met!

His hand—suddenly on my chin—tilted my face back up so I was looking at him directly in the eyes. He gave me a long and very serious look, the smile gone.

"Absolutely not," he said, his voice a hoarse whisper.

It was like minutes ticked by: he looked at me, and I at him, until finally I cleared my throat and smiled, his hand dropping back to his lap.

"Do you work out?" Ugh, that sounded dreadful. But I felt like I needed to change the subject.

He didn't seem bothered by my question. He confirmed that he worked out. A lot. It was his hobby. He and Michael—that was the name of the other chaperone—were workout buddies. I couldn't even put both my hands around his biceps, they were so big. He certainly wasn't a silly, scrawny high school boy. I couldn't imagine him ever pinching a girl like Lex had pinched me last night.

It gave me a bit of a thrill to know I was sitting with the chaperone of the ski trip—a twenty-one-year-old guy, in college, and more sophisticated than any of my brother's fumbling friends. I was thinking of one in particular who had labeled me a prude because he said I didn't even kiss him on our date, if you could call it a date.

I still couldn't believe Billy had started that rumor. Billy was the first guy I was allowed to go out with, after the continued series of steady refusals by my dad for the right to date. But by freshman year, he couldn't refuse me any longer.

Billy had taken me to see a musical in D.C. It was awesome—the show, that is. It was the Broadway production of *Dancin'* directed and choreographed by Bob Fosse, who directed *Cabaret*. How could a date go wrong when you're seeing a Fosse musical?

But it did. He barely talked and seemed much more interested in his car. He never even attempted to hold my hand. He drove me straight home afterward, and when he pulled up to my house, I just opened the door and got out. He stepped out and said goodbye to me from the other side of the car! That was it, so I walked on into my house without even looking back. Maybe I was mistaken, but I didn't recall him ever trying to kiss me or even walk me to my door. And he labeled *me* the prude?

The light was fading, and everyone in our group was getting up and going out to the parking lot to catch the bus back to the lodge where we were staying.

Steve stood up and held out his arm for me to take.

He offered me his arm.

I hesitated a moment. *He offered me his arm!*

I started to say something, but his gaze was so intense it made me look down at my feet. I held my breath and stood up, sliding my arm around his arm, my hand resting on that firm, strong bicep. I quickly shot him a glance, looking at him through my lashes, and he put his other hand on my arm and smiled at me, leading us out behind the rest of the kids. There were a few looks, with a couple of double takes, but I kept my gaze ahead for fear of grinning or blushing too hard. I could barely contain myself.

3 | PLAYING FRENCH

"Stairway to Heaven," Led Zeppelin

I woke up the next morning, yawned, and shook my head to release the sleep. Then I remembered the day before and everything that had happened. If it wasn't for my ski accident, I doubt I would have ever met Steve.

The whole thing felt crazy. He was so different from any of the other boys I knew. He didn't try to kiss or grope me. He just wanted to talk and get to know me better.

When we'd gotten back to the lodge the night before, I'd headed off with Marybeth to the room to get ready for dinner. Marybeth was so excited about Charles, she didn't even stop talking for a moment to ask me about Steve. I'm not even sure she noticed. But I didn't feel like sharing just yet. It just didn't feel real.

During dinner, he sat with his friend. I looked over at him a few times, discreetly, trying not to be obvious. But every now and then when I looked up, he would be staring at me with those intense eyes. I could feel the hot flush spread across my cheeks each time and would quickly look away.

After dinner, I headed out of the large dining hall. The long wooden tables and benches made the place look like a canteen and really contrasted with the log cabin feel. It was packed, and not just with our group. There were multiple groups from different high schools. Besides the chaperones, we didn't have anyone in charge. A few of the seniors had arranged the whole thing.

Trailing behind the girls from my room, I watched Marybeth as she made a beeline over to Charles, waving at me when she caught my eye. As I waved, I quickly turned around to look for Steve, and almost stepped right into him.

"Hey," he said, with a little grin playing around his lips. *Is he laughing at me?*

"Er ..." My face heated up again, a feeling I was experiencing a little too often since I met him.

"I have plans tonight," he started, a long, uncomfortable pause passing between us as some kids jostled past, separating us and then pushing us back together. "I already promised Michael I would go out with him tonight. But if you're free tomorrow ...?"

"Yeah, I mean yes," I said, a bit too eager. "Out drinking with the guys?" I was trying to sound natural, but it ended up sounding corny instead. "Um, that sounds great."

"I don't drink."

"Oh."

He gently grabbed my hand with his, and before I knew what he was doing, he'd brought my hand to his lips and kissed it.

"Then"—he winked at me—"until tomorrow." He turned and walked through the door.

I almost fell forward as somebody behind me slammed into my back. It hurt so bad that it reminded me I still had this awful headache since the accident.

"Ow, are you crazy?" I turned around, angry until I saw it was Peter, my best guy friend ever. "Oh, it's you."

"Now that's not nice! 'Oh, it's you'?" He frowned. "What's with the hand kiss from muscle man?"

"Ugh!" Exasperated, I turned around and huffed off, yelling over my shoulder, "You're such a child."

After a quick stop to see the nurse, I decided to turn in early. That was a feat unto itself, as it was really noisy with the continued partying from all the rooms. But the nurse said I could have a slight concussion, so it was better if I took it easy and went to bed early. I was super tired, so it wasn't too hard to follow her orders.

Lying in bed the next morning, still thinking about Steve while everyone else in the room was getting ready for breakfast and another ski day, I was interrupted when Marybeth stuck her face down in mine. "Come on! Get your ass out of bed. I'm ready to go eat. I'm so starved I could eat two plates of those hash potatoes."

I groaned as I rolled toward her. "Ouch! Wow, my neck even hurts."

"Yeah, um, sorry about that. I should have looked for you harder, but when I came down the slope looking for you, I ran into Charles ... and, well, you know how it is." She looked sincerely sorry as she sat down next to me, but also completely smitten. "Are you okay?"

"The nurse said I might have a slight concussion. She told me I should take it easy today, just in case. So I guess I'll just hang around here." I was sure there was a room somewhere with a television and some videos. That could be nice, especially now that I realized my neck hurt too.

"Do you want me to hang out with you?" Was that concern and hope mixed in her eyes ... hope that I would say no?

"No, no way. You go have fun. You're not ruining the little romance you've got going with Charles. Besides, you would have ditched me anyhow to hang out with him on the slopes, so be gone already!"

"Well, okay then." She stood up and pressed down her puffy ski pants. "Are you coming to breakfast at least?"

"Yes, I'm getting up, and I'll be there in a minute." I put my feet down on the floor and leaned forward, standing slowly. "Yeah, I'm good. I'm just going to throw on some jeans and a sweater and I'll be down. Save me a spot."

"Okay, great." With that, she nearly ran out the door.

Twenty minutes later I was headed to the cafeteria to grab a biscuit or something. I wasn't very hungry because I was too nervous about bumping into Steve again. Maybe the whole thing was in my head. Just a nice guy being nice to a girl who'd hurt herself on the ski slopes of Vermont. It just didn't make a lot of sense that he would be into me. Way older, way handsome, and way mysterious. With all the questions he'd had for me, he'd hardly shared much about himself.

Most everyone had cleared out of the cafeteria by the time I made it in, including Marybeth. And there was no sign of Steve. I went up to the food counter anyhow to see if there was anything left, and sure enough there were a few biscuits, so I grabbed one and decided to explore the lodge.

It was enormous, made from huge logs. The whole place had a golden-orange hue to it. A huge porch with long, deadly icicles hanging from the eaves wrapped around the entire building. It was everything I imagined an old lodge would look like in the snowy mountains of Vermont. But thankfully there were no soulless-eyed twin girls dressed in blue running around the long hallways at night, beckoning to me.

Most of the rooms had bunk beds, like the room Marybeth and I shared—brown-paneled walls with wool blankets and circular rope rugs. Thankfully ours had its own bathroom. Several other rooms had to share a communal bath in the center of the hallway.

I worked my way down to the basement where there was a huge room that looked like a space where they probably put on plays or dances. I didn't see a television, but there was a pool table and an old upright piano towards the back of the room.

I walked over to it, scanning the room as I went in; it was completely empty. And super quiet. Sitting down on the bench, I swung my legs around and touched the keys, testing them out, one by one. It was a little out of tune, but not too bad. Still playable.

I began playing the scales, starting with the C note. First the five-note scales followed by chords: flat, neutral, and sharp. Then the eight-note scales. I closed my eyes, lost in my rhythmic, repetitive dance.

"You play the piano?"

I jumped in my seat at the sound of his voice. My heart raced as I tried to compose myself. I turned around to answer and my breath sucked in as I looked at him. Thankfully, I was sitting; I don't think I could have stood. It wasn't just his eyes. It was his smile, the strong jaw, and his hair—softly feathered. He looked even better than I'd remembered. *What is he doing here, and not skiing?*

"Sorry, I didn't mean to startle you." He smiled.

"Yeah, no, I mean, it's okay," I fumbled. "Yeah, you just took me off guard. I didn't think anyone stayed behind."

He sat down on the bench, sliding in next to me, his shoulder touching mine.

"I ... I took lessons for five years when we lived in California. But stopped when we moved here. I don't practice much anymore." I looked at him from under a piece of hair that had fallen in my face. "What about you?"

"No. I never learned." He sounded wistful as he gazed down at the piano. I watched as he moved his fingers over the keys, touching them lightly. "This one's loose," he said as he tapped it a few more times, hearing it rattle among the other keys. He stood up, bent over the top, and started fiddling in the back. "I think I can fix this."

I couldn't keep my eyes off him. He was careful not to show his feelings or give himself away. For every question I tried to ask, he always managed to turn it around into a question for me. It made me even more curious about him.

Even though it was daylight outside, here in the big, dimly lit room, it felt like night. There was only a bit of amber light coming from old lamps placed about, next to couches, chairs, and one on either side of the old piano.

While he bent over the back of the piano—looking somehow vulnerable in the moment—I decided to take a chance and ask him why he didn't drink. It's not like I drank all the time, or smoked, for that matter. But I did like to drink at parties or sneak a smoke occasionally with my friends. Most kids did. It really wasn't such a big deal. I didn't know anyone who consciously said they didn't drink.

"Mmm ... well, my father is an alcoholic. Recovering," he finally said with a trace of disgust, as he continued to fiddle with something in the back of the piano. "I've seen what it did to him, and my mother, so I won't touch it."

He turned to me, looking down at me with serious eyes. The smile was gone, replaced with concern. "Drinking is not only harmful to yourself, but it also destroys the lives of the people that care about you."

Is he giving me a lecture?

"At least, that's what it did to mine," he said quietly as he stood up from the piano and placed his hands on his waist. He quickly twisted right, then left, and then sat down and turned toward me. He reached out and absently touched my cheek where my cut was already healing. My heart raced with him sitting so close, and his touch. But his tone held such a mix of sadness and ... maybe a touch of anger. I didn't know what to say. I just looked into his eyes, trying to quiet my heart.

"I have an older sister who was very sick when she was born, and now she lives up north in a place for 'special' kids. I haven't seen her since I was a child."

"Oh," I said, not knowing what else to say. I didn't understand why he would share such an intimate detail with me. But I felt it was very important that he had. And that "oh" just lingered like a softly spoken "sorry." But I didn't say sorry, because that didn't seem right. I just looked at him and tried not to fidget as he held my gaze. My mouth was so dry; I couldn't control the urge to lick my lips. His eyes dropped from mine and he turned his attention to my mouth.

Relief flitted through me as his intense gaze left my eyes, but now it was replaced by nervousness as he watched my mouth, which just made me lick my lips again out of sheer apprehension.

He leaned over slowly toward me. At first, I thought he was going to whisper something to me, but he didn't. Before I had a chance to react, his hand gently touched my chin, bringing me closer to him as he placed his lips against mine.

I hadn't expected it at all. He seemed so rugged, and yet his lips felt like velvet against mine. And warm. They were so warm. Before I knew it, his tongue had pushed between my lips, and I found my mouth opening, as his found mine.

As he kissed me, his hand moved from my chin and gently cradled the back of my neck, holding me gently yet firmly to him, while he continued to move his lips over mine. This felt like nothing I had ever imagined. I mean, I couldn't have imagined what I had never experienced before. I was warm all over.

Smiling, he leaned back and looked at me. That look held more than I knew; it was worlds ahead of me. Then he turned back to the piano. "Play me something," he demanded gently.

I let out my breath. I hadn't even realized I'd been holding it. No wonder I felt light-headed again. Oh my god, this was incredible.

My hands were shaking with excitement as I turned toward the keys and tried very hard to look natural while I played "Für Elise," the one nice piece I knew from start to finish.

4 | MY KNIGHT

"Nights in White Satin," the Moody Blues

Our private moment was interrupted when the doors to the room flew open and several kids spilled in. They filled the long, empty room with laughter, talking, and music as they turned on the old stereo and picked up the pool cues. As it turned out, the slopes had closed early because a storm had come in again.

"I'll catch up to you later," Steve said as he was quickly dragged away by Michael. "I promise." He shot me a wink over his shoulder.

Thankfully, I didn't have to sit alone, as Marybeth walked in just at that moment. She'd been looking for me so she could tell me all about her morning and afternoon with Charles.

"We rode up together on the ski lift, and—oh, he's an expert skier, so we went on some of the more difficult runs," she said, beaming. "We were sharing a hot cocoa after lunch when they told us they were starting to shut down the slopes, and I was having so much fun!" She frowned.

"Did he kiss you?" I asked.

"No. I mean, he was really sweet, held my hand on the chair lift, but no," she sighed. "I think he's really shy."

"Yeah, he is super shy. Remember I went to a movie with him once?" I remembered the date not all that kindly. He had barely spoken in the car. Sat next to me stiff, like a zombie. I just couldn't figure out why he'd asked me in the first place because it didn't seem like he liked me one bit. And after that, he never asked me out again. I don't know, maybe my dad scared the shit out of him like all my brother's friends. But I liked him much better as a friend than a date.

"Yeah, I do remember that. Well, he talks at least!" she said, hopeful.

"Thank god for that!" I said, relieved she didn't feel awkward or resentful that I'd gone out with him first. Marybeth just burped and yelled, "My burps are giving me whiplash, eh."

The day passed uneventfully—nothing could compare to that kiss. Everything else around me seemed to fade away. It was like I was watching a play, and I had a bit part in it. I kept my eyes out for Steve, but he seemed to have disappeared.

Dinner came and went with still no sign of Steve. I hung out with Marybeth and some of the other girls in our room, trying not to think about him. Eventually, Charles, Peter, and Tony came in and invited us to their room. They had beer so we eagerly went with them to hang out.

We were all sitting around drinking when Lex, the jerk, came in. He walked over to me and gave me this nasty smirk. I felt like a rabbit trapped in a corner, but then the door opened, and Steve walked in. I almost choked on my drink as my heartbeat thundered in my chest. It must have shown because Lex turned his head to see what I was focused on. Steve looked around the room till he spotted me and the serious look on his face faded into a welcoming smile. Like he was a magnet, I walked right past Lex and straight to Steve.

"Hey!" I said, way too enthusiastically. "Do you want to come in and hang out?" I almost asked if he wanted a beer, but thankfully I hadn't forgotten our conversation from earlier that day. I glanced down uncomfortably at my beer and casually set it down on top of the dresser.

He shook his head but smiled and said, "No thanks, it's way too smoky in here. Do you want to go for a walk outside instead?"

"Oh sure, why not." I was trying really hard not to show how excited I was about the idea of being alone with him. "Let me grab my sweater and coat from my room."

He waited outside my door while I went in and threw on my sweater and picked my coat up off the bed. I quickly looked in the bathroom mirror, checked my teeth for food, and then hurriedly squished toothpaste in my mouth and rinsed. If he was going to kiss me, I sure wasn't going to taste like beer!

The minute we walked out onto the porch, I snapped off one especially pointy icicle and turned to attack. "On guard!" I laughed.

"Oh, so that's how you're going to play it? I see." He reached up and grabbed one himself, then swiftly leapt off the steps down onto the packed snow. "Come, now. I dare you to attack me on the sacred grounds of these lands—where my forefathers and their fathers before labored, sweat, fought, and died." He held out one hand with his "sword," and the other beckoned me with a flick of his wrist.

"Oh, sir, you dare tease. You think I cannot take you to task? Think again!" And with that, I bounded off the steps and we fenced our way back and forth: a jab to his side, a jab to mine. He reached out with his icy blade, and I ducked just in time and spun around behind him. As I came up for a breath, he grabbed me by the waist and tackled me to the ground.

Laughing so hard, steam coming out of our mouths, we seemed to forget the cold snow all around us, which was soaked into our clothes.

"Get off me, you cad!" I demanded, feigning outrage. I was trying hard to keep up the act, but laughter was getting the better of me.

"You're not to get off so easy, my lady." He had me pinned, my back on the ground, his body hovering over me. All of a sudden, I was aware of the position I was in. My heart pounded so loudly in my ears, I was sure he could hear. My laughter suddenly caught inside me, and a small squeak escaped my mouth.

"Uh-oh," I said.

He grinned widely, well aware he had the upper hand. Our eyes locked and then he started to lean down toward me. But at that moment, the door to the lodge opened, and about a dozen kids came barreling out, including my brother, thankfully lost in his own laughter and conversation with his friends.

And just like that, as fast as it had all happened, it ended.

Steve rolled off me and stood up. Holding his hand out to me, he bowed and said with a grin, "My lady ... ?"

I took his hand, and he quickly pulled me up. Putting my hand to my head, I felt a little dizzy and a bit queasy.

"Are you okay?" he asked, concerned.

"Yes ... I think. I just feel tired all of a sudden, and a bit funny. I think I should turn in early tonight. I just don't feel quite right."

"That sounds smart after that fall you had. I'll walk you to your room."

But at that moment Marybeth walked up and said she was headed up to our room, so I said good night to him there. With no privacy left, our moment now gone, we just smiled at each other.

"Till tomorrow," he said, keeping up the act.

"Yes, sir. Tomorrow." I curtsied, and he bowed low. Then I turned, laughing, and dragged Marybeth with me through the door.

"What was that all about?" she said, looking back over her shoulder, a slight frown passing over her face.

"Oh, nothing." But inside, I was grinning all over.

That night when I got back to my room, I took my bag of pot and gave it to Marybeth.

"Are you crazy?" She looked utterly confused.

"Maybe, but I just don't want it. I don't really like getting stoned anyway. It makes me paranoid." I pulled my covers back and climbed into bed. "You know I just bought it to look cool. How stupid is that?"

"But I don't want it either." She frowned.

I tucked my feet all the way in, stretching my legs out under the cold sheets. I scrunched my pillow behind my head, ignoring her comment. "How cool is it that we both found boyfriends on this ski trip, or at least potentials?"

She bounced down next to me, her grin as wide as mine. "Yeah. Pinch me. I can't believe it. Let's all hang out together tomorrow when we go skiing. Can you believe we only have one more day?" She sighed. "Four days is just not enough!"

"No, it's not, especially since I only got to ski, like, two half days. So, yeah, let's hang out together. I'm sure Steve and Charles will get along. Charles is very sweet. Not your usual obnoxious high school boy."

"No ... you're right about that." Marybeth lay back with the silliest, dreamiest expression on her face.

"You hoser!" We both started laughing so hard my stomach hurt. "Go ... to ... bed!" I pushed her off onto the floor. "I need sleep!"

I decided to join everyone the next day and go skiing. And I got my chance to ski with Steve. Steve had only skied a few times before, so he wasn't quite as experienced as me. But he wasn't bad either. It was fun to ski together, but the best part was holding his hand as we sat on the chair lift. It didn't even matter if it was stuck and frozen in the air, suspended in time. Just being with him was perfect. A dream.

Sitting up next to him on the chair lift, I listened intently while he told me stories—stories about other people and other places, but never really about himself. I learned he was graduating from George Mason next year, he worked part-time as a security guard, and he did some construction work, but nothing more than that.

I looked down and saw skiers pass by. But I didn't feel isolated and lonely this time—not like that day when Marybeth and I swung hovering over the world. I think I even spotted Doug and Peter. But it didn't matter. Nothing mattered anymore. Now I felt wanted, secure. I had a boyfriend. I thought.

On the long ride home, I lay with my head in his lap, eyes closed, once again listening to the sounds of the Stones mixing with the soft murmur of voices. The music flowed through the space of the bus and over me like honey: soft, relaxing, and warm, the muted sounds of laughter and conversation never ceasing, even after the long week of activities.

I suppose it was the excitement of the week. New friends made; new relationships forged.

Steve ran his fingers through my hair and tickled my ear with a feathery touch. I sighed, opening my eyes, and he looked down at me and smiled a warm, comforting smile while he ran his finger down the bridge of my nose to the tip. "You have an incredibly straight nose," he whispered. "I like it." He leaned down and kissed it.

We kissed again, whenever we were alone. But we weren't alone often enough. Although he held my hand freely, and always had his arm around my waist or had me put my arm through his, he never openly kissed me in front of anyone. He just seemed so ... courtly. And very protective.

I wished the bus would just keep going, and not stop. I never wanted to say goodbye.

5 | TRANSITIONS

"California Dreamin'," The Mamas & The Papas

The day after I got back from the ski trip, I lay on the floor of my room, my stomach pressed into the thick and itchy shag carpet, listening to my new Go-Go's album, *Beauty and the Beat*, while drawing little spirals of images with my name entwined with Steve's name.

Our house was too remote for visits from my friends—deep in the woods, with no way to bike to each other's homes or play in the streets. I missed California and my old life.

It had been five years now, but it still didn't feel like home. I didn't know if it was a good thing, like a promotion, or if the people my dad worked for just couldn't stand working with him, so they would just transfer him somewhere else. Anyway, that's what my mom would say during one of their "nonspeaking periods." Which were becoming more and more often since our move to Virginia. I couldn't remember there being so many arguments when we lived in California—although everyone in the neighborhood could hear him from the garage, cursing at anything and nothing. But even so, I just remembered a lot more laughter, and sunshine.

Turning over on my back, I looked up at the ceiling while wiping a pathetic tear from my cheek; I felt so trapped, so helpless, and tired of day after day with my dad slamming doors and hearing the endless stream of curse words and insults that he threw at my mom. There was always so much yelling and screaming, anything could set him off. I could hide in my room for only so long before he would yell at me to come down and do another chore.

The chores! My brother and I felt like his little soldiers. Every Saturday and Sunday he had us at it, and not just taking out trash, vacuuming, or laundry. Nope. While my friends were off playing sports or hanging out at the mall or at their country clubs on the weekend, my dad had us heaving up piles of brush and dirt onto the back of the trailer that was attached to the little four-wheel mower and then hauling it into the woods to dump it. It didn't matter how cold, hot, humid, or gnat-infested it was. We worked. Every weekend.

One night, as I lay fast asleep in bed, the door banged open, and in the doorway, silhouetted by light from the hallway, stood my dad.

"Get up now," he ordered, with his gruff, alcohol-soaked voice, his glasses on the tip of his nose, his arms straight at his sides, and his hands balled into fists. He pressed his mouth closed, and the nostrils flared wide on his huge nose.

"What's wrong?" I yawned; not sure he was serious at first. But I knew. It only took a look, and you knew. "Why?"

"You left your wet clothes in the washer. Go downstairs immediately and put them in the dryer." He stood there, staring at me, leaning forward ... teetering as if he would fall over. Those scary eyes said, "I dare you to defy me," and that was enough to get me up and jumping and on my way past him.

That wasn't the only time. It was a recurring episode. Eventually, I was less scared, tried to pull the old, "Dad, even God rested on the seventh day" defense. But it never worked. And I still wouldn't dare defy him. But I was the only one who really would argue with him. Oh, my mother would, as strong and stubborn as she was, but then it would get really ugly.

Every morning, until just recently, he would fling open our doors wide and order, "feet on the floor"—that good old West Point training. Oh, how I used to want to go to West Point just so I could dress up in a trim gray uniform and be surrounded by cute boys. What an idiot I was. If his attempts at ordering me around were any indication of how life would be at West Point, well, that was not somewhere I wanted to be. If I were to ever hear "feet on the floor" barked at me when I eventually moved out, I would shoot the person who demanded it. No matter how defiant they were, I vowed to never say anything like that to my own children.

Although, the stories of the young plebes who had to stand at attention and be continuously hazed—bossed around and ordered to do ridiculous things—by the older soldiers struck me as funny. West Point was like one gigantic fraternity with a nonstop rush week. Dad even taught us how to make our beds so tight you could bounce a quarter on it, something he learned from his days there.

He earned a reputation from my friends as "the Great Santini" because of the way he ordered us around. He never quite bounced a basketball off my brother's head, but I think he did drop him or hit him on his head as a toddler for playing with his fancy model airplanes.

I stood up in front of my white-framed mirror with the thin gold trim, which hung over my childhood princess dresser set—I had begged dearly to have the princess furniture set four years ago, but at this age, it seemed childish—and proceeded to comb out tangles in my somewhat shagged, somewhat feathered hair. I couldn't decide on this New Wave look, or my love of all things feathered. Like, is it going to be Joan Jett, or Stevie Nicks? My hair was getting darker every year that we lived here. It was a dark honey-blond, with only a few traces of lighter blond streaks from last summer. I reached over to my jewelry box, picked out my feathered earrings, and slipped them on.

The phone rang and it was Bambie. Bambie was the nickname I gave Barbara. No particular reason except it just came out once, and it stuck. I couldn't wait to tell Bambie all about Steve.

I met Bambie at the beginning of the school year in biology class, my newest of friends. She was very different from the other kids. She had this purple parachute purse by Le Sports Sac that she put safety pins all over, and a button with a band I'd never heard of before called the Clash. She wore pointy shoes with black tights and a knit miniskirt dress that was black with a bold stripe of red going down the sides. Her hair was cropped very short, and she wore black Ray-Ban sunglasses. Most of the girls in my school had long, feathered hair and wore moccasins, Bass loafers, or high-heeled Frye boots. My school was a split between preps and grits—better described as the Southern Rock crowd. The term "grit" was much preferred over "redneck."

No one ever intentionally cut their hair short. It was usually because of some horrid accident after a perm gone wrong, like mine in the eighth grade. But Bambie looked really cool and edgy. Her difference wasn't accidental, it was completely intentional; it just grabbed me. Even though I still clung to my hippie relics like my feathered earrings, I was mixing it up with new looks inspired by her. I cut my hair myself because of my newfound interest in Joan Jett. And I didn't do a bad job. The idea of being a beautician was growing on me. But I preferred painting. I dreamed of being an artist. Or a model. Or a dancer. Maybe the other way around. A dancer, an artist, or a model.

Bambie's musical tastes were also completely different from anyone else's I knew. We were all slipping back to our rock 'n' roll roots after being bombarded with disco for the last few years. DISCO SUCKS T-shirts and pins were all the rage. I made a SAVE AN ALLIGATOR, KILL A PREP shirt.

But not Bambie. Besides the Clash, her favorite music were bands like the Jam, Duran Duran, and Madness—more bands I had never heard of. Let's just say she wasn't impressed with my Pat Benatar and Van Halen concert experiences.

The first concert I ever went to was the previous summer. Two concerts, back-to-back! First Van Halen, and then Pat Benatar, with Billy Squire opening for her. The summer of '81 was epic! I still wore the bootleg concert T-shirt I got from the parking lot that night.

But Van Halen. That was a concert! Pat Benatar was outside, in an amphitheater. But the Van Halen's '81 Tour was at the Capital Center. Huge. Powerful. Earsplitting. Literally, I couldn't hear for a week after. But it was fun. I went with my brother and his friends. And I am *not* making it up when I say David Lee Roth looked right at me. I nearly died.

Bambie said I needed a serious upgrade to my look and music, so a couple of weeks before we drove down to Georgetown in my little yellow Karmann Ghia for some shopping. D.C. was only a half hour from where we lived, and right over the Key Bridge. She took me to this little hole-in-the-wall punk rock record store called Penguin Feathers, and I bought my first punk album: the Damned, *The Black Album*. And then we walked up the street to the coolest store called Commander Salamanders, where they had all of this punk and new wave clothing and accessories. I bought my first official punk accessory: a thin, leopard-print choker.

"Oh my god, guess what? Oh no, you'll never guess! I met a guy on the ski trip!" I blurted out, excitement shooting out of me like fireworks. "He's so handsome and mature; he's twenty-one. And his name is Steve ... Steve Greene," I sighed.

Bambie understood. She had a boyfriend named Eric, and he didn't go to our school either. I mean, he was still in high school, but he played in a band. He seemed mature because he was very quiet. Not the grabby, show-off type, despite being in a band.

I told her all about the trip. Every detail. Every moment.

"Hold on a sec," she interrupted. "What did your dad say when you stepped off the bus with him? How exactly did that go over?"

"Well ... I kind of evaded all that."

"How? I mean, how did you 'evade' your dad seeing him?"

"Well, pretty easily actually." I sat down on the padded princess chair that matched the princess desk and reached for my nail polish as I wedged the phone between my chin and shoulder. "The bus dropped us off in the parking lot," I continued. "I said goodbye to him on the bus, explaining that it wouldn't be cool to just shock my dad like that ... to tell him, 'Hey, Dad, here's this guy I met.' Not to mention he's five years older than me." I laughed. "Which I'm sure my dad would figure out immediately. Somehow, I don't think he would approve of that. Actually, Steve was really cool about it."

And he was. As I'd stepped out of the bus in front of him, into the shelter of kids and parents, I saw my dad standing over by the car. Thankfully he hadn't spotted me yet, so I turned to Steve, motioning with my head toward my dad.

Steve smiled at me, reached out, and squeezed my hand. "I'll call you," he said. "I promise."

"So, that was it," I explained to Bambie. "I walked over to my dad, and I didn't even have to say anything."

"Hmph."

"I mean, he would totally freak out, don't you think? I'm not really sure what to say. He doesn't need to know. Ever."

"Oh, you're walkin' the line." She laughed. "But seriously, he's going to find out eventually."

I could tell she was concerned, but honestly, I would do everything to keep him from meeting him. I wasn't stupid. It took my dad long enough just to let me date, along with the third degree he gave everyone. I knew dating an older guy was way off-limits.

I could introduce him to my mom, though. Things were really getting tense with my mom and dad, so I knew she wouldn't tell my dad about him.

"Yeah, but my dad works late all the time," I said, blowing on my nails to dry them, "so he won't have to meet him. Not yet. Like I said, for now, he doesn't need to know. Besides he hasn't called me yet. So, it might not even be an issue." I sighed. I finished with my nails and plopped down on my back in bed, kicking my feet up over my head and touching the wall behind me.

"Don't be silly." I could hear Bambie's exasperation masked by her role as my supportive friend. "He'll call. And besides, it's only Saturday, and you all just got back yesterday. You remember what we read about guys in *Seventeen Magazine* ..."

"They don't call back until three days pass," we both chanted at the same time.

"That sucks!" I moaned. "Hold on, I hear my mom calling." I rolled my legs down, jumped up from the bed, and held the phone against my hip as I walked to the bedroom door. "Yeah?" I yelled down the hallway, hoping she could hear me from the kitchen. But there was no answer.

"Bambie, I gotta run. I'm supposed to go to the store with my mom. I'll call you later or see you in school Monday."

Despite what *Seventeen Magazine* says, I wasn't so sure if guys called on the first day after meeting someone, or the second day or otherwise. But if he didn't call me before Monday, I knew I would die. But he didn't call

Saturday. And Sunday I spent most of the day outside helping my dad and brother doing yard work.

When the day pressed on, and we were all getting thirsty and sweaty, I volunteered to grab some lemonade. As I ran into the house, my mom yelled from the sewing room upstairs that she had just made some lemonade and it was sitting on the kitchen table. *Mind reader*, I thought.

Just as I was about to yell back "thanks," the phone rang on the kitchen wall.

"Can you get that? I'm a bit tied up here," she hollered from upstairs.

"Sure."

I ran into the kitchen and plopped down on the built-in desk next to the cabinets where the kitchen phone hung.

Out of breath, I picked up the phone. "Hello?"

"Suzanne?"

It was Steve! My heart leapt up into my throat. I seriously doubted he was ever going to call.

"Hey," I squeaked.

"Hey yourself." A song was playing in the background that I didn't recognize, really mellow, yet interesting. "So, what are you up to?"

"Um, just sitting on the desk ... I mean, I was outside helping my dad and brother do some yard work and came in to get some lemonade when the phone rang. My mother's upstairs." It all rushed out too fast.

He chuckled and said, "Want to do something this week?"

"Ya, definitely!" Too eager. *Crap.*

"Okay, I'll pick you up after school Tuesday, okay?"

"Yeah, that'd be cool."

I was so excited that after hanging up I ran through the house and bounced out the door. My brother and dad were standing there amid a huge pile of weeds and branches piled high in the wagon of the tractor. They both turned and looked at me.

"Where's the lemonade?"

"Oops."

6 | CAT AND MOUSE

"Boat on the River," Styx

I stood outside the front of the school as kids passed by on the way to the bus or their cars. Steve pulled up front in a two-door blue Chevy Nova. It looked like a '70s hot rod. A bit dinged up, but it had a very tough-boy kind of vibe to it. I don't know what I expected him to drive, but in a way, this fit. With the engine still on, he got out, turned, and looked over the roof of the car, placing one hand on the roof while the other brushed back his hair, smoothing it. He grinned wide—just like I remembered him.

He was wearing brown tight-fitting cords with a V-neck velour sweater. I was wearing my best blue jeans, which were tight and uncomfortable, but they looked great, and I had on my maroon turtleneck sweater with just my blue down vest. It wasn't that cold for March, so I didn't need a huge coat.

He came around the car and opened the passenger door for me. I looked up at him and smiled, and he smiled back, as I sat down in the passenger seat, and then swung my legs in after me, just like I learned from Barbizon School of Modeling, a course I took in seventh grade: "a lady always keeps her legs together."

He walked back around to his side, and as he put the car in drive, he turned to me and grinned. "You look as pretty as I remember you."

"Thank you." I blushed.

I was flustered after his comment and couldn't seem to think of anything smart to say. We sat in silence for a few never-ending moments, but I couldn't take it.

"Where are we going?" I finally asked. The suspense was killing me.

"Well, I seem to remember you said you liked hiking, so I'm taking you to the park off the Potomac." He turned and smiled at me. There would hopefully be a point when I wouldn't constantly feel weak at the knees with his direct looks.

We turned off the main road into a gravel parking lot next to one of the trails that led back to the Potomac. You could hike for at least thirty minutes straight to the Potomac River if you wanted. But we started off slowly with no real intention of a serious hike. He grabbed my hand to help me up over a rock but didn't let it go after that. I just hoped he couldn't sense how nervous I was by touching me.

After hiking through the woods for what seemed like an hour but was probably just fifteen minutes, we stopped to take a break. He leaned back against a tree and pulled me toward him gently, sliding his hands around my lower back, pressing me lightly to him.

Our bodies fit together comfortably; he was at least an inch taller than me. I was that awkward six-foot girl in school, the one that towers over everyone. I always seemed to have friends who were between five and five seven. Most guys said they were six feet, and yet somehow, I was still taller than them.

He pressed me against him, his hands running up my back, pulling me closer, and kissed me, just like I remembered from our first kiss. It sent shivers and tingles right down to my toes. I didn't know how to react to this feeling, so I pulled away, grabbed his hand, and pulled him with me. "Come on you, let's keep going." He gave me a little wink, lazily stood up, and off we went.

After our first date, we saw each other a lot during the week. He'd pick me up from school, and we'd go to the mall and play video games at the arcade, or we would drive down to the river and hike up through the woods. He was quiet. I mean, not a big talker. He did talk about guy things: cars, bodybuilding, car shows, and the usual surface stuff. But mostly we just did stuff and talked about it. Or he'd ask me questions. But there was still so much hidden about him.

We talked a lot about music. He wasn't really into the new stuff I was listening to, but we bonded on the old stuff. Not old really. But classic rock, and rock 'n' roll. Like, he was into David Bowie. Bowie was his favorite singer. Big sigh of relief there. Bowie was my favorite too.

Each time we were together, we'd hold hands and kiss, like we did that first time on our hike. He never tried to do anything else, like shove his hands down my pants or up my shirt. He was a perfect gentleman.

I might have been a virgin, but I wasn't a prude. I'd made out with boys before. You know, kissing—all bubble gum and popcorn stuff. But boys always had these stiff mouths, dry lips, and sandpaper tongues. The boys that were interested in me were always older, even if by a year. But I'd never had a real boyfriend before, unless you counted eighth grade when I secretly dated a tenth-grade boy for about a month. But we only went out twice to the mall to see a movie. Our parents were friends, so the first time we made out was in his room when they were all having cocktails downstairs in the living room. It was super convenient. I thought he was cute, but he was so full of himself. It felt like he was just jabbing me with his tongue. It was uncomfortable and clumsy and made me feel like I was going to choke. Plus, he tasted like cigarettes. Cigarettes and braces. He was kind of a starter boyfriend. He dated almost all my friends.

During freshman year, on Monday afternoons, I would sneak down to my parents' liquor cabinet in the basement, steal a bottle of red wine, and mix a large screwdriver in a thermos. I'd put on my winter coat and trek through the woods to my friend Julie's house, a fifteen-minute walk. Her mom was studying, getting her master's, so she was out late on Mondays. Her sisters were in college, so we were all alone. Just the two of us. And my parents both worked late.

When I arrived, we would raid her sister's closet, putting on silky, slinky dresses and clunky high heels and throwing silk boas around our necks as a final touch.

Then we would head to the family room, turn on the record player—taking big gulps of our drinks—while dancing to KC and The Sunshine Band's "Shake, Shake, Shake" and Peaches and Herb's "Shake Your Groove Thing," creating our own dance routines to rival The Hustle.

One time, after drinking too much, we called her neighbor, Mike, also a few years older, and met him down in the woods. He had some pot, so we got high and took turns kissing him. He was super cute. But when he shoved his hands down my pants, I freaked out. Maybe I wasn't ready for all that yet.

Two weeks from our first date, I came down with a bad cold. I stayed home by myself, missing school, while my parents were at work. Most of the day I just slept—falling in and out of dreams. I felt clammy with a fever, but at least my throat didn't hurt anymore. I tried calling Steve's house to let him know I couldn't meet him after school that day, but the phone just rang and rang.

Sometime in the afternoon, I woke to the sound of the doorbell. At first, I thought it was in my dream, but the persistent ring of the bell finally pulled me out of my sleep.

Groggy, I sat up in my dark room—the window shades were down with just a dull light filtering in—and listened. There it was again. It was definitely the doorbell.

I crawled out of bed, dressed in my long cotton nightgown, and looked around for my robe. It wasn't on my chair. Maybe it was in the laundry, or downstairs somewhere. I loved the nightgown I wore; it was soft, light blue, with satin strings I had tied at the neck to keep it from falling open. I padded barefoot down the carpeted stairs to the entranceway and got a chilly awakening as my bare feet hit the cool tiles when I walked to the front door.

The bell rang again, and I jumped. "Damn, who could that be?" I muttered out loud to myself. As I reached for the handle, I looked up at the clock hanging on the wall and saw that it said three thirty. It suddenly occurred to me, as I started to open the door, that it must be him.

I opened it and saw him standing there, leaning against the door, with his jeans fitting so damn snug and his light brown leather jacket over his dark turtleneck. I started to feel a bit light-headed. Maybe it was because I just woke up, and hadn't been out of bed all day, but seeing him there, well ...

The look in his eyes was a mix of concern, and something else.

I started to say something, but he beat me to it.

"Hey, princess." I wasn't sure I loved the new pet name, but it sweetly brought up the memory of our faux fight in the snow. "When I came by to pick you up at school, your friends said you weren't there today, so I thought I would stop by and see if you were okay."

"I'm sick," I sniffed. "I've been in bed all day." I stepped back, and as I did, he stepped in, closing the door behind him and then leaning up against it. It occurred to me he had never been inside my house before. He'd dropped me off, but down at the bottom of the driveway. I didn't want to risk anyone seeing him.

"You ... you shouldn't be here, you know. I'm all by myself, and besides I'm sick. You don't want to catch anything." I wasn't sure if I wanted him to stay or go. It was really exciting to see him, but I was a little bit nervous for some reason.

"I don't mind if I catch anything from you." He reached out and grabbed my hips and pulled me toward him. I could feel the coolness of his hands through the thin fabric of my nightgown. "This"—his thumb rubbed the fabric of my gown—"is so soft and ..." His eyes grazed over me, from my hips up to my eyes. "You look so ... sweet in your nightgown." His voice was very low; he sounded almost cautious. There was a look in his eyes I hadn't seen before. His hands slid farther around my waist, enveloping me. He pressed me toward him until his stomach was against mine, one of his legs between mine. One hand went a little lower on my back till his fingers grazed the top of my bottom, and the other slid up my back, as if trying to caress the softness of the fabric, but with me inside. His touch sent goosebumps up and down my spine.

He looked deep into my eyes and said, "Kiss me. I want *you* to kiss me."

I leaned up and placed my lips on his mouth, gently at first, then harder. A wave of sensation passed through me, and then I kissed him without holding back. My hands slid through his jacket, between the warmth of his body, and the cold of the leather, feeling the muscles in his back, feeling every curve. I dared to let one hand slowly move its way downward. As my hand slid over his butt, his mimicked mine, and pressed me harder against him.

I had never done this before. I mean, kind of, with that boy in the woods, but it wasn't like this. We were just goofing around. We'd kissed, but not really kissed. Not with passion. And okay, he'd stuck his hands down my pants, but I had immediately jumped away. It was kind of a fuzzy memory, with all the pot and alcohol.

This was different. A new sensation washed over me that I didn't know what to do with. He was no longer grinning or smiling. The soft twinkling look of humor was replaced with something else. His hand on my rear pressed harder, while his thigh trapped between my legs pushed against me.

The contact sent a wave of heat, like a heartbeat, right between my legs. A small sound escaped from me, and he pulled back with my bottom lip between his lips, in a languid, sensual way, still pressing his leg to me. Then he let go of my lip and traveled along my chin with his mouth, a soft caress from my jawbone to my ear. When his breath hit my ear, my knees felt weak. If he hadn't been pressed against me so tightly, with his arms around me, I would have fallen right then.

"Mmm ... you smell delicious. Like lemon and flowers," he whispered into my ear, which sent shivers down my body again. But he didn't stop. His mouth trailed down my neck to my collarbone, and he kissed me there, lightly, and then leaned up to look at me.

"Show me your room."

"Oh," I said, catching my breath. I broke away from him and pulled my gown down to straighten it. I could feel the heat in my face, the flush. I turned away and started up the stairs, and I could hear him right behind me, close.

What am I doing, taking him to my room? What if Mom or Dad comes home early? Besides, I wasn't ready to go all the way, not yet. I didn't want to. But I couldn't bring myself to tell him to go. I didn't want him to go. *Maybe I can play a record or show him my photo albums. That's what I'll do*, I thought. *I'll distract him.*

I felt impossibly hot, and I wasn't sure how much of it was from all the kissing and how much could be from the fever. I had almost forgotten I was sick.

As I led him into my room, I quickly went over to my record player, found my David Bowie album, and put on side one of *Hunky Dory*. I turned around, and Steve was sitting at the end of my bed, looking around my room. I looked around quickly to make sure I didn't have anything embarrassing lying about and spotted my notebook sitting on my desk wide open, the one with the drawings of hearts and our names in the middle. I quickly went over and closed it before he even noticed it.

"I like your room, it's cute," he said, grinning.

"Uh, thanks. It's still got a lot of stuff from my childhood." Decorated in a color scheme of yellow, pink, green, and blue, it was really childish: the pastel-colored clay LOVE sign hanging over my bed in bubble type, the large ballerina posters, my toe shoes hanging from the side of the bed, the collages I made of all my favorite actors and actresses: Sean Cassidy, David, his brother, Greg Evigan (from *B. J. and the Bear*), Rob Lowe ... all representations of things I loved when I was younger. I still loved it all, but it wasn't till now, at that very moment, when a guy was sitting on my bed, that I realized how silly it all looked. How childish.

"It's kind of obvious I like ballet." I pointed toward my *pink pointe ballet shoes*. When I was young, I'd dreamed of becoming a dancer. But my mom was convinced I wouldn't stick with it, so she kept waiting. Finally at the late age of fourteen, she caved to my constant pleading. So now I was taking ballet classes three days a week, modern dance twice, and tap on the weekends. Unfortunately, in the ballet class, I was at least three heads taller than all the other younger girls. It was pretty embarrassing at first, but I enjoyed it so much, and the other girls were really sweet, so I stopped caring.

He patted the bed next to him.

I didn't move. Couldn't. I didn't want to sit next to him. I was scared of what might happen next. I grabbed my photo album sitting on the shelf and sat down farther away from him, closer to my pillows. I scooted up onto the bed and sat cross-legged, pulling the covers over my legs. The light from the window behind me tried to filter through the shade, but for the most part it was pretty dark in the room. I reached over and turned on the lamp sitting on the side table next to the bed.

He watched all this quietly, and then got up, walked around to the other side of the bed, and crawled up next to me. Close.

"What's this?" He reached over and opened the cover. The side of his thigh touched my leg, which made me feel a bit panicked. He still had one leg hanging over the side of the bed because my bed was really small, even though I was sitting as far to the other side as possible. He leaned over, his shoulder grazing mine.

"It's my photo album from when I lived in California." I turned a page where there were photos of me, some dressed in cute little dresses, with messy long blond hair, and others in dirty overalls. "I was a tomboy who liked to wear dresses."

"You look really adorable here." He laughed and pointed at the one of me with the hair in my eyes, holding up a ribbon. I had just won second place in a horse show. I rode Western in the canyons of Palos Verdes, not English. I wanted to be a cowgirl, like Jane Fonda in *Cat Ballou*, not Elizabeth Taylor from *National Velvet*. Barrel racing was more my style, not jumps.

I was about to say something when he leaned in farther and I felt his hot breath along my neck. I stopped moving and sat very still. He kissed my neck softly, and at the same time, picked the photo album off my lap and moved it over to the side table.

I didn't move or speak as he returned his hand to me, and I turned my head toward him. Then he gently kissed me. This time, as excitement welled up in me, something else emerged. Fear. I realized we were on my bed, and I was just wearing this flimsy nightgown.

Before I could say anything, he leaned me back so my head was on my pillows, and he climbed over me, putting his hands on my waist. He scooted me down and straightened my legs out. I just stared at him, not sure of what to say, the excuses stuck in my throat.

He lay down on top of me then, putting his full weight upon me, except for where he leaned on his elbows, his hands placed alongside my body. He looked down at me, and his eyes held mine. Whatever he saw in my expression made him grin, and then he leaned down to my neck. He kissed me along my collarbone, slowly, while his hands came up and untied the top of my gown. I held my breath as his hands slowly slipped down and caressed my breasts through the material. But he didn't stop there; he kept moving down, sliding farther down, so his head was level with my stomach. He turned his head to the side and laid his head on my stomach. I felt his hands find my thighs, and slowly move up my legs, pushing my dress up over my legs.

"Wait," I squeaked, a small, strangled sound coming from my mouth. "I'm"—his hands pushed my dress up over my hips—"not"—his head hovered over my now exposed cotton panties—"ready for"—he lowered his face over me, and then hot warmth from his mouth enveloped me, through the material. I could feel the heat from his mouth as he moved, caressing me with his mouth. I squirmed under him, and groaned, "I'm not ready for this ... please ..."

"It's okay," he said. "We'll just play a little."

I was torn between fear and pleasure. I went with pleasure, for now. "Okay ... but, that's it ... no sex."

He laughed, and the vibration of his laugh distracted me from my fear.

7 | CHERRY PICKING
"Expecting to Fly," Buffalo Springfield

I knew Steve wouldn't wait too much longer before he would want to go all the way, not just over my clothes. And well, other things. But I wasn't sure if I was ready to lose my virginity yet. Most of my friends had lost theirs, but I was still scared. Mainly, I was scared it would hurt. And there was something else, like the loss of something important. Something I had that was unique and I didn't want to just let it go without some serious thought.

Two weeks had gone by after that day when he unexpectedly showed up at my house while I was sick. Even though he didn't push me that day, every time we started kissing, the subject came up. He had made it pretty clear that if I wasn't ready to have sex with him, then I wasn't ready to have a real relationship with him. I wasn't mature enough for him.

I didn't want to lose him. He was so charming and gallant around me. He was always opening doors for me and taking me to the movies, paying for everything. And his kisses were amazing as well. He was this incredibly handsome, mature guy. And he really wanted to date me. He wanted me. And he was very protective, which made me feel safe and secure. Being with him distracted me from everything else that I couldn't bear: my miserable dad, boring school, and the penetrating quiet that settled in after school. As well as the voice that told me I wasn't good enough, not pretty enough, and not smart enough. The voices were the loudest in the quiet.

The light from his parents' house shone across the driveway, just barely touching the hood of the car, as we sat cozily, tightly entwined, kissing. The darkness held possibilities within in, while the glow from outside was soothing. He fiddled with the buttons on my jeans, and before I knew it his hands were pushing down into my pants. I jumped backward at the same time trying to remove his hand.

With his hand still between my legs, he growled, "I'm too old for games. You're either ready or not. Do you want to end it now because it really seems like that's what you want?"

"No," I stammered, "I'm—"

"Then stop fucking with me. Why am I wasting my time with you? There are plenty of girls that would be dying to have sex with me." He abruptly pulled his hand out of my pants and ran it through his hair, moving away from me.

A rush of cold ran through me, and I immediately scooted closer to him. "No, no, I do. I mean I really do want to. Please don't be mad," I pleaded. "I'm just scared."

"Oh princess, there's nothing to be scared of." His voice softened, and he moved to close the space between us, putting both hands on my face. He looked deep into my eyes. "I'll be gentle. I promise."

His house—his parents' house, that is—looked a little bit haunted. It was situated up a hill in the woods at the end of a long driveway. As you came to the top, the trees cleared away, and there sat the house. The garage was separate, off to the side. I think it used to be a barn. The house reminded me of an old farmhouse, with a pitched roof forming a triangle in the center, and smaller dormer windows to each side, creating the look of eyes. It felt like there should be more rooms in the house, but from the inside I couldn't quite make out where they would be.

In the driveway, there were a couple of old beat-up cars, one up on cinder blocks. Their place ... it kind of reminded me of our cousins' places in West Virginia. I don't think they had a lot of money. I didn't think about it before, but they didn't live in the posh parts of McLean, but on the edge. Closer to the city.

As we walked into his house, I could hear the television on in the living room. His parents were probably watching *Miami Vice* or *V*, this incredibly weird sci-fi show about aliens taking over Earth. But rather than join them, like we usually did, Steve quickly said hello from the bottom of the stairs, which led up to his bedroom, and ascended, pulling me along behind him. I just turned as I headed up and gave a small wave to his mother, who looked up for a moment and smiled kindly at me.

At first, I thought it was strange that he lived with his parents, since he was in college. My friends who'd graduated the year before had all left town. But I guess if you went to college in the same town where you lived, and maybe money had something to do with it, it made sense to stay with your parents. I was definitely going away to college—no way was I staying home any longer than I had to.

His brother, Shaun, lived there too, in the room across the hall. His twin brother. I would say that was creepy, but they didn't really look that much alike, at least I didn't think so. I figured when he graduated, he would move out; he was graduating that year.

I hadn't shown up that night expecting this was going to be the night we would "do it." But the threat of losing him encouraged me to move forward. *"If you're not ready, then maybe you're not ready to have a relationship with me"* kept playing in my head. I did pretty much think I was ready. But I also didn't feel like I had a choice. I didn't want to risk losing him. What difference did it make in the end? Better to do it with someone like Steve than someone who was inexperienced and clumsy. Surely Steve wouldn't be clumsy. He said he would be gentle, and he would know what he was doing.

This wonderful, new, tingling sensation was growing in my lower belly. I wanted more of that. I wanted to know what the mystery was all about. I also didn't want to upset him by refusing again. I knew he wouldn't wait much longer.

His room was smaller than mine, but mostly it just seemed like that because of the slanted ceiling. There was only one window, one of the "eyes," which didn't really let in a lot of light. A circular, handmade rug sat in the middle of the wood floor. There was a small single bed pushed up against the wall with a side table and lamp. Albums were neatly organized on a little shelf, a record player sitting on top. The back of the room was dark and hard to make out, even with the overhead light on. He had a couple of posters up, one of a very pretty girl, naked, sitting on stone steps eating grapes. I think she was from Playboy or something. She was really pretty with this feathery blond hair. Perfect breasts. And there was a poster of some band called the Alan Parsons Project. Resting against the wall next to the side table was a Cherie and Marie Currie album, *Young and Wild*, with two cute blond girls posing in lingerie. I recognized one girl from the band the Runaways.

I sat on the bed, twisting his bedsheet with my hand, while he went over to his stereo and put on an album. It barely registered that music was playing ... something by Meatloaf, I thought. My mind was racing, and I couldn't look at him. I just kept twisting the sheet.

After he turned off the overhead light, leaving only the bedside lamp glowing, he walked over to the bed and sat down next to me. I couldn't look at him, I just couldn't. I was so nervous. I looked down at my hands, which sat lifeless in my lap, and closed my eyes.

His fingers brushed my arms as he pulled my shirt up and over my head. He gently pushed me back onto his bed so my head rested on his pillow. He didn't say anything as he unbuttoned my jeans and slid them down over my legs, leaving my socks on. After he tossed my pants to the floor, he reached back up and pulled my underpants down. I automatically put both my hands over my crotch.

He grabbed my hands as he scooted up the bed over me and brought them above my head. I could hear his watch ticking by my ear as his hands pushed my hands down, pinning them. His breath directed his deep whisper in my other ear: "Don't move them." An involuntary shiver ran down the base of my neck.

Then he reached down and snapped my bra open. I was wearing the kind that opened from the front, white, with lace. As he opened it, he pulled it up, so the straps were around my wrists, and left it like that.

I was about to say something, but I didn't think it was a good idea. I felt really exposed. No one had ever looked at my bare-naked chest before. I felt him slide off the bed, so I peeked through my lashes to see what he would do next. He stood staring at me from the end of the bed, his dark eyes scanning me from my feet to my hands—slowly. He looked satisfied. Then, he pulled his shirt over his head and tossed it where my clothes lay. He looked so strong, and it was sexy. It was so different than what I thought I was attracted to. I liked wiry, lean muscles. I didn't think I would be attracted to a bodybuilder's body.

Then he unbuttoned his pants, looking straight at me—right in my eyes, daring me to look away. I blushed while he pulled his pants down, with his underwear following, and my heart raced.

Now he was naked, as naked as me, yet he looked completely comfortable. Whereas I felt like a canary trapped by a hungry cat.

I opened my mouth to say something, but he put a finger to his lips, and then leaned over the bed, first placing his hands on it, then crawling up, walking his hands along my side, until he was directly above me.

He leaned down and kissed me, hungrily. That's the only way I can describe it. Like he wanted to devour me. Then he stopped, hovering over me. A small smile played on his lips, but his eyes were dark and piercing. I shivered under his gaze. He brought his finger to his lips. I thought he was going to shush me again, but instead he put it in his mouth like he was going to suck it, but then he removed it and brought it all the way down and then, not so gently, slid it between my legs.

I lay in the dark afterward, a dried tear on my cheek, staring up at the ceiling. This was not what I had imagined. This wasn't like the gentle caresses from my room, and the many nights making out in his car. Instead, from the beginning—the force of his finger, and then of him inside me—it wasn't gentle. I felt ... I just didn't have the words to describe it. It hurt. It was painful. And I felt disconnected from it and my body. Was this the way it would always be?

He said it wouldn't be so painful the next time, and I would start to enjoy it. I just needed to do it more. Like exercise.

Painful yes, but the weight of it all is what I hadn't expected—the emotional and physical weight. The way he stabbed at me, everything inside me felt like it was resisting, even though nothing came out of my mouth. It was too late to say no. My heart felt ripped open, and raw.

"It will get better, I promise. And I'll show you how much fun it will be," he said as he drove me home, his hand on my leg. He turned to me and winked.

"Yeah, okay," I said softly as I ran my fingers along the side of the door, looking out the window, the darkness enfolding us. The drive was long and felt even longer this time as we swerved down the long and winding road surrounded by shadowy trees. Everything about it seemed ominous and forbidding.

"It will, I promise." He pulled up my long driveway, put the car in park, and turned to look at me. "Look at me."

He gently pulled my face toward his with both hands. His eyes burned holes into mine. There was concern in them. Worry, I think. I nodded, shutting my eyes, and he leaned in closer and kissed my forehead.

Taking his hands away, he reached down into his pocket and pulled out a chain, and then slipped his huge college ring off his finger. He opened the latch to the chain and slid it on. Turning to me, he said, "I want you to wear this now."

Without waiting, he just put his hands around my neck, clasping it shut, and then slid his hand down the chain, over my chest, picked up the ring, and held it, inspecting it. Then he lay it down.

My hand instinctively went up to feel his ring, so heavy and full of masculine energy. Steve's energy. In that moment, for just a minute, I felt there was something wrong. But I couldn't place why I felt that way.

"I'm serious. I want you to wear it always." He looked at me seriously, with a little furrow in his brow. "You're mine now."

8 | DOUBLE TROUBLE

"Our Lips are Sealed," the Go Gos

Shaun, Steve's brother, lifted weights too, and although they were identical it was easy to tell them apart. Shaun was a bit smaller framed and had more scars on his face than Steve did. I guess it was teenage acne. He rarely smiled, but when he did, it was more of a sneer than a charming smile, like Steve's. To me they looked very different. Looking at Shaun, it was as if Steve was standing before one of those mirrors at the circus. The ones that warp you.

I couldn't put a finger on Steve and Shaun's relationship. Sometimes it seemed hostile, yet other times the way they communicated felt like they shared some secret. They'd spit nasty comments at each other as we'd pass each other in the hallway, Steve always pushing me ahead of him, like he didn't want Shaun to look at me.

I was spending more and more time at his house. I mean, I couldn't have Steve at my house. He was my secret boyfriend—at least from my dad. My mom knew, but not my dad. Not yet. And they both worked pretty late. Besides, it was always easy to say I was at a church event or spending the night with a friend. I didn't want to be home anyhow.

Sometimes when I went downstairs to get something to drink from the kitchen, I would stumble upon Shaun. He'd look up from whatever he was doing—reading a magazine or pouring some juice—and then his look would transform from grim to a grin: a distorted version of Steve's smile. I can't explain it, but that smile really creeped me out. It made me feel like I was naked, and like he knew exactly what I was doing up in the bedroom with Steve. I'd quickly smile and turn around and hurry right back up the stairs.

One afternoon, I was headed down the stairs with Steve behind me. When I arrived at the bottom, I turned around, expecting Steve to be there, but he was still at the top of the steps, in front of Shaun's bedroom. Hushed, angry voices that felt cold, like a strong draft, filtered down the stairs, inaudible. Their heads were bent like two rams locked in a power struggle.

When he came down the steps, I asked him what was wrong and he answered, "Nothing. Don't worry about it." He pushed me ahead of him. "Let's go." And he led me out the front door.

Shaun's girlfriend, Sara, was the same age as him: twenty-one. But she looked twelve. She had a boyish figure—no hips, just a hint of breasts. We never hung out with them. Didn't double-date, go to the mall or the video arcade, one of our favorite places. We just bumped into them at their parents' house, coming and going, and when we hung out with their parents.

Steve didn't have a TV in his room so quite often we sat downstairs with his parents and watched with them. Occasionally Shaun and his girlfriend would be there too. She was nice. But quiet. I didn't really notice her that much because I spent more time avoiding Shaun's gaze.

I babysat on the weekends, and one afternoon I decided to take Chrissy, who was about three years old, to the mall. Her parents trusted me and let me take her places, like the park or the mall on occasion. I loved to pretend I was a teenage bride with a baby. Not that I was stupid enough to do that. I just liked the idea.

I drove to Steve's house on the way to invite him to come along and show Chrissy off to his mother. His mom was really sweet. A tiny little woman with short brown hair and a round body.

When we got there, I knocked on the door and Steve opened it. He smiled brightly and pinched Chrissy's little sneaker.

"I can't wait to show Chrissy to your mom. She was asking about her the last time I was here," I said as I hopped past him and headed toward the living room, which was all dark except for the dim light coming through the flower-covered curtains. But it didn't look like anyone was home.

"She's not here," he said as he started up the stairs. "I think she went to the store. Just wait here, I'll be back in a moment."

I went into the little living room area with Chrissy and sat down on the couch. There was a TV in the corner next to the window. Another couch sat across from the one I sat on. And then there was the Archie Bunker chair that sat directly across from the TV.

I heard a creak on the floorboards and looked up as his brother walked into the room.

"Who is this sweet little girl?" He walked over toward us, a very charming smile spread across his smug face, resembling the Grinch when he patted Sally-Who on the head and scooted her back to bed. "You're so cute," he cooed as he bent over, hands on knees. He reached out and touched her cheek.

"Uh, she's one of the kids I baby-sit. This is Chrissy. Chrissy, this is Shaun, Steve's brother." Chrissy just sucked her finger and looked at him, then burrowed her head into my neck.

"What a pretty little girl," he said, and his hand moved from her cheek to her little knobby knee, like he was going to squeeze her chubby leg. She had on a cute little cotton white-and-blue-checked dress, and her little legs seemed vulnerable to his touch.

At that moment, Steve came bounding down the stairs, two at a time, and he stomped into the room, whisking Chrissy up and out of my arms. He stood there and glared at Shaun. Shaun cocked his head to the side with a sneer on his face, and they just stared at each other.

"Um, what's going on?" I said, standing up, confused.

"Never mind, let's go." Steve grabbed my hand, leading me out of the house.

As we drove away in his car, his expression was stony, and he kept his gaze hyper-focused out the window. His voice was tight but quiet when he said, "Stay away from Shaun. Don't ever let him near the kids you babysit. Okay?"

"Why? What's wrong?" I was holding Chrissy on my lap. I looked over at him, but he still wouldn't look at me. Eyes straight forward, jaw set.

"Just do what I tell you." He said it in a hard voice. Then, softening his tone, he added, "Please. Don't ask why."

I filed this away, for now. There was something wrong with Shaun, and this was just too creepy. Something was up.

That was it, that's all he would say about his brother. I couldn't imagine why he was so upset, but I quickly learned that talking about him was off-limits. I never brought Chrissy with me again to his house.

9 | CHURCH GIRL

"Sunday Girl," Blondie

When we lived in California, we didn't go to church on Sundays, and neither did my friends, except one. She was Catholic, which I experienced when I went to her confirmation when we were eight. But God was in our life, in some form or another. When I was very young, and we lived in Concord, Massachusetts, my dad was in the hospital for back surgery, and I prayed to God for his safe recovery. But other than that, Easter was our only formal audience with God. Even Christmas didn't seem like it had anything to do with religion. For me, God was this old man with a long white beard, sitting up in the clouds (which represented heaven to me), and he looked down on us, watching and listening to everything we were doing or thinking. Which kind of creeped me out. My only real education about him came from Hollywood and the children's books at the doctor's office. He seemed like Santa's more powerful brother. But a little less giving.

My dad was raised Catholic and my mom was Episcopalian. Somewhere along the way, between the military, West Point Academy, and education in engineering and science, my dad turned his back on the church. Actually, I think it was when the Catholic Church turned its back on him and wouldn't let him marry my mom in the church because she was a divorcee. I'm guessing that must have been it.

I actually didn't find out my mom had been married before until I was about ten. I was very upset when I found out that she had kept this huge secret from me. It was as if she had led this other life, one that didn't include us. I know it was unreasonable to be mad. She probably didn't think a little kid would understand. And at the time, I didn't. It's like she had betrayed my dad. Ridiculous, I know.

We moved to Virginia between fifth and sixth grade, and after we settled in, sometime around seventh grade, I started yearning for some kind of connection. I was looking for answers that I couldn't get at home.

When I was younger and still taking naps on occasion, I used to hear an angry voice in my head. It was when the room was dead silent. Suddenly this energy would fill the room, as if a little man were talking to me. I imagined him as a little green gremlin. I couldn't quite see him, and I could never make out any particular words exactly, but it was a low, fast, mumbling rant in a terrible gargling voice. It was the only time he would come out to me. I'd get so scared, I'd run down the hall to the kitchen where my mom and dad sat; I'd cry, trying to explain it. They didn't believe me and thought I was making it up because I didn't want to nap.

I knew for a fact there was something more out there in the world. Stuff that we couldn't really see in our daily lives, and I wondered, hoped, I could find the answer in church. Of course, that didn't happen. When I finally had my chance, I just couldn't bring myself to ask about the little man. I knew they would think I was a freak. Besides, I hadn't heard from him since I stopped napping. Maybe he'd stayed in California.

In seventh grade, I asked my mom to take me to church on Sundays. It didn't matter which one, what denomination, group, or whatever you called it: Presbyterian, Episcopalian, Catholic, or Baptist. I made her take me each weekend until I found the right one. My brother didn't go with us and neither did my dad. It was me and my mom. We did this for several months, until one day, my friend Moe invited me to her church.

Moe's church was Presbyterian. All that meant was that it wasn't super ritualistic like Catholic or Episcopalian. We didn't do the crossing thing. But you still took communion on Sundays. What was extra special, and ultimately the reason I chose to go with her and join the choir and fellowship, was that it meant I got to hang out with her every Wednesday after school. Every Wednesday, we would carpool to the church for choir practice, followed by fellowship meetings. That's where you sit around in a circle and talk about ideas, philosophies related to religion, or just school. Basically, life. Sometimes we played games and various activities. And because I'd joined the choir as well, I was now obligated to go to church every Sunday. Not just when I felt like it.

But honestly, church ended up being more of a social hangout, which distracted me from my quest. My original curiosity faded fast, which pretty much started with the first time Moe and I smoked pot before choir practice. We decided it would be the perfect opportunity, as we usually took a walk in the woods after we did our "homework." Later, when our carpool arrived, we'd try to climb into the backseat as if everything was normal, but we'd soon find ourselves slinking low into the seats, giggling our asses off while our fellow passengers raised knowing eyebrows at us.

And practice was ridiculous. I'm surprised our choir director didn't toss us out! If anyone knew how we raided the kitchen before choir started, savoring the sugar donuts meant for Sunday's after-service snacks, they'd probably have thrown us out.

Thankfully, the pot would wear off before fellowship began and Reverend P showed up. He would definitely not be amused. We were fourteen, in eighth grade, and we thought we were the coolest.

Reverend P was never amused with us. Especially after the time we were on one of our church retreats at Camp Glenkirk over Halloween and we decided to dress up as punks. I didn't think we were slutty, but I guess with our torn short dresses and dark eyeliner, we might have looked a bit that way. We got style ideas from shows like *Quincy* and magazines: heavy eye makeup, dog collars, ripped stockings, and short, tight dresses.

Nope. He didn't approve at all and promptly told us to put on pants. I was so outraged. I argued that girls on beaches wore less. Heck, even the girls in costume for our *Daniel and Friends* play wore less! Bikinis with *I Dream of Jeannie* see-through tulle over it? But he squashed my protests with a "do it or leave" order.

It wasn't lost on me how ironic it was that religion and getting high were connected: the greatest means of escape. Anything I could do to get out of the house and away from the yelling, the screaming, and the shadowed stench of fear that lurked in the walls of our house was an easy choice.

Soon after I started going, I decided I wanted to become a member and get baptized. Because of the confusion with my parents' experience, they just never got around to doing it for me or my brother. I started staying after on Sundays for Bible study. In the spring of my freshman year, I got baptized, and I became an official member of the church with my very own Bible and a certificate. I was so proud.

Peter, my friend from the ski trip, went to the same church Moe and I went to. Although he was in the same grade as my brother, two levels above us, he wasn't really a close friend of Joe's. When I first met him at a fellowship meeting, I completely fell for him. He was so cute, with this thick, dark, wavy hair and pale skin. He reminded me of some French character from the 1800s. I could just picture him in a white blouse with long billowy sleeves, open at the neck. But he didn't even notice me. I was all braces and bad perm. He was always nice though, and Moe knew him, so we all eventually started to hang out together during our free time at fellowship.

During one of these free times, when I was still crushing on him, we were all outside horsing around in the graveyard behind the church. It was a few of us, running around playing tag games, when all of a sudden, I found myself alone with Peter, and from out of nowhere he grabbed me and kissed me. I knew immediately by his expression that he was just teasing me, so I slapped him. He laughed and ran off. This just confirmed my suspicions: boys sucked. I don't think he really knew how much he broke my heart by not taking me seriously.

By freshman year, my crush was over, and he was busy drooling over Moe, but she was dating Bob the drug dealer by then. Instead, the three of us became tight friends.

Steve didn't like the way Peter always ran up and hugged me or tackled me. He was like a brother to me now, and we were always horsing around. It was just who he was, a very touchy-feely guy. But of course, Steve didn't like that. I just kept trying to tell him he had nothing to worry about. Peter and I were buddies. My crush on Peter, which I did not tell Steve about, was long ago crushed, and he was more like an overgrown Labrador puppy to me—albeit a gorgeous Labrador puppy. But as of a few months before, Moe and Peter had started dating, so there was nothing for anyone to worry about. That ship had long ago sailed. But Steve didn't need to know any of that.

It was still cold out, so I bundled up in layers, tired of the same down jacket I'd worn all winter. I wore two sweaters with my corduroy jacket, jeans, and a cute red knit hat. Sitting in the passenger seat of Steve's car, I babbled on and on about Joe and his friends. I tried to describe them, and explain Peter, and our relationship.

"We're all such good friends now, and Peter and Moe are finally together. He had a crush on her for-eve-r." I continued, "I used to like him but that died off a while ago." I laughed, then turned to look at him. "No really, it's totally cool. We're just good friends."

Shit, I thought, *I didn't mean to say that. I meant to keep that to myself.*

Even from his profile, I could tell I had made a mistake. His jaw had set into a firm lock. The muscles twitched.

"No, really, Steve, we're all just such good friends." I pulled my jacket down at the waist because it kept riding up, and uneasily looked away. "I can't wait to introduce you to the gang," I said, more with hope than conviction.

We turned into the supermarket parking lot and immediately I saw the group—the usual high school kids hanging at the outer edge of the lot, the very back corner. The supermarket was closed, but there were always some cars still parked there that belonged to the diners at the adjoining Pizza Hut. My brother, Peter, Lex (the pincher), and some other kids were all hanging around someone's opened hood, looking at the engine.

"Well, actually you met all of these guys on the ski trip. Well, almost all of them."

We pulled in right next to them, and, zipping my jacket all the way up, I got out. Peter looked up and saw me, and with a big grin, came running over and jumped on me, like he always did with that happy, friendly hug.

"Get the hell off her!" A shout came from behind me as Steve came around the car lightning fast and shoved Peter off me. "Don't touch her!" His voice had lowered to a nasty growl. "Ever." He looked twice his normal size. It was as if the anger had transformed him into this other person. His muscles seemed to strain in his neck.

Peter backed off. "It's cool, man." He looked at me, raised his eyebrows, and turned away with a shrug.

I opened the car door and got right back in, sitting there looking straight ahead. I was humiliated by his aggressive possessiveness, but at the same time, weirdly, I was kind of thrilled that he was jealous. It meant that he really did care for me a lot. He would even fight for me.

But I couldn't go out there. I didn't look up. I didn't see what he did or said. I just heard the murmur of voices.

I flinched when I heard a knock on the car door window. It was Joe, motioning me to roll the window down. Frowning, reluctantly, I put it down.

"You okay, sis?" he said. His straight brown feathered hair fell forward as he leaned over. All my friends wanted to go out with Joe at one time or another. He looked a lot like Richard Hatch, aka Captain Apollo from *Battlestar Galactica*. That's probably why I was more into Starbuck ... it would be way too creepy to crush on Apollo.

This was probably the first time Joe had been nice to me in ages. All we ever did was fight. But now, he looked concerned.

"Yeah, I'm good," I lied.

"Okay, cool." He stood up. "See you later," he said, and sauntered off.

Such brotherly love, I thought as I rolled the window up and waited for Steve to come back and get in the car.

10 | PLANS

"Messenger of Love," the Pretenders

My afternoons of sitting around on the couch watching black-and-white romance movies or soap operas, fantasizing about having a boyfriend who would sweep me off my feet, were a thing of the past. I finally had my own boyfriend, one who was literally strong enough to do just that.

I would laugh so hard when he picked me up and threw me over his shoulder. Mostly he was just trying to show me how strong he was; he really liked to show off his biceps. I didn't care about that, but I loved it when he picked me up and tossed me on the bed. I just had a hard time keeping a straight face, it sent me laughing uncontrollably. Thankfully he loved my laughter unless it was directed at him. Not that I ever did that. But he was sensitive to what he perceived as people laughing at him.

Overall, things were going okay with us. He wasn't too subtle about his jealousy and overreacted when he thought some guy was looking at me or paying any attention to me. But it didn't bother me too much. He paid it back by hugging me and kissing me, and well, just paying a lot of attention to me.

Even sex had gotten easier. It didn't hurt so much anymore, and he was being gentle ... or maybe I was just getting used to it. The only thing was, he liked to do it a lot, like, every time we were together. And more than once. Several times. Back-to-back. Sometimes I just didn't want to,

I just wanted to lay in his arms and talk, snuggle, or listen to music. But those were all things that led right back to sex.

My brother's prom—and consequently Peter's, and all of my friends who were seniors—was only a month away.

Moe was going with Peter and my brother was taking Marybeth. Yeah, that was a bit of a drama scene for a moment when she broke it off with Charles and then started dating my brother, especially because Charles and my brother were best friends. But the drama seemed to have died down. Unfortunately, now that she was dating my brother, I didn't see her so much. And double-dating was not an option—my brother and I did not get along.

In the fall, long before I met Steve, Joe's friend Scott invited me to go with him to the prom. We were just friends, so it wasn't a date. Although, I kind of suspected he liked me because he seemed super bummed out when he learned I was dating Steve. But, unlike most of my brother's friends, he didn't actually ask me out. Besides, I didn't see him like that, so I was relieved that he never asked. I didn't want to have to officially say no.

A lot of my friends who were sophomores like me were going with my friends who were seniors. It wasn't just that they didn't want me to feel left out. It was what we did. We hung out together, did things together, like when we all went to the Van Halen concert. I didn't see why dating Steve now had to change my plans. I had made a huge effort to continue to hang out with them and include Steve. But it was so uncomfortable. Steve was unpredictable. In the end, I thought it was better to separate these worlds.

I was still scared to tell Steve about the plan to go to the prom with Scott. I knew he would take it personally and get angry. But I wanted to go so bad that I decided to take the risk and tell him. I wasn't going to miss out on this.

"It's not like I'm going with Scott as a boyfriend!" I whined to Bambie over the phone. "And he knows it. I can't go with Steve. He's not a senior, and neither am I, and he doesn't even go to our school!" I was trying to convince myself there was nothing wrong with this plan. "I really want to go," I continued. "Both Moe and Marybeth are going, and my brother, and all his friends! I mean, we're all friends. Just because I'm dating Steve, I don't see why I have to change my plans." I sucked my breath in sharply.

"Okay, take a breath," she laughed. "And don't be silly, of course you don't have to change your plans. But what did he say about it when you told him? I can't imagine he'd be okay with it, considering the property tag you have around your neck." I could picture her sitting on the floor of her bedroom with the phone wedged between her head and shoulder, leaning over her toes, polishing them a deep shade of red.

Ignoring her comment, I said, "Well, he seemed hurt, and maybe a bit angry. But he seemed to understand after I explained how we'd planned this before we started dating. But it's actually kind of hard to tell how mad he is. He gets really quiet." I frowned. Bambie wasn't going; her boyfriend didn't even go to our school. And besides, prom wasn't her thing.

"Ooooh, oh, listen, I love this song!" Jumping up and down, I reached over and turned up the volume on my record player. Chrissie Hynde was singing that song about how it or "he" makes her wanna do it.

I was dancing around in my underwear with the phone cord wrapped around and tangled in my legs. "I feel kind of bad, but I don't understand why I shouldn't go, really. And he doesn't seem that upset." I hoped.

"So, go. *Fuck!*" she groaned.

"What?"

"I just smudged my polish."

I drove over to Moe's Wednesday after school, our usual routine before choir. Blasting "Messenger of Love" by the Pretenders, I pulled into her driveway, noting Peter's car parked next to her mom's. I could have gone around to the back, but you never tried to sneak anything past Mrs. H. Besides, I reminded myself, I was supposed to be here. This was officially church business. Moe and I no longer smoked pot. I had officially quit, so there was nothing to be sneaking around about, or be guilty about, for that matter.

"Hi Mrs. H, how are you?" I asked cheerfully as she opened the front door.

Mrs. H reminded me of those stereotypical housewives from the '60s with her simple buttoned-up cotton dresses and the tied sash around the waist. She was fairly tall—not as tall as me, but she stood straight and had a very strong presence. Her hair was short, red, and curly. She wore cat-eye glasses. Her skin was pale, which enhanced her freckles. She could be pretty darn scary at times, rivaling my father, but she was always nice to me. I just wanted to stay on her good side.

"Hello, Suzanne, it's nice to see you. How are you doing today?" She smiled, letting me in. "Is that another one of your famous creative endeavors? Maurine has been telling me all about it." Maurine was Moe's given name. Everyone called her Moe, except her mother.

Like I said, nothing got past Mrs. H. She was referring to my jean jacket with the ballet shoe and rose I'd painted on the front pocket. I had been painting band names, like The Outlaws, Lynard Skynard, and Van Halen on the backs of jean jackets for a small price since freshman year. For Moe, I had carefully painted the Grateful Dead on the back of her jacket with a red rose. I loved the way the rose looked, so I repeated it with a wood-burning tool onto my leather purse. It wasn't a band I listened to so I didn't understand the reference when the girl at the checkout counter at Dart Drug asked if I was a Dead Head. I just blankly looked at her and mumbled, "Mm-hm."

"Yes, it is." Smiling, I tried to maneuver past her so as not to give too much opportunity for questioning. "Moe and I have a lot of studying to do."

"Well, I don't see how much studying you'll get to with Peter down there," she said with a trace of sarcasm. I think Mrs. H knew a lot more about what we were up to than Moe wanted to admit. But if she did, she didn't let on.

"Oh ... right." I faked a frown. "Don't worry, he won't stay long." I headed to the door at the end of the entryway. Opening it, I said, "Thank you, Mrs. H."

I don't know why I said thank you. I just felt like I needed to say something. She didn't respond; she had already gone into the kitchen.

It sounded pretty quiet downstairs as I ran down the steps. *They're probably making out*, I thought. *I'm definitely knocking.*

Although I did knock, I only gave them two seconds before I burst open the door to see Peter scurrying off Moe. Mimicking her mom, I loudly burst out: "What are you two doing down here!?"

"Oh my god, Zanny, you scared the shit out of me," Peter choked out.

"Oh my god, what the heck?" Moe was less freaked out; instead, laughter filled her smile. "You're such a pain in the ass."

"Oh please." I bounced over and jumped on the bed, lying across Moe, who had now scooted up so she was sitting with her legs stretched out.

"Ouch, be careful of my feet," she said. She'd had some kind of foot surgery the previous fall, but seriously, they were way recovered by now.

"Seriously?" I looked at her with my eyebrow raised.

"Well, don't break them again." She picked up her mint lemonade off her bedside table and took a sip. "Peter and I were just planning prom."

"Oh really, is that what that was?" I grinned. "You plan with your lips locked?"

"Zanny, you wanna help us?" Peter jumped on the bed between us. "My lips can do double time."

"Ew, don't be gross." I shoved him closer to Moe.

"For real?" Moe frowned at him.

"So, what's the plan exactly?" I changed the subject.

Peter lay one leg across Moe and the other across mine.

"We're like a sandwich." He grinned.

"Yea, an egg salad sandwich," I teased.

"No, a meatball sandwich." Moe grinned.

"Hey, why is everyone being so mean to me?" Peter whined. "I'm a salami sandwich! Super tasty."

"You're gross," I said. "Seriously, what's the plan for the class of '82 prom? Are you two coming with me, my brother, Scott, and Marybeth to Dominic's?"

"No, Peter is taking me to—"

Right at that moment, someone knocked on the door and then opened it. In stepped Steve, leaving me no time to untangle myself from the ridiculous position we were in on Moe's bed.

"What the hell is going on in here?" Steve burst out, his face darkening.

"Nothing." I struggled to get up as fast as possible. "What do you mean?" I stammered.

"Dude, we're just planning the prom," Peter added as he moved his legs off me.

I turned to look at him with a glare, mouthing, "What the fuck?"

He shrugged, innocently.

I stood up and started over to Steve, but he walked over and shoved me to the side with one arm, not even looking at me.

Meanwhile, Peter and Moe had also climbed out of bed and were now standing next to it.

"Dude, relax," Peter ventured. "It's all good."

"'Dude'?" Steve grabbed Peter by the collar of his shirt, pulling him in close, leaning his face in. "Do not fucking call me 'dude'!"

I couldn't believe he'd said that. What was he doing? His face was turning purple, and the veins were bulging on his neck.

"Steve, please stop it, let go of Peter." I reached to grab his arm. Peter started giggling, to my horror. It was a reaction he had when he felt uncomfortable. Although it could also have been a reaction to the ridiculousness of Steve's behavior.

But this just pissed Steve off even more because he went for his throat.

Peter's eyes raised in disbelief, and Moe shrieked.

"Stop it right now, Steve!" I yelled.

He dropped his hand from Peter's neck and turned to me. "We're leaving now."

"No, I am not," I said, standing my ground. "You're leaving. I'm staying. Peter will leave too, but I'm staying."

He raised his eyebrow at me, and for a minute I thought he was going to challenge me, but instead he turned back to Peter, who by now had backed up, with a more serious expression, the laughter gone.

"Don't ever touch my girlfriend again," he said in a controlled, quieter voice. "Do you understand?"

"Yeah, dude. I do," he said in disbelief, looking over at me and giving me a sad look.

"What's going on here?" said Mrs. H, who had appeared at the door. She looked irritated more than anything else. "I thought I heard shouting."

"Nothing, Mom, it's fine. Actually, both Steve and Peter are leaving." Moe grabbed Peter's hand and led him out, passing Mrs. H.

Steve looked at me and said, "We'll talk later about this."

"There is nothing to talk about," I said defiantly.

"Oh yes there is." He turned and walked past Mrs. H, who looked from me to him with a raised eyebrow. I thought she was going to say something to me, but she just sighed, turned, and followed him out.

I turned around and flopped flat on Moe's bed with my head buried in her covers. There were no tears to be shed; I was too stunned. The jealousy had to stop. It was flattering, but it was humiliating. Maybe he would just stop after a while when he realized I didn't want anyone else.

I didn't know what Steve was going to say or do later when I saw him the next night. But oddly, when I did, he didn't say anything. He was quieter than normal. But I could see that he was holding something back.

"That was fucking crazy," Moe said when she came back into the room and lay down next to me. "He must be really crazy about you to act like that." But her eyes betrayed what she was really thinking: *Fucking psychopath.*

"Ugh," I groaned, pressing my face deeper into the covers.

"Come on, stop it. We have some planning to do." Cheerfully, she poked me where she knew I was ticklish. "Come on, sit up."

I relented to Moe's persuasive maneuvers, and we continued with our plans. While we were not going to go to dinner with them, they would meet us after, on the way to the actual event.

"This is going to be a night to remember!"

11 | PROMISES

"Hold Me," Fleetwood Mac

My mom had a closet full of formal gowns and cocktail dresses she'd collected over the years for events that she and my dad went to. Working at Hughes Aircraft meant entertaining or being entertained. I had always loved dressing up in her outfits, although I never had a chance to wear them out. Except in sixth grade, I did wear her polyester purple-and-white-striped suit to school. It had the widest and pointiest lapels ever, with flared hems. I knew people thought I was a freak, but dressing up or down was my way of expressing my mood, and I'd been doing that since I started dressing myself as a kid. My style was forever changing, day to day.

This wasn't my prom, and I wasn't going with my boyfriend, so I didn't want to buy anything new. I dug deep into her closet and chose a long silky and stretchy bright green halter top dress. It tied around my neck, leaving the back bare. It was cut kind of low, but not too bad. It hugged my body yet was loose enough to flow around me, brushing the floor when I spun in a circle. I was with my mom when she bought this dress when we still lived in California. It was probably from 1976. Six years old.

I left my hair down; it was nice and wavy from sleeping in little braids that I had woven the night before. I liked the new punk shag I had, but as my hair started to grow out, Steve kept saying he liked it when I curled it, so I was trying that out.

Standing there looking in the mirror, I was reminded of the image of Olivia Newton-John on her first album cover and the song "Have You Never Been Mellow." It came to me in a soft whisper. Squinting my eyes, I imagined the sun glowing from behind me. A gently focused lens. Suddenly, I had an idea.

I turned around and started rummaging through my closet, and after some digging, I found what I was looking for: my Renaissance Faire wreath I picked up back in California. I think I was maybe ten years old when I got it.

I placed it carefully on my head. With my dark blond waves and the wreath pushed back a little, the ribbons cascading down my back, I looked very ... pre-Raphaelite. *Hmmm. Cute*, I thought.

"You look beautiful."

Startled, I turned to my mom, who had been watching me from my door with a look of nostalgia, like a weeping willow, beautiful yet somehow at a loss. She was so beautiful herself. Sure, now she was heavier, which on her short frame made the extra pounds look like more than they were, but when she was younger—even a couple of years before, in California—she was a bronze tennis goddess. Strong and tan with a killer smile. All dimples, with her brunette hair. Well, sometimes it was blond.

"Thanks, Mom." I smiled at her. "It's not my prom, so I can have fun with my look."

"What does Steve think of you going with Scott?" She walked over and sat at the edge of my bed. "I can't imagine he's happy with it." Her brows knit together as she fiddled with the bedspread.

"It's fine." My voice sounded a bit off-pitch—too loud. "No really, he's fine about it." She didn't look convinced. "Mom, he's fine, trust me. He acts all protective and tough, but he's very understanding." I said this more to convince myself than for her.

"Come on," she said, standing up and brushing my hair behind my ear. "Your brother's waiting downstairs." I quickly pushed my hair back over my ear and we headed downstairs.

As Joe and I started out the front door, my dad appeared from the study and handed Joe fifty dollars for the evening.

"Have a good time." He smiled and raised an eyebrow, which seemed to say, "Don't get into any trouble."

We both said "thanks" at the same time, confused by this rare show of generosity. He held the door open for us, and we walked down the path toward Joe's blue van, glancing back and waving bye.

My dad didn't easily give up money. Trying to get money out of him was like pulling teeth. Even though he yelled and screamed, he had these moments of silly and small bits of generosity. But I hadn't seen it in a long time.

"Wow, Joe, that's a first," I said as I climbed up into the passenger seat. We headed down our driveway toward Marybeth's house.

"Yeah, that must have been really hard." Sarcasm dripped from him, like sour milk.

Scott was going to meet us at Marybeth's place, where her parents planned to take photos of us all before we left.

When Scott walked in, he stopped short and looked at me. "Wow, you look great."

"Thank you, Scott," I said, mock batting my eyelashes.

Marybeth's parents gathered us together and took a few photos before we all piled into her father's white Cadillac, which he had lent us. With Joe at the wheel, we headed off.

Joe pulled off the road once we left the neighborhood. Scott cracked open a bottle of champagne that he pulled from behind the seat and began to pour it into little plastic cups, handing us each one.

I sipped my drink nervously as I looked out the window while they laughed and talked—sounds I didn't hear because I was lost in my own thoughts.

I had called Steve before I left our house, just to say good night, and to tell him I would come by tomorrow afternoon. I was still trying to show him there was nothing to worry about, that he was first and foremost on my mind.

He sounded suspicious, though he asked, "Why don't you drive here in the morning?"

"Well ..." I wasn't sure what to say. And I was still tiptoeing around the unspoken episode that had happened with Peter.

The plan was to go to Moe's house in the morning for brunch. I didn't feel comfortable telling him that. I was sure he would get angry and it would hurt his feelings that I hadn't included him. But he wasn't going to the prom with us, and I knew that would make Scott feel awkward.

No one ever said anything directly, but I just had this feeling my friends didn't like him. Maybe it was because he stood in front of me when there were guys around. Or because he never wanted to hang out with anybody. Oh, and he always shook hands really hard, making my friends grimace.

He was always bear-hugging Joe, who I could tell didn't like it. He'd tell him to get off him, but never in an angry way. Joe seemed careful around him.

"Well," I said cheerfully, trying not to make a big deal out of it. "I'm going over to Moe's house in the morning for breakfast, so I'll just drive over after."

I figured if I didn't say anything more, I wouldn't need to lie. I didn't want to lie. But I was scared to tell the truth. Completely.

"Okay," he said in a quiet voice, which made me nervous. I knew he was holding back. But I didn't ask. Hopefully, it was just my imagination and living with my dad too long.

That night we had so much fun. I think because Scott wasn't really my date, I was able to just be as silly as I wanted. And for the first time in a long time, my brother and I got along. We went to Dominic's in Georgetown before we headed to the prom. A very fancy, upscale French restaurant. At the very end, the waiter brought out a huge Baked Alaska Pie that was on fire! When we were getting ready to pay the bill, the waiter said it was taken care of: my dad had called and paid for the meal ahead of time.

Prom itself turned out to be a bore because the prom "guards" wouldn't let us bring our photography teacher inside. His name was Keith—we were on a first-name basis with him—and he was super cool, lots of fun, and wasn't just our teacher, he was friends with a few of the seniors, including my brother. He was dressed in a white tux, but with his long blond hair and mustache, he didn't pass as a student. Sneaking him in wasn't an option.

Instead, we all drove back to D.C. and this time headed to the 9:30 Club, a punk club where live bands played. We were very self-conscious and uneasy about going in wearing tuxedos and long dresses, but Keith urged us on. When we walked in the door, instead of sneers, people told us we looked cool. I think our dresses looked pretty "retro" so they ended up looking cool. There were a lot of laughs as we explained that we'd ditched our prom.

The evening couldn't have been better. I just hoped when I went to my prom in two years it would be just as great.

I climbed out of bed the next morning with a foggy head and slight headache, stumbling to the shower to get ready and head over to Moe's. I didn't want to miss anything. Last night was so much fun, and my memory was a bit fuzzy on what we did, so I couldn't wait to reunite with the gang and find out more about it.

I dressed quickly, throwing my yellow sweatshirt over my jeans, my hair all flat now, and headed over to Moe's. The whole crowd from the night before was there, already sitting around the table, looking the worse for wear. Marybeth and my brother were there; boy did he look bad. Doug and the redhead were there too; somehow, she still looked perky and fresh. Charles and his date Nancy, and of course Peter and Moe. And Scott was there too. He gave me a kind of sheepish look. Not sure what that was, I just smiled nicely and sat down at the other end of the table.

Wow, pretty much everyone looked tired, or like they were barely holding on to their insides. My headache seemed mild in comparison. Way too much drinking the night before!

Mrs. H could really entertain. The dining room was set up all fancy for us with a whole spread of yummy food: eggs, bacon, waffles, and toast. And I was starved. She even made us coffee.

"So, what happened last night, after you dropped me off at home?" I stood up to load my plate with some delicious food, looking over at Moe. She put her finger up to her lips and nodded her head toward the kitchen, mouthing silently, "She can hear everything. I'll tell you later."

At that moment, as I started loading up my plate, the doorbell rang.

Mrs. H went to answer it. *I guess one of Moe's friends is late*, I thought and turned around to see who it was. Standing there as if it were perfectly normal and as if he'd been invited was Steve. I almost dropped my plate. I felt the color drain from my face.

No, no, no, I thought. This wasn't right. This wasn't normal. It was awful, so awkward. My mouth must have fallen open as he looked at me and smiled. I knew that smile. It was just temporary. It was a secret message that only I understood.

I sputtered, "Whaa— um ... hi!" Ugh. *Great*.

"Mrs. H, this is Steve, my boyfriend." I recovered as I introduced him. I didn't know what else to say.

"Yes, we've met before, honey," she said. My face flushed red in the memory of that day, only a month before. I could see the disapproval on her face. It was more than disapproval. It was a look of concern. But she turned and went back into the kitchen, while Steve just walked right past me into the dining room where everyone was hanging out. He didn't even wait for me.

The rest of the brunch went by in a fog, or most of it. I felt terrified inside but acted like everything was normal. I remember some conversation, laughing, but it felt forced. I watched Steve from the corner of my eye, joking with everyone. I studied him. He wasn't the like the others. The way he talked, it was like he thought he was better than everyone else: smarter, just because he was older. Like he knew something they didn't. He was so much bigger than everyone else, too. Not just taller—my brother, Scott, and Charles were just as tall. But he was so muscular that it made him seem bigger than life.

He didn't let me out of his sight. When he sat down, he grabbed my hand and pulled me onto his lap, like a little girl. And I felt like a little girl by the way he looked at me, and the way he held me in his lap. It was so embarrassing. I bowed my head, feeling little inside as I withdrew deeper into myself.

When I ventured to look up, nobody was paying attention. Maybe they didn't see my discomfort. Maybe they thought it was normal. I mean, maybe it was.

If I was being honest with myself, I knew deep inside that I had blown him off. I'd gone without him. He was hurt. And he was upset. This was all my fault. I should never have gone.

I can't remember when we left. I just remember driving to his house, following behind him in my car. And the next thing we were doing was sitting in his room, and that's when it happened.

I didn't know what I expected. But I didn't expect what he said next.

"This is all Moe's fault," he said in a very even voice.

"What?" I didn't know what he was talking about.

"She's the one that told you to go to the prom with Scott. She organized it so you wouldn't be with me. She didn't even want me to come to her house for brunch."

"What are you talking about? That's not it. She likes you."

"So, you're saying you chose to be without me? You chose Scott over me?"

"No, that's not what I'm saying. I didn't choose anything. I told you, if I didn't go with him, I couldn't go to the prom with them. And I really wanted to go with my friends."

"So, you would rather be at the prom with your friends than be with me? You like your friends better than me?!" Now his voice was different. He wasn't yelling ... but he was angry and upset. And there was a threat in his tone.

"No. I don't like my friends better than you, I just really wanted to go. It wasn't about you. I ... I would have taken you if I could, but it's not my prom." I tried to make him feel better. I was wracking my brain to figure something out to make this all stop.

"Then it's her fault. I know that she talked you into it," he began again, his voice menacing. "I saw you all. You were conspiring, and more. She ... and her, her boyfriend, they have you wrapped around their little finger."

I didn't know what to say, and he was looking at me with so much anger. This was not the same guy I knew. I was scared he was about to break up with me. I just couldn't bear it, going back to the way it was before. Alone. Nothing to do. No one to hold me. No one to love me.

"If you want to keep me as your boyfriend, then you have to stop being her friend."

"What?" *Huh?* My mouth fell open in disbelief. I searched his face, his eyes, to see if he was serious. But I could tell. He never joked like this. "You're kidding, right?" I tried.

"I'm serious. Choose." And with that, he stood up. "Go home and think about it. Call me tomorrow and tell me your choice. It's me or her." And he walked out of the door and crossed the hall to the bathroom.

I sat there for a minute. Stunned. He was serious. Very serious.

I bolted out of the room, almost tripping down the stairs as I ran to my car and drove home with a mask of shock and tears. *What am I gonna do? What am I gonna do?* was all I could think.

When he called me the next day, I still wasn't sure what I was going to do. But I knew what I couldn't do.

The phone rang, and quietly, I answered. "Hello?"

"Did you make up your mind?"

"Are you being serious?" I said with quiet tears running down my face, my voice shaky.

"Yes, I'm very serious. It's either me or her."

I knew right then there was no way I could change his mind. He was serious. He meant everything he said.

"Okay."

"Okay, what?"

"Okay, I'll end my friendship with her."

"Then call her and tell her. And then call me back." He hung up the phone.

I did call her that day. I don't know what I said. I don't think I was even able to explain it. But I begged her to understand. *He had changed my life. He was the only boy that had ever noticed me. He wanted to protect me. He would take care of me. He was my escape. He was just really hurt, and this was the only way I could make amends. It won't be forever. He'll change his mind. He just needs me to show how much I care about him.*

"It isn't like we still can't be friends," I reasoned. "We can talk on the phone; we can see each other at school—he doesn't need to know that—but we just can't see each other outside of school, except church of course. We can still see each other at church."

I really wouldn't have been surprised if Moe never wanted to talk to me again. But she just quietly listened. I knew what she thought. I could tell she thought I was weak, that he was an ass and that I was desperate. Pathetic. She didn't need to say that out loud. She accepted what I said, and then we hung up.

Was I making a mistake? What choice did I have? I didn't want to choose between them. *But what choice did I have?*

I couldn't lose him.

12 | AFTER SHOCKS

"You Got Lucky," Tom Petty and the Heartbreakers

It was becoming more and more challenging to go to fellowship and choir, which seems absolutely crazy. I mean, how could he be jealous of church!? But the late-night Wednesday choir practice followed by fellowship and hanging around with Moe and Peter was pissing him off.

Over Easter, I'd invited him to come to church with me. I knew church wasn't really his thing, but I'd wanted to share all my world with him. I was so excited when he said yes. He looked very handsome all dressed up in a suit. I wore my lightly patterned blue cotton cowgirl dress with a neckline full of ruffles that came up under my chin. Just like a cowboy shirt, it had ruffles on either side of the neck that went down into a V at my waist, with buttons on one side. I wore a cute leather belt around the waist that had a silver saddle buckle, which paired perfectly with my cowboy boots. The sleeves were puffy at the shoulder and long, with more ruffles at the wrist. The skirt was full, with a larger ruffle on the bottom. My hair was honey blond and feathered. The whole look said *sexy cowgirl with a dash of innocence.*

My mom had come, and Moe had too. But that was all before prom. Now it was different. But the pictures came out great, showing a handsome, happy couple.

Now I just tried not to talk about church. I spent so many afternoons at ballet and jazz, I hoped he'd forget where I was heading.

But the stress was getting to me. I couldn't hang out with Moe anymore before church group, so Wednesday's fellowship and choir were nearly impossible unless I drove by myself, which I did at first. But I knew I needed to let something go. *Besides*, I told myself, *my voice sucks*.

A lot of our friends—the seniors—were moving on. They wouldn't be in choir or attending fellowship. Probably even church, except on holidays. So, it wasn't like I would be missed. No one would even notice I wasn't there.

But it was one more thing I felt bad about telling Moe. I could tell she was disappointed. Maybe even worried about me. That's probably the only reason she didn't completely hate me.

I still went to church on Sundays, but I stopped singing in the choir and going to fellowship. Eventually, I stopped even listening to Reverend P's words. I mean, I listened, but they didn't register. His words just went into one ear and out the other. I felt like I was living in a Charlie Brown world. It was as if he was speaking a different language. The connection was lost, and I felt like an imposter.

I felt left out when they talked about the trips they were planning, which I knew I wouldn't be able to go on. All those weekends at Camp Glenkirk and the trips down south touring while performing the church musical. They were epic. When we put on *Daniel and Friends*, we drove all the way to North Carolina. We stopped on the way down, performing at other churches, then we'd pair up and spend the night with some family willing to host us. Moe and I were always together.

Everyone seemed to enjoy our performances, except maybe this one Southern Baptist church. The looks on their faces when they took us in, little white kids singing on their stage dressed in Babylonian costumes … well, I'm not sure they liked us or our singing. But they were super nice to us afterward at their potluck dinner.

The next morning when we were treated to their soulful and joyous singing voices during the church sermon, I guessed it wasn't us so much as our singing that had raised an eyebrow. We were just a bit amateurish in comparison.

I sat in the doctor's office in shock with tears running down my cheeks. Steve just sat there in the chair looking pissed off, as if I was responsible.

"So, it's herpes," the doctor continued with her slight Southern accent as she slid Steve a dirty look. "And it's transmitted during sex." She was probably in her early thirties. Her curly blond hair and thin, wire-framed glasses gave her the look of a frazzled scientist, but the warmth in her voice put me at ease.

"But I've only had sex with you," I said, turning to Steve.

"Well, I don't have it. So you didn't get it from me," he growled.

"It's not uncommon. It's easily transmitted, and more and more people have it. And"—she turned to him, her left eyebrow raised—"quite often you don't even know you have it, especially men. You can transmit it easily."

I had been in pain for the last two days and had no idea what this was. Unbearable burning pain. It felt like I was on fire. Finally, when I said I couldn't have sex because it was so painful, Steve took me to the clinic. Now he looked at me as if I had lied. He questioned my virginity! I was mortified.

She turned to me with pity and worry written all over her expression, continuing, "And then you can expect the occasional outbreak. Don't worry, just use the cream. It will go away in a few days to a week. Just use the cream two to three times a day, or as needed." She handed me a package and glared at Steve again as we walked out of the office.

Over the next week, Steve would call to check in on me to see if I was doing better. I said we could go to a movie, but I wasn't completely healed. He said he was busy right up until the first time I said I was all better. The first thing he did was take me back to his place.

Long rays of sunshine warmed my body as I lay stretched across the floor of our family room reading "The Portrait of a Lady." Saturdays were glorious, especially when my dad wasn't around. No chores! I just loved to lie in the sun and read.

The sound of the doorbell roused me from my fictional world, and I twisted around and bounced up to get it. I knew it was Steve, but he was a little bit early. My mother was home in the kitchen, baking, and thankfully my dad was still away on a business trip. He knew I had a boyfriend, but my plan to keep them apart was working.

Still lost in the fictional world of Henry James, I skated on the tiles in my socks, pretending to be a graceful dancer, with a smile and excitement to see my mysterious lover—my Lord Warburton.

As I opened the door, barely responding to my smile, Steve grabbed me by the arm and steered me directly into the bathroom that was to the left of the front door. He sat me down on the toilet—on top of the closed lid—and unzipped his pants.

I could hear the clanking of dishes in the next room, running water, as my mom cleaned up in the kitchen all while tears streamed down my cheeks. But he was oblivious. My discomfort, the noises of the other room—none of it interrupted him. Not even a little. And as abruptly as it began, it ended.

13 | FATHER'S LITTLE GIRL

"Eye in the Sky," The Alan Parsons Project

This is really no surprise, but Steve and my dad hated each other from the start. Steve wasn't scared of my dad. He stood up to him. I loved that because I was the only one who had stood up to my dad: talking back to him, not showing him fear. I was the "belligerent one," as he liked to call me. Everyone else was scared of him, but not Steve. He wasn't even fazed by his dark scowl and his intimidatingly large, flared nostrils. On occasion my mom's stubbornness would fuel resistance. But it didn't happen enough.

When Tony, my brother's friend, asked me out in eighth grade, he asked my dad, not me. Even with that courtesy, my dad said absolutely "no way." Right there in our garage, he actually asked my dad, to his face! He didn't even try to sneak out with me. Instead, he thought if he approached Dad with courtesy, with old-school respect, and asked him, he would say yes. But no, my dad refused, telling him I was too young to go out with him and he'd have to wait till next year when I was a freshman in high school.

I was livid. I stomped after my dad and confronted him in the backyard while poor Tony sulked in the garage.

"How could you say no! I'm old enough to date, Dad," I demanded. "All of my friends are dating!"

"You're too young," he barked back at me, while at the same time poking me in the shoulder. "Stand up straight, like a soldier. You have terrible posture."

"What?" I flushed with anger. "What are you talking about?" I took in a big breath, then said, "I'm a lady. I stand with my chin up and shoulders back ... *if I choose!*" I shouted. "I'm not a soldier."

What was he doing yelling at me about my posture when I was trying to make a point about being old enough to go out on a date!

He's so fucking crazy, I thought.

"Ugh!" I said in frustration, stomping my feet hard on the ground; I turned around and stormed off to my room.

He didn't budge one bit and called me a belligerent daughter. I know I mentioned this before, but it's worth repeating. He made me wait a whole year before I could go out with that boy! But by the time I was allowed, I wasn't interested in him anymore. I mean, it wasn't the point of the who. It was the point of the when.

Sure, I had a few "kissing" experiences without dear old dad's permission—in the end, I just had to go behind his back. Eventually, I did go on a couple of dates with my brother's friends at the beginning of my freshman year: sweaty palms, long silent drives, shy awkward conversations, and cigarette-breath kisses filled with braces. They weren't so bad, it's just, no one asked me out a second time. Except Tony. But I'm sorry, crushes die out.

Steve was my first everything. And he was someone who wouldn't back down from my dad. Who wouldn't be intimidated by my dad?

My dad was hardly ever around anymore, and when he was, he was yelling at us, slamming doors, and being nasty to my mom.

One day, I was sitting at the desk in the kitchen working on my homework, and I could hear him out in the garage, cursing at my mom. A steady stream of nasty: "fuck, bitch, cunt ..." She was in the kitchen with me, nowhere near the garage. And she was quiet as a mouse. She would wait like me, to see if it would teeter off. Go away.

The door slams, and the volume of his rage increases. The walls around me feel like they're closing in. The sun goes from bright to dark, as heavy clouds descend around me. The curses are now unrecognizable as he comes in and sees my mom, who's sitting behind me at the kitchen table. Hateful, ugly words vomit out in her direction. But she, stubborn and proud as she is, rises to meet his challenge.

I can feel it—they're standing behind me and screaming at each other. I can't figure out why he's so mad at her. None of it makes sense. I'm missing something. How can he be so angry?

Wait, he's looking for something, something misplaced, broken, not finished. I don't even know.

She says something I can't quite make out. Something about him losing his memory, or eyesight.

"You fucking bitch, I ought to shove a broomstick up your cunt."

I put my fingers in my ears and placed my head down on my homework and imagine being back in California with the sun shining on my face, playing in the canyons, listening to the rustle of the wind through the leaves of the trees.

Now that I was with Steve, I could avoid my dad ... most of the time. I usually left to meet Steve somewhere else or just drove to his house. I avoided having him near my house when my dad was around. It was a carefully organized plan centered around "the two paths shall never cross."

But that day, when I went downstairs, prepared to meet him in the driveway as he insisted on picking me up, there Steve was—waiting for me in the front hallway.

I hadn't expected my dad to be home so early. It was rare.

As I walked up to him, my dad came out of his office.

Shit. I had hoped we could sneak out before he realized Steve was there.

His eyes darted to Steve standing in the hall, his whole body got all rigid, and he strode right up to him.

"I don't like you seeing my daughter," he said in his angry, military-dad voice. They were eye to eye. I just retreated into the background, resigned to the fact that this would be the last time I saw Steve.

But Steve stood up really tall, like he wasn't scared of anything, and retorted, "As long as your daughter wants to see me, you can't keep me away from her. You can't tell me what to do, and you can't keep her from doing what she wants to do."

Oh my god, I couldn't believe he said that to my dad. I was thrilled—absolutely thrilled! He would fight for me!

Red-faced, my dad seemed stumped, and sputtered, "But I can forbid you to be in my house."

"Dad! Don't." I grabbed Steve's hand and steered him out the front door. I looked back at my dad, throwing him a defiant look.

I could stand up to him, and so could Steve! He couldn't tell me who I could or couldn't see any longer! I wouldn't let him tell me what to do ever again!

So what if Steve couldn't come to my house? I could go to his.

And I did. I spent more and more time at Steve's house. I even started to sneak out and spend the night there, only to come back the next morning, very early, and pretend I was just up early to get to class on time.

That night, after the encounter with my dad, I lay in Steve's arms and he whispered in my ear, "I love you."

14 | LOST LITTLE GIRL
"Mad World," Tears for Fears

Steve started showing up at school out of the blue, a lot. Not just after school, but right in the middle of the day. It started soon after prom. He'd find me outside by the smoking lounge hanging out with my friends. Maybe he thought he'd catch me smoking. But I didn't smoke. I mean, sure, sometimes I had a cigarette with a friend, but I didn't "smoke."

At first, I was flattered when he showed up, and excited; I liked showing him off. My handsome, mature boyfriend, with this amazing body. But it began to make me nervous, his hostility to any guy that would approach me. But what I really disliked was how friendly he was to girls. Pointing out how nice they looked. But then if I dressed the way they did or wore the same lipstick, he'd make me wipe it off.

I quickly figured out he was there to let everyone know that I was his property. I also suspected he wanted to catch me hanging around Moe, or even Marybeth. Even Marybeth was getting the "treatment." Especially anyone from prom, except my brother.

One day when he showed up, we sat on the edge of a windowsill, behind the entrance to the stairs, so it was kind of out of eyeshot from the halls. It was me, Steve, my classmate Karen, and her boyfriend, Dan. Steve was telling some joke—I wasn't really paying attention—his hand on my leg, when Dr. M, the principal, came around the corner.

"Get your hand off her leg." He was a big, imposing man himself—not one to back down from anyone. I pictured him in the military, not as a principal of our high school. "I don't allow that kind of thing here in my school," he said in his deep, authoritarian voice.

He figured out right away that Steve wasn't a high school student. I guess it was kind of obvious. He did look way older. Definitely too old to be in high school. But he probably looked too old even when he was in high school.

Steve didn't move his hand, just glared back at him.

Uh-oh, I thought.

This just made Dr. M angrier. "You're not a student here, and I don't believe you have permission to be here." His face was burnt red, his eyes bugged out, and the veins bulged in his neck. He then ordered Steve to get off the school grounds immediately and told him not to show up again.

My face turned a furious shade of red, and I quickly disappeared into the bathroom and hid for the whole next period, skipping PE. Probably not the best idea, because I was already failing it.

I always disliked Dr. M, but this was too much even for me. I was completely ashamed and embarrassed. My idea of getting through high school was to go unnoticed. I'd already fucked that up last year, taking credit for my then "friend" Cindy, who had stolen a down jacket (which turned out to be the coach's) off the fence during the first and last Friday-night football game I attended. It's a long story, but let's just say, I got detention for that, even though it was finally revealed that I didn't steal the jacket.

Even though I was mad at Dr. M for making a scene, I was relieved Steve was forbidden to come to school. He'd gone too far this time. I was confused by his behavior—not just the possessiveness, but his aggressiveness toward others. What I'd perceived as romantic before—this chivalrous knight—had somehow turned into an ugly, overpowering possessiveness. But I didn't want to push him away by telling him this. I mean, I'd rather have that than no attention.

I know my friends thought I was crazy, or maybe brainwashed, because even with all that, I told them he made me feel special. I knew his behavior, his actions, were his way of showing me how deeply he wanted me. All of the other stuff, the jealousies and bullishness, were just more proof that he loved me beyond everything. I would pay almost any price that he asked of me because he filled this emptiness that had engulfed me for so long. I needed to fill that dark, unknown void. The space between here and there that seemed so dark—he filled that. I couldn't be alone again. He saved me from the chaos at home, and he, well, he just made me feel safe and stable.

Living way out in the woods where we did with no friends nearby, with my parents arguing and fighting daily, I felt alone most of the time. Everyone was wrapped up in their own relationships now. Julie was no longer around—my one friend in the "neighborhood." I mean, who calls living in the woods high up on a hill with a fifteen-minute walk through the woods to your friend's house a neighborhood?

I couldn't talk about any of this to anyone. I didn't want to talk to my friends about my feelings, my true feeling about Steve. Even Bambie. They wouldn't understand anyway. Hell, I didn't even understand. He made me happy; he made me sad. He filled me up, he drained me. But without him, I had nothing.

And more and more, all I had was Steve. The more he pushed my friends away, the more room he took up. And I was feeling more and more desperate to keep him, so I wouldn't be completely alone again.

But I had to start admitting it to myself: I didn't like everything he did, and I didn't know how to make it stop.

15 | THE BIG BAD WOLF

"Playground Twist," Siouxsie and the Banshees

I loved playing video games at the arcade with Steve, especially Tetris and Frogger, and he loved Tempest. Most Friday nights, that's where we ended up.

"Mom," I yelled up the stairs, "Steve's here." Looking out the window, I could see the headlights of his car as he drove up our steep, winding road. "I'm leaving ... I'll be back later." Thankfully, my dad was out of town, so I could stay out as late as I wanted; my mom wouldn't say anything about it, so Steve could come over to get me without worry.

Not that she *could* say anything about it. She seemed happy for me. Sometimes, she expressed worry that I spent all my time with him. But at the same time, even if she didn't like him, I didn't care. She couldn't make me stop seeing him. And she wouldn't dare tell my dad because he would get just as angry at her for letting me go off with him, as he would be angry with me for seeing him. No one was going to be able to stop me from seeing Steve. Definitely not my mother.

"Okay," she yelled back down, "have fun."

As I ran toward the front door, I made a quick stop in the bathroom to check myself in the mirror. I wanted to make sure my hair looked just right and touched up my lip gloss too. "Cute," I said, talking to no one but myself, and pulled my sweater down. It was a fuzzy white thing. Sort of half angora and half synthetic, although it was a bit itchy and made my cheeks red. The jeans were nice and tight—my new Jordache Jeans that I'd saved up for last summer. They were so tight and dark blue that the summer heat and humidity made my legs turn blue when I wore them the first time. It didn't occur to me to wash them first.

"Hmm." I smacked my lips together and blew a kiss at myself in the mirror. *I'm sure Steve will think I look sexy* I thought to myself, as I gave myself one last check.

I could hear him walking up the steps, so I hurried and grabbed my purse and darted out the front door before he rang the bell.

"Hey," I said, as I ran up to him and hugged him.

"Hey yourself." He leaned down, gave me a kiss on the forehead, and grabbed my hand. As he led me to the car, I noticed his eyes slide down my body, lingering on my jeans. He raised his eyebrow and an expression passed over his face that I couldn't read. He courteously opened the door, and I scooted in.

Usually, we would go to Time Out at the mall. They had a great selection of games, but tonight he took me to a different place. There weren't as many kids and it was super dark—just the bright lights from the video games and pinball machines.

After we picked up some soda at the counter, we scouted out some games. Luckily there was a pinball machine right next to the game Steve wanted to play. He didn't like leaving me alone, which I appreciated because most of the guys there seemed a bit on the creepy side.

I pulled the little lever out and released it as I leaned over the dazzling lights and images of mermaids and pirates. It was mesmerizing. I watched the ball ricochet from one lever to the other, making a racket of noise. I was lost in the game when I heard Steve's voice, threatening and angry: "What are you looking at, buddy?"

I turned around and there was this guy who looked scared as shit, face red and sputtering, "Nothing, man, I'm just waiting for a turn."

Steve seemed to get larger by the minute. His already massive chest seemed to puff up even more as he stepped in front of me and the guy and blocked him from my view.

My notion of how romantic his jealousy was had turned to embarrassment in a heartbeat, but also fear. I never knew if he would do something more. Like, how far he would take it?

Mortified and angry, all I could come up with was: "Steve!"

This, I thought, *is just too much*. I picked up my purse and walked around him to the door. He caught up to me fast and grabbed my arm and put it through his and directed me out, as if this was his intention all along. I knew better than to say anything. My dad had given me a lot of training on dealing with unreasonable people who overreacted to small things.

"Why the hell did you pick those pants?" he growled. "You need a good spanking."

I looked up at him to see if he was serious or joking. The look that I saw was neither.

In the beginning, there were only a few times that Steve and I had what he liked to refer to as "high school sex," and because he was five years older than me, I believed that's what it was. It's not like I'd had a lot of experience. He told me people did "special" things to make their relationship and their sex life last longer; otherwise, they would grow bored with each other.

Role-playing, he called it. While I still spent my time in class daydreaming and writing out our names in the shape of elaborately drawn hearts, he most likely spent his time imagining roles for me to play the next time we were together. I was kind of into it at first. I always liked acting and used to imagine myself being famous one day.

So basically, he was the director, and I was his star. It was exciting, I never knew what to expect. "You dress up as a nurse, and I'll be the patient," he suggested. Which soon became, "You pretend you're driving a car ... You're a naughty teenage girl, wearing cut-off shorts and a tube top, just asking for trouble. And I'll be the cop that pulls you over. You're such a bad little girl and you don't want to get in trouble for speeding, so I tell you to give me a blowjob, and I'll let you off the hook."

He even had me bring over clothes for the part.

So, yeah, it was fun in the beginning. But then one night he grabbed me by the hand and led me down the stairs into his parents' bedroom, which was right off the living room. He told me they were out at the movies that night and wouldn't be back for hours. Shaun was nowhere around either, so we had the house to ourselves.

"Come on in here," he directed—the room was dark, no lights on, just the glow of the hallway light filtering in.

"Lie down on the bed and close your eyes and pretend you're asleep," he commanded. "I'm going to go out, and when I come back in, I'm going to pretend I'm a burglar who catches you asleep. I want you to struggle and fight against me while I rip your clothes off, yeah? You get the idea." Without waiting for an answer, he walked out and shut the door and left me in the dark.

I wasn't shocked by his words. I knew that was his thing. I was used to it. I mean, it was just role-playing, like he said. It wasn't real. But my heart raced as I lay there. My eyes slowly adjusted to the darkness with the help of the little bit of light coming from the window. A blue light cast itself across the room and spotlighted a long dresser that sat next to the bed. On it sat a wedding photo of his parents. Their gaze looked down at me as I lay there on the bed. They seemed to be telling me what I already knew—I had no business being in their room.

But I had no choice; at least, I felt like I had no choice. So I just lay there in my underwear in that dark room and closed my eyes hard, pretending to be asleep. I became "the girl asleep who is awakened by the burglar who is raping her."

Some time passed, and then the door slowly squeaked open. I heard footsteps quietly approaching the bed. I rolled over onto my side as if reacting to a ripple in the air that disturbed the quiet of the room. He was fully dressed in his leather coat and gloves as he tried to silently crawl across the bed to where I was. Goosebumps climbed up my body.

I didn't move an inch, pretending I was now in the deepest sleep as he slowly began to pull the covers back. My fear was more than an act. My cue to wake up was when, after the covers had been slowly peeled off, his hand firmly clapped over my mouth and the full weight of his body was on top of me.

Later, when he drove me home, I wrapped myself in a cocoon of silence. My eyes were glued to the road ahead, focused on the center line as it disappeared with the headlights into the darkness beyond as if pointing to an unknown future. My whole body felt weightless. Insignificant.

I'm just a piece of a puzzle that I can't find, I thought with the frustration of just not knowing who I really was and what I really wanted. The radio played some over-orchestrated Jethro Tull song, covering the silence between us. *What is the puzzle?*

16 | WHO PROTECTS US *from the ones that love us?*
"Hell Is for Children," Pat Benatar

There was never a time when my parents got along for more than a few weeks. Ever since I could remember, there was yelling and screaming. But in the past few years, it had become so bad that my mom moved out of their bedroom and into the guest room.

My brother and I wanted her to divorce our father; it was the one thing we could agree on. It was awful being at home with the fighting that went on every night. When I heard the garage door open in the evening, dread would creep over me. If the fights started after dinner—and yes, my mother prepared a sit-down dinner anytime he was home, even though he criticized every morsel and complained he could have made it better—I would hurry to my room, hoping not to get in the way or even be seen. But if it happened before dinner, which was often, we would hide our heads in our hands as we hurriedly ate. Everything made him mad, so the less interaction, the better.

My mom never wanted to break up the family, and she refused to talk badly about our dad. That all changed the night he tried to choke her.

The sweat trickled down my back as I stared out over the hill watching the lightning bugs dance across the lawn. Another hot, humid Virginia night had set in. It should have been beautiful. My dad had invited some friends and co-workers over for dinner. It was late, and we were all outside waving goodbye to the guests as they got into their cars and drove down our long and winding driveway from our house in the middle of nowhere, back to their friendly suburban neighborhoods.

Luke, our happy-go-lucky German shepherd, was running around barking, and he walked right in front of my dad, almost tripping him. My dad cursed and kicked him hard. My heart ripped open for poor Luke, who whimpered and ran off around the side of the house. I was about to say something when I was interrupted.

"Tom! Don't do that!" my mom scolded as the guests continued down the driveway. No one seemed to notice, or they just looked away and acted as if nothing happened.

This was how it usually started. I bowed my head and, as fast as I could, I hurried up the walkway into the house. Making a beeline into the living room, I sat down at the piano and began to play. Playing piano was the only way to relax, to enter a different world and escape from the one I was in.

When I was confused—about Steve, about the unknown—or feeling so low I didn't want to be alive ... well, I just played the piano. When I focused on the notes, the sound, the rhythm, all other thoughts were pushed aside.

They had been arguing all night, even in front of the guests. My dad hated it when she interrupted and didn't care what other people thought, especially after he'd had a few too many drinks. His "party drink" was a Gibson with gin, dry vermouth, and a pickled onion. But normally he drank something out of a short glass, probably whiskey.

He had no trouble telling her to "shut your trap" in front of our guests. There were a few awkward looks, but nobody said anything or defended her. She didn't know when to stop. It wasn't her fault. She was strong, independent, and stubborn. *Why can't she just keep quiet? She knows he'll get angry.* I squeezed my eyes harder, trying to concentrate on the music.

The living room was a quiet place. We were only allowed to hang out in the basement, which had been redone into a TV room, with a big, sprawling, modern U-shaped couch. One of those soft couches that comes in square sections. Modules. We were also allowed to hang out in the old family room, which was now the music room—that's where my dad kept his stereo—or even in the sunroom. But never in the living room, unless we were entertaining, or I was playing the piano.

My mom had picked out all the furniture. When we first moved to Virginia, at the end of an awesome summer in California, we made a temporary home living in a hotel in Washington, D.C., for a month or two. I brought my cat, Sprite, the only animal I was allowed to keep. The horses (Kaleb and Star), our other cat (Frisky the 1st), and dog (Buffy) all went to the new owners of our home. It's like they got to keep our life, while we were off looking for new lives. The life of ocean breezes, fragrant eucalyptus trees, and dusty canyons was replaced by fresh-cut grass and hot, humid, buggy summers.

The first thing we did in Virginia was go house hunting. Just me, my mom, and Joe, while my dad worked. We met with a real estate agent named Jim who quickly took on the role of grandpa as we explored the neighborhoods of McLean with him, looking for our new home.

We'd always lived in old, comfortable homes, such as an old colonial house in Concord, Massachusetts, and then a 1970s rambler-style house in the hills of California. But now, my parents—or maybe it was my dad—wanted a new home.

My dad came from a strict Catholic family. His parents were Polish immigrants and had been merchants in Poland. But in St. Paul, where he was born and where he grew up with two sisters, one older and one younger, he was the spoiled son. And while they worked hard and didn't have a lot of money, they were not poor. His older sister was a concert pianist who married a judge, and his younger was a nun and an amazing artist. She later left the convent, got married, and became a schoolteacher.

My mother, on the other hand, came from a very poor but happy West Virginia family. And when I say family, I mean my grandma had twelve brothers and sisters. Boots was her nickname, and she had my mom at eighteen. Her daddy refused to acknowledge the college boy (or sailor, it was never clear) who knocked her up. He and my great-grandma (whom my mom called Ma and Pop) raised her along with their other children. My mom was the same age as my grandma's youngest sister, Betty Jo. My grandma (who I called Grams) took off with her new love, later marrying him, and sending for my mom when they finally settled out west in Washington.

Mom survived all this with her beautiful, dimpled smile and stubborn strength. She was a knockout, the captain of her cheerleading squad, and always had a lot of admirers. She married right out of high school to her football player boyfriend, and thankfully didn't get pregnant. Instead, he got another girl pregnant. So soon there were divorce papers, and then a move down to Los Angeles, where she started over again, and eventually met my dad, a young pilot in the air force who flew jets and was a newly hired aeronautical engineer at Hughes Aircraft. An unlikely pair, from their backgrounds. But they made a beautiful couple on the outside.

I never knew my dad's family very well—my grandparents died before I was born—but my mom's I do. I adore Grams. And my grandpa, the one she ended up marrying, was the sweetest man. He passed away when I was in eighth grade.

One of the benefits of living in Virginia, I guess, was its proximity to West Virginia so we could visit the rest of the aunts and uncles. I adored my uncle Bud, who had long sideburns and was the captain of a coal barge. He taught me how to fire a gun and eat a freshly grown tomato from the garden, like an apple. You just sprinkled salt on it. Prior to that moment, I'd hated tomatoes.

The point is, my mom probably thought our new Virginia house was paradise. All brand-new and everything. And it was so close to her family. Not to my grandma; she lived in California. But I think I was closer to Grams than Mom was. But Virginia was close to the people she grew up with. Those who felt like brothers and sisters to her.

So that's what we found: a brand-new house. One of those revival houses meant to look old. But it's not. And inside was everything new you can imagine, including a garbage disposal, trash compactor, and microwave. And there was even a little spout on the side of the sink that boiling-hot water came out of.

So, why not get new furniture too? But it was new "old-looking" furniture—just more colonial revival stuff. The living room was all white, with scalloped edges, and fancy tapestry curtains. I really missed our old place and its modern ranch style.

Lost in the music, I barely heard the door open and footsteps behind me. I peeked up to see her as she passed. A vision in her gold-threaded dress. She was a petite woman, buxom and curvy. Her hair, recently died blond, was short and wavy. Even now, she was striking.

She walked over to the far side of the living room and sat down on a chair in the corner, her cocktail in her hand.

And that's where she sat, in her lovely, quiet, petite chair, when my dad stormed in after her, slamming the door behind him.

Immediately I tried to tune it out, but it's hard not to hear someone yelling "bitch, cunt, stupid woman." The abuse that poured out of his mouth was ugly and scary. It was always the same argument: she embarrassed him, she interrupted him, she talked over him, she gave her opinions, which he didn't ask for.

"Can't you just learn to keep your fucking mouth shut?" he spat, taking her by the shoulders, shaking her. I didn't want to hear what they were saying, so I tucked my head lower, trying to concentrate on the piece I was playing, trying to tune them out, pretend I was somewhere else. He would stop, he always did.

But then, in a very quiet and strained, choking voice, I heard my mother pleading, "Tom please ... stop it ... please let go." Her words trickled through my wall of defense, breaking the shield protecting me. I suddenly realized what was going on: he was actually choking her, really choking her. I jumped up, knocking over the bench.

"Stop it, stop it!" I screamed. My voice sounded shrill to my ears.

To my surprise, he stopped immediately and backed away from her. He looked at his hands as if he didn't recognize them as his own and then turned and left the room.

"Mom, are you okay?"

She nodded, but it was obvious she was struggling to speak. I crouched down, kneeling in front of her, and wrapped my arms around her waist, laying my head in her lap.

"I'm so sorry," I cried. "I should have done something sooner."

"Shhh." She ran her hands through my hair and wiped the tear from my cheek. "This isn't your fault, honey. Everything's going to be fine." It was hard for her to speak; it came out quiet and strained.

"Stay here, Mom, I'll be right back."

I jumped up and ran into the kitchen and called my brother, who was at his friend's house. "Come home right away," I sobbed. "Dad hurt Mom."

As soon as Joe arrived, we talked her into coming with us to the police station, determined to have her file a report. All the way there in the car, she nodded in agreement. But when we arrived, she refused to sign anything.

"Mother please," I pleaded. "You have to do something. He can't just get away with that!"

Once a beautiful, vibrant woman, now a broken shell of her former self, she looked up at me with those sad eyes. "No, this isn't how I will handle this. I'll do it my own way."

The bruises on her neck were getting darker and you could see the shape of a handprint. The officer said she had an ambulance outside of the station, and she wanted us to take my mother over to the hospital to have her looked at. But she said unless my mom pressed charges, there was nothing she could do.

I sat in the front seat of the ambulance with angry tears running down my cheeks. *An ambulance! I'm in an ambulance, with my mom in the back*, I thought. *How can I ever look my dad in the eye without thinking he's a monster?*

A dark thought entered my mind and spread like a disease throughout my body: had I done enough to protect her? I'd just sat there, playing the piano ... doing nothing.

17 | DARK, UNCERTAIN MOMENTS

"Tained Love," Soft Cell

Summer blossomed before us with its oppressive, predictable heat while crickets played their orchestra in the night and relentless gnats danced to their frenetic rhythm. Shirts were sticky, clinging to the body from the humidity. There was no escaping it, except to escape into the air-conditioned walls of one's home. Our home was always "under" air-conditioned, as Dad liked to conserve energy.

Just like a teenager running away from home, one night we would do just that: sneak away in the dark, leaving our old life behind. In the end, that was my mom's way of handling the problem of Dad.

Before that, not long after "the incident," he came home and announced his job was finished here, and we were all moving back to California. Mom followed him into his study where behind the closed door you could hear their voices talking, but we couldn't make out what they were saying. Oddly, there was no yelling.

Later that night, my mom came into my bedroom and sat on the foot of my bed. I had been reading *Madame Bovary*, and my head was all wrapped up in how similar Emma and I were—yearning for luxury and romance inspired by reading popular novels.

"What's that you're reading?" she said, pulling the book from my hands and reading the back cover.

"Oh, it's actually quite melodramatic." I laughed. "Not sure why I'm reading it again. I just love the time period and getting lost in it. But really, everyone dies, and it's really mean-spirited; there are no redeeming characters." I pulled it back from her hands. "Mom, what's going on?"

"Well, your dad said he has a job opportunity in L.A." She looked sad, wistful even. I knew that she wanted to move back to California just as much as I did. But I knew she didn't want to go with him. "Honestly, I don't think he's getting along with his boss again. This just keeps happening. I don't know." She paused, clearly bemused by his abrupt news. "He doesn't really tell me the details, but I don't think they can fire him; he's too smart, and good at what he does. So, I guess they transfer him." She shrugged her shoulders. "It's quicker this way, and it looks good for them, and of course for your father."

"But Mom," I began, panic setting it. I was just stunned. This was my dream—the only thing I had wanted since we'd moved to Virginia five years before. And now, here was my opportunity. "I can't. I ... I want to finish high school here. I don't want to leave my friends." *Or Steve*, I thought. "And ... more importantly, we just can't go with him."

There, I said it. I'd needed to say it. She needed to know how I felt.

"I know. I know." She pushed my hair behind my ear, a gesture that normally drove me batty. But under the circumstances, it made me feel better. "Don't worry, we're not going to go with him," she whispered. I raised my eyebrows at her. She had something planned. I could tell.

I think it didn't even register that we had no intention of going with him. He soon left again for another business trip to L.A., maybe to scout for houses like he'd done in the past three moves. I don't know. It didn't matter.

With some very quick decisions and stealthy planning, we all packed up, just taking the essentials, and moved in with my mother's friend Jane. She was Charles's mom, tall and lanky with short, wavy hair, and a good friend of my mom's.

When I wasn't sleeping over at Steve's, I slept in a sleeping bag on her living room floor with my brother nearby. Sometimes it felt like a slumber party, what with Charles, his girlfriend, Joe, and Marybeth sprawled out through the living room and dining room.

I refused to feel bad about it. He had done this to us. The never-ending screaming and yelling. The huge fights between him and my brother. The constant cursing and swearing at anything and everything.

And especially the way he treated my mom. Then that night, "the incident," when he'd started to choke her.

I knew deep down he didn't mean to. That he was out of control. But it wasn't bearable anymore. Not for me, not for my mom, and not for Joe. We had to leave.

It was like we were on an adventure that summer, running away from home, living in this strange house, surrounded by people who kept us busy and distracted. I knew we wouldn't stay long. My mom was already looking for a rental for us, and soon we would sneak back over to the house and move everything to our new, unforeseeable future.

Jane's house was so big, and it was fun to explore. One afternoon, sitting in the shade of an umbrella on the deck with Steve, I tried to describe to him how I felt, the weight that had fallen off my shoulders. He leaned over and pulled me close to him, giving me a warm hug.

He made me feel so secure in his arms, I just knew he wouldn't let anyone hurt me. And yet, I understood that with that came the acceptance that he was sometimes cruel and unapologetic about his needs. But I craved his attention. It didn't matter what kind. Fear and pain became an acceptable caress.

In some ways, being with him made me feel less scared and distracted from the events surging confusingly within me. He stepped in and filled the dark shadows, even though, at times, he frustrated me with his own shadow.

He could be very romantic, fulfilling my fantasy of what I always thought true romance looked like. He'd show up with red roses and take me out to dinner. But then he'd ruin it. He'd grill me, wanting to know everything I did that day, every detail. Every place I went to.

Sometimes, everything was so sunny and bright. And yet, other times when he'd show up, I'd start feeling uncomfortable. It was like he always felt he had to outshine everyone. I didn't understand why. He was fine the way he was. I don't know why he tried so hard. But there was some crazy competition thing he had stuck in his head.

It was complicated. I wanted to be with him, but not all the time. I was beginning to feel suffocated, and with school out, I didn't have that as an escape.

One thing was for sure: now that we were free of my dad's anger and punishing curses, there was a huge weight lifted off our shoulders. I was looking forward to moving into our own place with my mom and Joe, where we could enjoy the quiet that life could offer.

The summer crawled along: long hot days and tired, humid evenings. Not even the shade from the droopy old elm tree could rescue me from the heat. Thankfully Jane had a swimming pool. It was freezing, but a quick dip cooled the heat from the body fast.

I flopped on my stomach next to the pool, leafing through the large glossy British and Italian *Vogue* magazines that I'd picked up when I was in Georgetown with Bambie last time.

Jane was one of the only people I knew who had a swimming pool in Virginia. Most people just joined country clubs that had pools, golf courses, and tennis courts. She was originally from California and sat out sunbathing any chance she could. She was super tan with long legs and short cinnamon-brown hair.

It felt like the hottest week yet, and it was just the beginning of a long hot summer. I made a point of lying out by the pool with her between time with my friends and time with Steve.

The sweat beaded, then dripped down my forehead. I brushed it away for the trillionth time as I played my two favorite songs of the summer, "Sweet Dreams" and "Tainted Love," over and over again on my kick-ass Aiwa Walkman cassette player that Grams had given me the Christmas before. Out of the corner of my eye, I watched as Jane turned her little white kitchen timer to another twenty minutes and rotated a quarter of a turn. This way, she managed to get the insides of her arms and legs as tan as the rest of her body.

It was nice to do just nothing for a change. Between Steve, going to dance class, and now the gym, I had limited time to just chill. At least school was out, so I had time to breathe. But during the school year, it was hard to juggle it all.

Since I'd started ballet classes, I thought I had gotten into pretty good shape. But Steve said I was getting fat, and weak, and should lift weights. I thought he was going to take me to his gym, but he said he didn't want me there, it was filled with too many guys. He didn't want me looked at. He had a better gym for me: Spa Lady, a woman-only gym.

I asked Krissy, my classmate, to join me so I would have a workout partner. Then Steve wrote up a personal workout schedule for me, so I would alternate muscle groups.

I was there three times a week, at ballet three times a week, and at jazz twice a week—I dropped tap at the beginning of the summer. There was just too much going on. Next up, I was interviewing for a job at the record store in the mall. Besides needing the money, keeping busy allowed for a lot more independence.

The sweat trickled down my back as I reached behind me and pulled the swimsuit Jane had loaned me down over my butt again; it kept riding up uncomfortably. I flopped over on my back, mimicking Jane.

The lyrics to "Tainted Love" felt true, something familiar. I played it over and over, memorizing each phrase. Sometimes I did want to just run away. "Mm-mm, run away ..." I started to sing as I swatted a bee away. "Get away!" I pushed myself up. "Seriously, get away!" I shooed the bee away with my magazine. "Mm-mm ... Ouch, what just bit me?"

The summer reprieve at Jane's house was coming to an end. My mom rented a house out past Great Falls, in Sterling. The final move happened fast when Dad was out of town on a business trip again. We had our stuff moved, hoping not to run into him in the process. We grabbed everything we wanted. I didn't even know if he knew about it. We left all that to my mom. I didn't ask. I hadn't seen him since the night he came and told us we were moving. That was a couple weeks ago. It felt like months.

After the movers left, I ran through the house, looking around to see if anything had been left behind. In my parents' room, my mom had left a big box of photos. I briefly looked at them, stunned that she would leave them behind—a full history of the whole family. I quickly grabbed them, ran downstairs to my car, threw the box in my little car's passenger seat, and drove off, not looking back.

Life wasn't going to be the same anymore. No more doors slamming. No more cowering. No more yelling and screaming. I couldn't wait to live in a quiet house. I knew it would take me a long time before I stopped jumping when a door closed.

18 | THAT'S SO PUNK

"Christine," Siouxsie and the Banshees

As junior year began, Bambie and I grew even closer, especially now that I wasn't allowed to talk to Moe except secretly.

Bambie was becoming a massive influence on me. She was so cool, with her short pixie cut and bold-colored tights worn under short, mod-style skirts.

Together we dyed our hair, tinting my hair in places with food coloring and doing hers all black, while we planned our escape to college together. Two years wasn't so far away, and yet it felt like a million.

She was one of my only friends who understood my loyalty to Steve, and he liked her, which helped. She wasn't in the same circle as all my other friends, even though everyone got along great. I guess her not being direct "friends" with Moe made her safe.

"I'm so excited." I leaned a bit closer to the mirror as I continued painting orange food coloring on little sections of my hair. Next up was red. "I got hired at the record store at Tysons." Now I'd have extra money. I'd looked everywhere and somehow, I cut a break with the old guy running the store.

"Oh wow, that's so cool!" Her voice trailed out the door of the bathroom where she was dyeing her hair. "Guess what?"

"Hmm?"

"Me too! Well, not at the record store. I am now a salesgirl at Woodys, not far from where you'll be working."

"What? That's awesome! We're practically neighbors. We can time it so we can have breaks together!"

Tysons was pretty cool. I'd spent so much of my time there wandering the mall with my friends since seventh grade: the movie theater, Farrells Ice Cream Parlor, and a pretty decent record store, where I worked now. We used to have our parents drop us all off, get pizza, then head to the theater, jumping between movies to see as many in one night before we got caught. Which we never did, thankfully.

"Steve is going to hate this, but who cares, he can't force me not to dye my hair. Can he? I mean, at least I didn't cut it again. He hated when I did that. He likes it long and sweet." Steve wasn't too sure about my interests in music and clothing either. But for all the things I let him control, I still resisted in small ways.

I put *Halloween* on and danced around in my underwear with red and orange food coloring painted on random strands.

I didn't tell Bambie about some of the stuff Steve and I did. It was too ... freaky. I wasn't sure what she would say. I couldn't imagine any of the other girls I knew doing the stuff we did. But at the same time, I didn't feel good about it either. I couldn't put a reason on why it felt wrong. I figured it must just be me, since he said it was normal.

"Oh! No, no, no! I'm so sorry!!" Bambie squealed from the bathroom.

The sink was covered with black spots. "Don't worry." I laughed as I headed down to the laundry room, adding over my shoulder, "I'll go grab some 409 and paper towels, it works magic."

After we rinsed her hair out and dried it, we stood there staring at our reflections in the mirror.

"Wow, you look really cool. Very Chrissie Hynde, verging on Siouxsie." I turned to look at her jet-black hair. Bambie liked to call me Siouxsie, with the singer's spelling, S-i-o-u-x-s-i-e. I hated being called Susie, but when she did it, I knew she was saying it with it being spelled our way.

"Thanks. I like the way the yellow and red streaks look in your hair. Very punk." She grinned.

Later that that week, I was in for a big surprise: apparently Bambie didn't have permission to dye her hair black, even though she'd told me she did. Would I have dyed it if I knew she didn't have permission? You would need to have met her mother to know why I would never blatantly disobey her. She scared me almost as much as my dad did, or Moe's mom. But of course, I was to blame. Somebody had to be the scapegoat. Her mother forbid her to hang out with me anymore. Like that would really work.

How ironic, really. Steve forbid me to hang out with Moe, and Mrs. C forbid Bambie to hang out with me. Terrific! Karma's a bitch.

I was very careful not to tell Steve about this, of course, because he was already acting funny around all my friends, and not just Moe. He was either too friendly with them, or completely dismissive. But he liked Bambie, and acted normal around her, so I was very careful not to ruin that.

I loved the bits of color in my hair. Every time I looked at myself in the mirror, it made me feel a little bit more free ... Something he couldn't take away. I knew he wouldn't break up with me for dyeing my hair.

19 | THE LAST DANCE
"Let's Get Physcial," Olivia Newton-John

When I wasn't with Steve or Bambie, I was at the gym, working my new job at Variety Records, or taking dance classes—the one place where my mind was focused on something other than the drama of life. Especially my confused feelings toward Steve's ever-tightening restrictions. Dance just freed me up from any thoughts, instead allowing me to focus only on the moment.

At first Steve seemed to take an interest in it. He liked the idea of me as a dancer. But lately he seemed like he was trying to discourage it. Not so much by anything he said, but by his lingering presence.

He'd show up at practice and stand in the corridor watching from the window. I thought he was being supportive and interested. He even brought me flowers once, which was incredibly sweet. But I soon realized he was there for one reason: to make sure there weren't any other guys hanging around.

One afternoon, after I had arrived and was practicing at the ballet barre with some other girls, I glanced over to the long window and there he was, standing like a statue, watching over me, with a hard cold stare chiseled out of stone. The hair on my arms stood up and a shiver went up my neck.

I reached my hand up and waved, trying to smile, but the whole thing made me nervous. Behind him, the door opened, and a boy walked into the small room followed by his younger sister, Anna. She hurried in, late for class, as her brother sauntered over to the window and stood next to Steve, looking out at all of us, with a curious yet bored expression.

Steve turned to the boy, said something, and then stepped in front of him. The boy looked at me from around his shoulder, with his eyebrows knit together, and then turned and left. Steve continued to hover in the corner until class was over.

At the end of class, Theresa, the dance instructor, and owner of Theresa's Dance Studio, came up to me. "Suzanne, could you please tell your boyfriend not to hang around here during class anymore? It's distracting, and quite frankly, he's intimidating."

My face turned bright red, and I quickly stammered out, "Sure."

She reached over and put her hand on my shoulder and in a softer voice said, "It's okay, it's not your fault. But I noticed you hold back more when he's here." Her eyes showed concern. "Is everything okay between the two of you?"

I quickly glanced over at Steve, but he wasn't looking, he was looking at all the girls going into the changing room putting on their sweats. He was definitely flirting with them, and while I was turning seventeen in a few months, the rest of the girls were closer to fourteen and fifteen.

"Yeah, everything's fine. I'm fine. Thanks though." I smiled weakly and hurried out, throwing my jacket on, grabbing his hand, and dragging him out fast.

I stood my ground despite his negative presence. Even if the girls in my ballet class were my age, which they weren't, being extra tall even for my age, I pretty much towered over everyone in the class, which made me stand out when we danced. That's why I tried extremely hard to be good. I figured if I was going to stand out, it should look like it was on purpose. Quite often Theresa put me in the center of our numbers so it would just look like I was lead dancer.

My feet and my body were sore as I exited the backstage door of the Community Center. It was the studio's third and final night performing, and I was in two of the performances. Thankfully, Theresa had put me center stage in the ballet performance, so I looked like the star, even though I wasn't.

My modern dance class did this really fun number to "Let's Get Physical" by Olivia Newton-John. We all looked like we could have been a part of the cast of her video. And at least with this group, we were all around the same age, so I didn't stand out too much.

As the door shut behind me, I saw Steve standing over by his car in the parking lot. He was leaning up against the car door, watching me as I walked over toward him. He had this superior expression written all over his face, like he knew something I didn't know.

My feet hurt, and I was tired, but my apprehension about what he thought about my performance could still not dim the exhilaration and excitement I had from being on stage. It was everything I thought it would be.

"Hi." I beamed, ignoring his look. "Did you enjoy it?"

"You looked ridiculous up there," his voice hammered out flat. "You're taller than any of those other girls, and you stand out like a giant."

I was stunned. My heart dropped to the pit of my stomach.

He grabbed me by the arm and pulled me aside, lowering his voice, but now it seemed like he was pleading with me, and yet there was something else I couldn't quite define.

"People are laughing at you!" he said through clenched jaw.

As if to emphasize his point, a group of dancers exited the building and walked by deep in conversation, laughing at some joke. I suddenly felt sick to my stomach.

"I don't like it at all. You're practically naked up there in those tights."

He was agitated and upset ... and angry.

Then his voice dropped even lower. "Some boys from your school sitting in front of me said really vulgar things about you, about your long legs ... and where they'd like to wrap them."

My face burned, as if he had slapped me. I held back my tears as I felt the red creep up across my face.

I didn't sign up for dance company again after the season ran out. We had a few more performances in other places, but I didn't mention them to Steve. I just quietly went, and quietly left.

My heart wasn't in it. I was too fat, too tall, and a joke.

I picked up more shifts at work. Steve wasn't allowed to hang out there and watch me work, so I had a place to myself.

20 | ON THE COVER OF A MAGAZINE

"Girls on Film," Duran Duran

I sprawled on his bed while Steve went downstairs to get a snack for us—like he usually did after we had sex. I don't know what came over me, but I leaned over the side of the bed and looked under it. I just had this feeling. Maybe it's because I remembered one night he showed me a photo of Heather Thomas, the actress from *The Fall Guy*—the one of her in the tiny pink bikini. He showed it to me and asked if I thought she was hot. Well duh, of course I did. I would kill to have her body. He said I had a decent body now that I worked out, but I could still stand to lose some weight. I had baby fat, he told me.

After he showed me the photo of her, he put it under his bed. So now, left alone in his room and holding on to that memory still lurking in the back of my head, nagging me ... I had to take a look. It was too dark under there, so I climbed out of the bed, still naked, with only a sheet wrapped around me, to take a closer look.

There, in the dust and dark, were stacks and stacks of magazines; *Playboy*, *Penthouse*, *Hustler*, *Qui*, all stashed under his bed. This was no small collection—but at least a hundred, maybe more, stuffed in that small space beneath the bed and the floor.

I sat back, stunned. I didn't know what to do. I felt sick to my stomach. I felt betrayed ... insufficient. Yeah, insufficient was a good word to describe the way I felt.

My eyes drifted over to his closet—the closet with the padlock on it. He had told me before it was off-limits. Under no circumstances was I to go into it. Now I sat there wondering how many more magazines he had stuffed in there. Or were they just magazines? But I knew better than to ask or even mention the magazines.

When he came back up and entered the room with a tray of crackers, cheese, and apples, I just lay back down on the bed and closed my eyes—holding back the tears.

"Hey, what's wrong?" he said, coming over, laying the tray next to the bed. He climbed in, still in his jeans, his shirtless chest and abs still covered in a light sweat, and curled his body around mine, hugging me to him. His strong arms always made me feel safe and secure. Even when the thing I feared most was him. It was confusing. Everything was confusing. I didn't know where to begin. I just shoved it away, buried it deep. *Don't think about it*, I told myself. That's how I'd get by.

He squeezed me tighter and whispered in my ear, "Hmm, what's wrong, baby? You're shaking."

A small, strangled sound came out of my voice as I tried to control myself. "I'm okay. I'm just feeling kind of nauseous. That's all."

"Okay, then just lay here in my arms." He reached over and switched the lamp off and pulled the covers over us. "You'll be fine," he said softly as he buried his face in my hair.

But as we lay there, with him pressed up behind me, his naked chest against my body and his legs entwined with mine, I could feel "him" pressed against my back. A tear escaped as his hand reached between my legs.

Not long after I discovered those magazines, he asked me to pose for some Polaroids. Some with clothes, some without. He convinced me it was all in fun—everybody did it. He would have something to look at when I wasn't there. Nobody else would ever see them, he promised. He even encouraged me to take some on my own, although he instructed me, "Never use a regular camera with film that needs to be developed. Only use the Polaroid."

Anything to get him from needing to look at one of those magazines, I thought.

Motivated by that thought, I eagerly embraced the idea. So, I wore a blue silk negligee with lace, a red-and-white candy striper uniform, a suede fringe bikini—anything I could find, make, or afford to buy.

I sat innocently, provocatively, or indifferent. I smiled coyly, I licked my lips, and I leaned forward and pouted. I was seventeen, but that didn't stop me from knowing how to be sexy. I just did what I remembered from those magazines. Plus, I grew up watching and dreaming of looking like Anne Margret and Raquel Welch, so I could pretend. It was just acting, after all.

He reached over to his nightstand and grabbed a magazine, or book. The cover had two girls on it and said something like *Dreams of a Young Girl* by David Hamilton. This wasn't at all like his *Playboy* magazines, which I expected him to grab. It wasn't that at all; it was more like young girls in French fields and farmhouses, innocent looking, yet teetering on womanhood: flowers in their hair and their dresses, thin, see-through fabric. It was innocent, yet it came across as very provocative.

"Here, get on the bed on your knees. Yeah, like that. Now, wait." He leaned over and pulled my strap off my shoulder, revealing my breast. "Yeah, just like that ... good."

I did as he instructed, ducking my head, pouting as I held my top, trying to look modest while also revealing myself.

"Yeah, that's it. You got it baby," he said laughing. "Hold still ... now that's sexy!"

Behind him, I saw that the door to his closet was unlocked, and the padlock dangled open, the door slightly ajar. That's where he had grabbed his camera from. And that's where he would lock it up after.

More and more, Steve started to tell me what to wear or what not to wear. His heavy high school ring around my neck wasn't enough. He also wanted me to wear high collared necklines and baggy pants.

He'd call me sometimes in the morning and ask what I was wearing. The first time I thought it was cute, that he just wanted to picture me in his mind. Then one time, he showed up at school—this was before he was banned—and peeked through the classroom window to see what I was wearing. I was mortified. Thankfully only Moe saw it. But still.

When I first started dating him, before he got all possessive on me and before he started telling me to "cover up," he took me to meet his high school friend Ray.

It was a typical hot and humid day. I had on cute cut-off jeans and a white tank top with lace scalped edges in a soft peach and wore flip-flops. The little flowers on the straps of my bra poked out from the straps of the tank.

He didn't say anything about my outfit when he picked me up, and when he introduced me to his friend, it seemed like he was showing me off, with questions like: "Isn't she sweet?" It made me feel like I was there as his prize, with him beaming his approval in my direction.

When Ray looked me over a few times, Steve didn't even get mad or jealous. It wasn't until later that I figured out he was just showing me off to his high school buddy—to prove something that he didn't share with me.

After, as he pulled up to my house, he looked at me with a very serious expression and said, "Next time, don't wear shorts that short. They're too short on you; you're too tall and your legs too long. And your top ... it's too revealing. I don't want anyone gaping at your legs and tits. You look like a tart."

He could have slapped me, and I wouldn't have been more shocked.

"But ..." I stuttered, my face getting hot. But his expression told me not to contradict or argue. "Okay, I just thought you would like it."

"Of course, I do. But just for me." He leaned over and kissed me aggressively. A possessive kiss. Then he reached over and pulled the handle on the door, opening it for me. I stepped out of the car and stood there watching him drive off, confused.

I tried as much as possible to stick to his rules, especially when I was with him, but I didn't always get it right. And sometimes, I just didn't listen. And when he'd catch me, he'd get really mad—if not then, he'd hold it in till we got back to his place.

21 | SUMMER DREAMS
"Peaches," Stranglers

As spring approached and summer plans were being made, I longed for something fun to do. To just get out of town. There was no traveling to California like I used to do in the summer as we didn't have the money. We all had jobs and had to chip in however we could.

Steve kept promising to take me somewhere. I tried to talk him into going to the Bahamas with a school friend of mine and her boyfriend, but that never amounted to anything. He said he didn't know them well enough. I thought he just didn't have the money.

He was working as a security guard now. Still doing construction part-time as well. I got the feeling he wasn't making much. But he wouldn't tell me.

I was working a lot after school and still taking a few dance classes a week, but I wasn't in the dance company anymore, so no performances.

Marybeth and I were planning to take a summer course at the Corcoran School of Art in downtown D.C. That was one of my top choice schools that I was applying to in the fall.

But other than that, it was just going to the gym, a few dance classes that I refused to let go of, and work. And Steve.

Moe was going on a trip with her parents to California, and Bambie was going on a cruise with hers. The summer loomed with very little prospects of a reprieve.

I liked living at the new place in Sterling, although I knew it was temporary. My mom was still looking for a permanent place because we had to be out by the end of the year. But as a transitional home, it was great.

There was a heavy weight that had been lifted and while I could tell my mom was still stressed out, we were all very relaxed at home. No shouting, no slamming doors. Sleeping in late and staying up however late we wanted. No one was telling us what to do, not even my mom.

I had just finished packing my small suitcase and was brushing out my hair when I heard Steve honk from outside. He had stopped coming to the door. I don't know why. It wasn't that my mom made him uncomfortable, even though she seemed to clearly show that she didn't approve of us dating anymore. But she couldn't intimidate him. Hell, if my dad couldn't, certainly she wouldn't be able to.

She used to approve of our relationship, but something changed. She never said anything. I could just tell that she felt uncomfortable around him. She seemed worried. But I shrugged it off. Another adult "issue." What did she know anyhow?

To my surprise, the week before, Steve had called and said he had a surprise for me. He was taking me to Ocean City. We hadn't gone away together anywhere before, except car shows and stuff like that. I was so excited to finally be doing something like this with him. It would be so romantic sleeping in a tent together! It was Friday, and we had the whole weekend.

I ran down the steps with my bag, excited to be going away for the weekend, and nearly ran into my mom at the bottom of the steps. She stood there with her coffee in hand and her fuzzy slippers, looking at me with a worried expression.

Ugh. Here we go.

"Bye, Mom!" I pleasantly burst out, trying to skip around her.

"Honey ..." she began. But no way was I getting any lectures.

I stopped short and arched my eyebrow. "Mom, I'm fine." I leaned over and kissed her on the cheek. "I'll see you Sunday night, or Monday. Don't worry about me!"

And with that, I bolted out the door, leaving her and all her worried clouds behind.

His car had this sort of tent on wheels attached to it. Well, it looked like you were pulling along a long steel rectangular box with wheels. But it popped open and became a tent; we were going to stay in a campground off the main strip, just a few blocks from the beach. It wasn't quite as sophisticated as an actual camper like my family used when we went to Nags Head in the summer, but kind of cool in an adventurous sort of way.

We arrived in a reasonable amount of time despite the weekend beach traffic. The only problem was that we got pulled over by a state trooper for speeding. Steve was still fuming at me later because he said that I had "flirted with the officer." But I insisted I hadn't. I was just being nice. It always worked for me: if I was nice, they let me go with a warning.

When the trooper bent down to look past Steve to see his passenger, I leaned forward, with a big smile, and said, "Good morning, Officer." I was being formal too. I figured if I were extra polite and courteous, it would be better for Steve. He gave me a big smile and winked! I attributed it to my adorable dimples.

I think that's where the problem started. His reaction to me set Steve off. Steve just gritted his teeth, his face set in stone, very serious, and looked straight out the window.

But he really let me have it as soon as we drove off. Accused me of flirting. The usual. I don't even know. It spoiled the rest of the drive. I sat slumped down low in the corner of my seat, holding back angry tears, and feeling hurt.

The two guys that had their camper parked right next to ours, Jim and Dave, were college boys. Jim was my height with sandy blond hair and gray eyes. Dave was shorter and had dark brown hair, a mop of curls.

They were really nice, but Steve made it clear he didn't want me near them. Of course, he joked with them and hung out late talking to them by the campfire while he shoved me off to bed.

I had really looked forward to this trip, but instead, I was miserable. When we went to the beach, he left me on my towel by myself a lot as he walked through the crowded sardine-layered beach looking at all the other girls through his mirrored aviators.

I just lay there stunned. Was I being paranoid? Was he really ogling and flirting with girls on the beach, right in front of me?

When he came back, I asked him what he was doing, and he told me to mind my own business; I should worry more about the fact that I was starting to look fat in my bathing suit. I was so glad I was wearing dark sunglasses to hide the shock and tears that were forming. I rolled on my stomach and buried myself in my magazine.

That night after we ate and I was putting my stuff away in the corner of the tent, I tried to talk to him about it.

"I don't understand what you're doing. Aren't I enough?" I pleaded pathetically with him as I sat down on the sleeping bag.

"Stop nagging me about it." He turned to me, the fading light from outside and dark tent giving me no indication of his expression. "I'm bored and just looking. Flirting—whatever you want to call it—makes me happy."

"But I don't like it." My voice was louder, but on the edge of a whine. I sounded so weak and pathetic to my own ears.

"Stop worrying so much about it. It will make our relationship last longer." He abruptly stood up. "You're just a child, you couldn't possibly understand how any of this works."

And with that he turned and left to go hang out with the guys outside by the fire.

What had changed? He was becoming more and more like this. Hot and cold. *I just have to try harder.* I silently cried into the pillow, eventually drifting off to sleep.

The next morning, I was sitting by myself eating a bowl of the Pac-Man cereal I'd brought with me. Another one of my crazy diets. I loved to experiment with just eating one thing. This time it was Pac-Man. Counting calories sucked, but this way I didn't have to think too much about it.

Steve had gone off to pick up some aspirin for his dad. They were staying at a hotel somewhere nearby, and we were going to have dinner with them that night. I didn't even know they were there until he'd mentioned it that morning. He had to have known; how else would he know where to call them to check up on them? And now he was getting aspirin? *Does he ever plan on moving out? I think he likes living with them, taking care of them.* King and Queen. That's what he called them. I thought it was odd. But, whatever.

As I sat there munching on my cereal, lost in my thoughts, Jim walked over and sat down next to me.

"Hi," he said shyly, as he brushed some invisible dirt off his jeans.

"Hey, what's going on?" I tried to sound cheerful. I knew I must look terrible with big puffy red eyes.

"Um, is everything okay? I heard you both last night and ... well, are you all right?" I hadn't noticed before, maybe because I hadn't had a chance to talk to him up so close, but he had these beautiful gray eyes with long lashes. They looked serious and yet gentle; it was like he could look right into my soul and see my pain. Yeah, I know that sounds corny. But that's how it felt.

"Yeah. Um, I'm fine. But ... thanks," I said, as I turned away embarrassed, a flush of heat spreading up my cheeks to my ears.

"You know," he said, quietly, looking down at his shoes, "you deserve better than him."

Stunned, I stammered, "Um, it's not what you think. It's okay, we just got in a fight. We do that sometimes. Everyone does. He really loves me. I mean, he takes care of me. Last night ... that was just ... stuff."

I stood up and he stood up with me so fast we almost bumped each other. He was the same height as me, and we were eye to eye. He placed his hand on my shoulder, gently.

"I'm sorry, I didn't mean to say anything to upset you. Here." He took out a little piece of paper from his pocket and put it in my hand.

"My number. Call me if you—" He looked away, then back again into my eyes, and smiled. "If you need to talk or something."

I took the note and turned away, climbing up the steps to the tent. At the top of the steps I stopped, turned around, smiled at him, and shoved the note in the pocket of my jeans.

"Thanks," I said quietly and went inside.

22 | BETRAYAL

"I know There's Something Going On," Frida

School was starting in two weeks. I would finally be a senior. So far this had been the worst summer ever. Steve was working a lot of late-night shifts recently at his security guard job. He was also applying to be a police officer for Fairfax County, so he was pretty stressed out and nervous about that. There were loads of interviews and stuff he had to go through. He was pretty busy, but he still showed up during the day between jobs, when he knew I was home. Yet, he was impossible to get a hold of at work. It wasn't like he was pulling away because he was still everywhere in my life, but it was like there was this part of him I couldn't touch.

"I'll be right back," he said, and headed to the bathroom. It was the middle of the day, and he had stopped to see me before he headed to work, knowing my mom was at work.

As the door closed behind him, I stood up and put my clothes back on. As I slipped my T-shirt over my head, I noticed his wallet on my dresser. Without thinking, I picked it up. I loved looking at the photo of him on the driver's license, and at that moment I just had this urge to see it again, so I opened it.

There, tucked in the slot next to the license, was one of those photo booth strips of him with another girl. There they were, the two of them, four times, with four happy expressions, totaling eight happy smiles. I could tell it was very recent; the shirt he wore, I had given it to him for his birthday this year, was a dead giveaway. The girl in the photo, pretty, but not that pretty, was definitely in high school. But I didn't recognize her, so she wasn't from my high school. She looked kind of sleazy, to be honest.

Tears welled up in my eyes as he walked into the room. I held up the pictures; a question formed in my eyes.

Instead of backing out of it, apologizing, or even lying to me, a cloud crossed his face, and the veins on his neck strained as his voice snarled with accusation; "How dare you go through my wallet!"

"But I didn't mean to, I was only looking at your license," I stammered, stunned.

"You have no right to do that!" His face was distorted with rage. "I can't trust you, snooping around my things like a thief."

What have I done? I was so confused. Was I the bad guy because I went through his wallet, snooping, and not trusting him? He wouldn't even address what the photos implied.

He jammed his wallet into the back of his jeans, leaned over and grabbed his T-shirt off the back of my scalloped gold-and-white princess chair, turned, and walked out of my room, taking two steps at a time down the stairs.

I ran after him, almost tripping because the tears were blinding me, making it impossible to see.

"Please don't leave," I blubbered, "let's talk about it."

He turned around, his hand already on the doorknob. "I'm not putting up with this bullshit." He opened the door and walked out. I ran to the window and looked out as he started up his car and drove off.

I could barely navigate myself to the kitchen. I stumbled across the hallway to the kitchen sink where I saw a pair of scissors. I picked them up and stared at the sharp edges.

No, no, no, I silently screamed. *What just happened?* I began slowly dragging the edge of the scissors across my wrist. The pain felt surprisingly good. It took me away from my thoughts. It redirected the pain. I felt numb inside, so numb from everything, I needed to feel this physical pain. A different kind of pain.

I leaned back against the counter and slowly slid to the floor, the cold tile beneath me. I slumped down, curled up in a ball, and closed my eyes, hugging my legs to my chest, rocking back and forth.

The scissors weren't very sharp and the only damage they made were these pathetic little marks with only a bit of blood welling up in bubbles. But they were deep enough that I knew I would be reminded of this day forever.

Some hours later, I dialed him at home. When he answered, I sobbed into the phone and begged him not to break up with me. I told him I didn't care about the photos and apologized for looking in his wallet.

He listened to me quietly, not saying anything as I cried and begged. Hating myself as I did it. Then, finally, he broke his silence.

"I want to see other people." There was no emotion in his voice. He was very cold, and it sounded empty.

I sputtered, "What? What do you mean? We should see other people?"

"No, that's not what I said. Me. Not you. I'm going to see other people. Not you." His voice was low and menacing. "I want to see other girls because I'm getting bored with just us. If you don't like it, then it's time we broke up. And if I hear that you're going out with anyone else, I'll break up with you."

I sat there shocked, holding the phone to my ear. Panicking as the tears dried on my cheeks.

Of course, I wasn't allowed to see other guys. I was his: his property.

"All right," I heard myself whisper. "Okay."

I can't let him go, I thought, feeling desperate and pathetic. *I don't want this. It's not fair, and I don't want to share him, but I can't let him go. I won't have anyone. I'll be alone.* Alone.

"Then we're fine." And with that, he hung up the phone.

23 | SENIOR BENEFITS

"Sweet Dreams," Eurythmics

The August heat carried on through September and into October. My jeans felt heavy and sticky against my legs from the humidity. And the air-conditioner in school did little to cool us off. The second week, it completely died. But they didn't shut the school down, we just sat at our desks with the sweat dripping between our shoulders and slugged back and forth between classes.

But nothing could bring me down. I was finally a senior. The excitement of finishing school and moving on was unbearable. Even my long drive to school didn't dampen the bubbling excitement that was growing inside of me. It took me an extra twenty to thirty minutes every morning to get to school from Great Falls. It was out of my school zone, but the administration was sympathetic and had let me continue at Langley, even so. I'm surprised they didn't say no as my grades were pretty low, except art. A's in art, possible D's in biology, and it was only the beginning of the year. I just didn't study. I didn't have much time.

As October passed, right as I turned eighteen, my mom signed a consent form that allowed me to sign myself in and out of school, the 18-Year-Old Declaration Form. It was simple: my mom worked full-time, and my dad wasn't around, so no one could sign notes for me if I had to leave for a doctor's appointment or if I came in late for any reason.

My goal was to just coast through senior year. Most of the time I wasn't really aware of what was going on around me within the walls of the prison we called Langley, with its gray stone hallways and security guard at the front gate.

We had to sneak out if we wanted to go off campus for lunch. Freshman and sophomore year, we didn't have to sneak, but then there were too many incidents, like car accidents with students during school hours. But now that I had my pass, I was free to go whenever I wanted. When Julie was still at school, during freshman year, she drove her parents' camper on the days she had a doctor's appointment. Then we'd all cram into the tiny bathroom and drive through the front gate without a problem.

School didn't interest me, except art. There were so many cliques at school. Each one always thought they were better than the other. Moe and I seemed to slip between a few of them: like the preps, grits, popular girls, or creatives, without being exclusive to one. But never with the jocks or the theater crowd. They were just too "special" to even notice anyone outside their scene. I made a friend freshman year who was new to the area, but she ended up joining theater sophomore year. Soon she was walking down the hall with this snarky group of theater girls, looking down their noses at me. As if we never had been friends.

Bambie and Moe were constantly annoyed at me because I was always coming in late. I'd be signing myself in and look up to see Bambie standing there, hands on hips, shaking her head with a grin.

I didn't even show up on my birthday. Now that really pissed them off; they had decorated my locker. When I got to school the next day, they had taken everything down, just to punish me for my lazy attitude. No one had ever done that for me before. I was so happy, and at the same time, I felt guilty.

I saw Moe a lot more now. Steve didn't seem to make a big deal about it. I guess he was over the whole thing, or my punishment period was over. I guess I had a different kind of "punishment" now. We never spoke about it again—the prom, Moe, or the girls.

I didn't question where he was when he wasn't with me; instead, I started going out with one of my friends that I worked with. Not all the time, just sometimes. She was a tough girl from Boston named Caroline. She was my "untraceable" friend. That just meant Steve had no idea who she was, and I kept it that way.

She was older than me, and a bit of a loose cannon, with a "strwong Bawston" accent. I adored her and the freedom it allowed me to hang out with her. She said she liked hanging out with me because she could understand me: "All the wrest of these people ahround heeuh sound weihd."

I explained that I thought it was because I had lived outside of Boston for three years when I was a little kid, and I'd picked up a strong accent. The more time I spent around Caroline, the more it rubbed off on me.

I really did pick up an accent when I was a child and we lived in Concord, Massachusetts. Concord was all farmland, fields, and colonial homes. My brother and I were like Huckleberry Finn, running around in cut-off jeans, poking lily pads with sticks, catching bullfrogs, and rummaging through old stuff abandoned in the woods. Pieces of cannons left from a time we had thought didn't exist except in movies. And an empty army trailer filled with rusty, empty first aid bins. So many things to explore. We'd come home tired and red from the sun, let my mom pull off our dirty clothes, and jump in the tub together—the last days of innocent childhood before the sibling fights began. Later that night when my mom did the laundry, she would find traces of our adventures: little baby peepers long forgotten in my pockets.

The kids that went to the kindergarten in Concord, and later grade school, were from hardworking farmers, mechanics, engineers, artists, and poets. An eclectic mix. I'm told my best friend at the time was from the city.

When my grandma came to visit from California, she was shocked to hear how fast my accent had changed, how much I'd absorbed everything around me. Later, when we moved to California, a few years in it was scrubbed free from me. The teachers thought I had a speech impediment, so they sent me to speech therapy in third grade; I had to practice saying my "awe's"—um, "R's," over and over again.

Caroline was tough. She had a proper handmade crucifix tattoo on her wrist. But she was sweeter than sugar to me, maybe because I was the youngest working at the store. I was the sweet kid, or better yet, green. She took me under her wing, and she definitely did not like Steve one bit. The beauty of him not knowing her, and that I carefully never talked about her, meant that drinking and sneaking cigarettes wasn't a problem when I went to see her. What he didn't know couldn't hurt.

Steve's jealousy was getting to me so much that in a way I felt like punishing him by going off and doing things I knew he wouldn't like.

Now that we were eighteen, Bambie and I could drink legally in D.C., so we drove to Georgetown in my little yellow Karmann Ghia, with Caroline too, and went to the bar on the corner of Wisconsin Ave and M Street. You had to walk up this long set of stairs to get to it, and it had a long L-shaped bar. The best part was it had a great dance floor. It was filled with jarheads (marines), and the DJ only played pop music, but it was danceable. I discovered I loved White Russians. The drink.

"You know you just do this to piss him off." Bambie paused, took a sip of her drink, and continued, shouting over the music and the throng of noise. "But he doesn't even know you're here! He just thinks you're spending the night with me and my ultra-strict mom." She rolled her eyes. "You're so passive-aggressive."

"Cheers to that!" I laughed. "I just need to blow off steam. I need space sometimes." I licked the edge of the glass. It really was sweet-tasting. "And I'm not sure that would be the definition of passive-aggressive."

"I get it, you don't have to explain anything to me." She looked at me, and started to say, "But—"

I felt a tap on my shoulder and my stomach lurched into my throat as I spun around. But it was only this tall, sweet marine boy. I threw my hand to my heart.

"I'm sorry," he said, "I didn't mean to startle you, I just wanted to see if you would dance with me." *Wow, what a nice, polite guy,* I thought.

"Sure," I grinned and leaned over, whispering into Bambie's ear, "There are so many cute jarheads here."

"Shhh, don't call him that to his face," she teased. "Where is Caroline?"

We both looked around and there she was at the end of the bar, already making out with some guy.

"I think she's okay," I said and turned to my dance partner, who was politely waiting. *Oh yay, "Let's Dance" is playing*, I thought, and gave him a huge smile.

It was always fun, and always innocent. Nothing happened except for a drink and dancing. But it still felt good. Like I was taking back a little more of me.

"This was so much fun," Bambie said over her empty plate of pasta.

After my shift ended at the record store, I walked over to Bambie's work to see if she was getting off work too, and it turned out she was, so we decided to go to Pizza and Pasta. The name sounds cheesy, but it was my favorite Italian restaurant. Their fettuccine Alfredo with garlic bread was the best. I'd taken Steve here, my mom took us here, and, well, everyone came here. It was the classic spot. The waiters were really nice, very polite, and extra cute.

We drove separately as we both had our own cars and lived in opposite directions. It wasn't even that late, but we were starved.

"I know, I'm so glad you got off at the same time. What a great coincidence."

The waiter came over and handed us the check and winked. We looked at each other and grinned.

"What's Steve doing tonight?" she asked.

"Oh, I think he's working. He wanted to meet, but I told him this morning I was feeling tired, and I was going straight home after work. I wasn't lying, I was tired. But not anymore." I shrugged. "Maybe a food coma though."

We both paid at the register and headed out to our cars. As we walked around the corner to the parking lot, I stopped dead in my tracks. There was Steve, standing by my car with his arms folded, looking really pissed off. I walked over fast, trying to gain some distance from Bambie. I didn't want her to hear.

"What's wrong?" Bambie stayed back and didn't follow me.

"What the hell are you doing? You said you were going home. You lied to me." He grabbed my arm and pulled me closer to him. "Why are you sneaking around?"

"Ow. What are you doing?" I tried pulling my arm, but his grip got tighter. "I'm with Bambie. It's fine, it wasn't planned, we just spontaneously decided to go to dinner. I was hungry."

"I don't believe you. You did this on purpose." His face was all twisted and angry.

"Are you okay?" Bambie called from her car, a worried look on her face.

"Yes." I shrugged his hand off my arm, for the moment. "I'm fine, it's just a misunderstanding. Go ahead, I'll see you tomorrow at school."

She looked like she wasn't sure. She hesitated, then said, "Okay," and ducked into her car.

"You're coming home with me," he growled. "Just follow me in your car."

"I have school in the morning, I don't want to be late—" I stopped suddenly, because he gave me a look so swift and so venomous, so threatening, that the words caught in my throat, and I shut my mouth.

"You're doing it, just follow me."

Reluctantly, yet dutifully, I got into my car and followed him home. Twenty minutes to imagine what was in store for me. I recognized the fragility of my current existence and came up against a brick wall.

It was still light out when he brought me up to his room; his parents were downstairs watching TV. But that room, his room, was always dark.

There were no games. No role-playing. It was just his punishing anger. My only revenge was to be quiet, not give him anything. It wasn't easy to swallow the tears. They wouldn't come anyhow. I felt so cold and closed up.

When it was finally dark outside, he left me alone while he went to shower. I got up, quickly put my clothes back on. My legs ached; my arms hurt; I basically hurt everywhere.

It was dark downstairs, so I was sure I would be able to sneak into the kitchen to get some water. The kitchen had a small light on, so I was able to find my way to it. I was filling up my glass with water when I heard a noise behind me. I whipped around, expecting it to be his creepy brother, but it was his mother.

"Are you okay?" she whispered. She was so tiny, so small. She didn't fit in this place ... this dark little house with hidden closets, closed doors, and dead silence. I didn't fit in. I fought the tears, feeling a growing lump rise in my throat. My eyes burned.

"I'm fine," I whispered back, bowing my head, averting my eyes. *I will make her a clay teapot for Christmas*, I randomly thought.

"I am so mad at him, I'm really over his paranoid behavior. I don't know what to do."

"I'm worried for you," Bambie said. "He really scared me, acting like that. Why was he so mad? You were just eating dinner with me."

"He thought I was tricking him, or lying or something," I whispered. I didn't want anyone else to hear us. We were in art class, sitting over by the windows. "That I planned to go out without him on purpose. I don't know. Maybe he's just hurt, and that's how he reacts. I don't know."

"Okay, well, your next revenge is coming soon."

"Huh?" I didn't know what she was on about.

"The New York trip!" Her smile widened when she saw my expression.

"Yes, I forgot, I almost forgot! I can't wait. I can't believe our fashion class is going to New York!"

New York was amazing. Our whole fashion merchandising class headed to New York on a bus, and we stayed four nights at a hotel in Times Square. Our teacher, Mrs. A, took us to visit Estee Lauder, *Mademoiselle* magazine, Cole Swimwear, and more. We saw CATS performed on Broadway, went to Mama Leones for dinner, and Benihana, where they chop up the meat right in front of you on the table.

Bambie and I snuck off to St. Mark's during our free time to a punk shop called Trash and Vaudeville and looked for an underground record store. Times Square had huge billboards of the Calvin Klein campaign with men and women wearing his new unisex-looking white briefs. I even saw a man in a fur coat holding a bag with a little dog in it right outside this tall, gold building on Fifth Avenue.

We shared a room with a girl named Samantha. She was a broken thing. She was the one who had been in a horrible car accident during freshman year. She and another student had snuck out during lunch. I don't exactly know what happened, but the rumors were that they went to get high, and she drove off the side of the road into a tree. He was instantly killed.

It must be so horrible to live with that—that guilt. So, Bambie and I took her under our wing and decided we would all have fun together. We snuck out late at night, which was forbidden, to walk to a liquor store in Times Square and get a bottle of alcohol. The bright lights of the porn theaters shone down on us, while the men that worked them beckoned us in. We just laughed, arm in arm, and made our way to a place where they sold us a bottle of vodka without blinking—the best thing to buy because you can mix it with so much and it doesn't reek.

The whole trip was a dream, and I didn't think once about Steve.

24 | DIAMONDS AND DANGER

"Burning down the House," Talking Heads

Variety Records was run by a motley group of people. John Senior was the senior manager; he was a sweet old guy, short, thin, with a slight hunch to his back. He seemed to really like me. I was hardworking and polite. But Debbie (I liked to think of her as Drusilla), the assistant manager, was a bitch. I have nothing good to say about her. And she definitely didn't like me either. She had this short spiky bleached hair and was rail thin. I'm sure the term "skinny bitch" was created with her in mind. I don't think she could have been pretty if she tried, and believe me, she tried. It was more the personality that made her so ugly.

Then there was John, the other assistant manager. He was the hippy. Heavy, sloppy, long-haired, and smelling like farts.

The only thing that saved the place, besides John Senior, was Mary Carol and Caroline.

Mary Carol was frail and mousy. She really did look a little like a mouse. She had these big eyes, a tiny, upturned nose, and a bit of an overbite. She was cute and sweet, but you could barely hear her when she spoke. She was quiet. She had a very tragic story that followed her everywhere. Some time ago, long before I met her, her brother had been murdered. Somewhere deep in the woods. And they'd never found the killer.

I liked Mary Carol a lot. She was kind and never judged anyone. But I didn't like her fiancé. He was very strange. But who was I to judge? Just because he looked a lot like Richard Simmons, with his afro blond hair. I mean, he really did look like him. And he was super controlling and demeaning to her. He was one of those guys, if you touched his hair, he would freak out.

Working at Variety Records during the mad holiday rush was a nightmare. The mall was packed, and parking was insane. I had to give myself an extra half hour just to circle the place until I found a spot.

I volunteered to work Christmas Eve because I needed the money, and I didn't want to sit around at home doing nothing. The air was a heavy cloud of stress with shoppers buying last-minute gifts. Everyone was supposed to have good cheer; instead, they were nasty and rude.

The store was packed, and I only had one more hour before we closed. I was at the register, Christmas music blasting over the speakers, and Caroline was across from me on the button counter. I'd look up in her direction as some guy turned and walked away from her, and she'd catch my eye, wink, and make some crude tongue gesture. She cracked me up constantly.

The button counter was always fun to work. For every three buttons you sold, you could easily drop one on the ground when you were pulling them out of the case and then scoot it under the cabinet so you could pick it up later and pocket it. So far, I had a good thirty buttons I had collected. Tapes were easily slid into pocketbooks and when you bought one record, it was easy to slide another in with it ... two for one.

I was in mad register-girl mode; each purchase you rang up you had to write the serial number, name of the artist, and the album in the ledger, so you would know which one you needed to reorder. Normally this wasn't a big deal, but when you had fifteen people in line on a last-minute Christmas Eve shopping spree, you tried to keep it moving. And moving wasn't so easy when you had to write everything down. If they gave you a credit card and the purchase was over $100, you had to phone it in and get approval!

I had just finished putting a credit card in the carbon copy gadget, placing the form over it and swiping the imprinter mechanism to imprint the numbers and name onto the paper. I was about to record several tapes and records in my ledger for a customer when a gruff, irritated voice interrupted my progress: "How long is this going to take?"

"Sorry, sir, but I have to record—" I looked up to see who was giving me attitude and recognized the man before me. He was a fairly famous news anchorman, Sam Donaldson. I'd heard he had a terrible reputation. And this just proved it.

"Just make it quick, please." He said "please" like his teeth were permanently glued together. It took an effort.

"Yes, sir," I said with my chirpy Christmas voice. I would not let Mr. Donaldson get me down.

I only had twenty minutes to go before we closed up. Steve was picking me up; he said he wanted to take me to dinner and give me my Christmas present early. I was going to meet him in front of the movie theater down at the other end of the mall, but he wasn't allowed to come near the store. It was mainly a rule to all boyfriends and girlfriends. John Senior said he didn't want any distractions, but I had a feeling when it came to Steve he didn't like how possessive he was of me; because the rule started soon after the first time Steve came to pick me up.

In my mind, things were the same with us. He never acted any different, so I pretended the whole "seeing other girls" thing wasn't real. As far as I knew, it wasn't.

After Debbie let the last person out, closed up the glass doors that separated us from the throngs still mulling out in the mall, and pulled the latch, John Senior went to the back of the store to do the books.

"My turn!" I yelled, running to the back of the store, quickly shuffling through the stacks of LP's. I found what I was looking for ... Talking Heads. I gently placed the needle on the track I deemed perfect for closing night— my favorite "catwalk" music.

"Burning Down the House" started up slowly and then, gaining some volume, full throttle, it turned our empty store into our own runway show. Caroline, Mary Carol, and I all strutted up and down the aisles between the records, pretending to be long-limbed sexy models. Mrs. A had said I could be a model and had given me a list of names to call. I never contacted anyone because I knew deep down Steve wouldn't let me.

We never got entirely through a whole song without somebody turning it down. There were just too many of us with different tastes.

This time it was John Senior who emerged from his office to turn the volume down.

"Oh well. That's better than off," I said under my breath to Mary Carol, who smiled sweetly.

I grabbed my purse and went to the bathroom in the back to fix my face. The mirror there was a bit dirty, but the lighting was okay. I reapplied my eyeliner and lip gloss and ran a brush through my hair, sliding a little comb to the left side so it would sweep up at an angle. I had put a little bit more black dye to the under-layer of my hair, but the rest was more of a golden honey blond now. It had gotten pretty long for me, down a bit past my shoulders, all layered and curled with care.

I pulled my favorite blue jeans down by the crotch, as they tended to ride up a bit. They weren't too tight, just well fitted. I readjusted the thin gold belt, sliding the clasp toward the side—I liked that asymmetrical look. I ran my hands over the soft texture of my fuzzy boat-necked sweater. The turquoise and black threads were woven into the blue, creating a sweet and sexy, but also funky look. Satisfied, I headed back out into the dark little office-slash-storage-room.

I grabbed the long white coat I had bought on layaway with my hard-earned money and slid my purse strap over my shoulder.

"Good night, John." He was sitting hunched over his record keeping, lost in his thoughts.

Skinny, old, crooked John. He was so lovely to me. Always seemed concerned. I sensed he didn't trust Steve by the way he furrowed his brow. I was glad I had to meet him somewhere else; I couldn't stand to see the disapproval in his eyes.

"Have a merry Christmas, Suzanne," John said over his glasses, the accounting books spread out before him, the harsh table lamp casting odd shadows on his face. "Don't let anybody change that beautiful smile you have."

Wow, that just made me feel sad and happy all at once. I could feel the flush creep up my face. "You're so sweet, John. Thanks. Have a lovely Christmas too," I said, and then turned fast and headed out.

Someone had put on Jethro Tull. A few of the gang were getting on their coats, while hippy John was closing out behind the register and

Caroline was vacuuming in the back. No one wanted to hear any more Christmas music. That was all we'd had to play all day.

I hugged Mary Carol and Caroline goodbye, we all wished each other a very merry Christmas, and I went off to look for Steve.

He was sitting by himself on the wall that wrapped around the indoor garden, right in front of the movie theatre. He looked somehow lost there, all by himself.

"Hey." As I sat down next to him, it occurred to me that I never used a nickname for him. A lot of my friends had nicknames for their boyfriends. I just didn't. I didn't say honey, babe, darling ... whatever. He was Steve to me. But at that moment, I felt like I should have one.

"Hey, kitten." I guess he had one for me. I always had one. In fact, I had so many nicknames from different friends it was ridiculous.

He was in a really good mood despite my initial impression that he looked sad. He grabbed my hand and pulled me in for a kiss. He was a good kisser. I felt kind of bad because so many of my friends didn't like him. Even the ones who used to like him had been saying negative things about him or acting more distant when he was around. It made me angry that they didn't understand or see his good side.

We walked away and out of the mall to find his car. He took me to a Chinese restaurant around the corner, one of our favorite places. The meal was fairly uneventful and for the most part, quiet. I kept expecting him to give me my present, but he didn't. And I didn't want to ask.

Heading home, I couldn't bring myself to ask him about it. I don't know why, but something was nagging at me. It just felt ... wrong. Sometimes things felt so right. But lately, I just wasn't sure. I was second-guessing everything. I didn't know if he was still seeing other people. I never asked, and he never said anything to me. Thankfully, if he was, he didn't feel like he needed to rub it in my face. Nothing else seemed to have changed.

He pulled into our driveway and put the car in park but didn't turn off the engine.

Frustrated that he wasn't going to come in, or say anything, I put my hand on the door to open it.

"Wait," he said quietly.

I turned around and looked at him. He looked so strange. All hunched over, like he was scared of something. But then, as I looked at him, he changed before me. He sat up a bit straighter, puffed out his chest, like he usually did, and turned to me, with a renewed confident look on his face.

He opened his hand and revealed a little black box. I hadn't even noticed that he had it in his hand.

"What's that?" I said, confused.

He looked me in the eyes. "It's for you."

"Oh!" Relief and excitement washed over me. He hadn't forgotten! *I bet he got me some cute earrings, like the ones I pointed out to him in the window of that freshwater peal shop*, I thought.

He leaned over closer to me and slowly opened the box. There, inside, was a ring with a tiny delicate diamond. *A diamond ring.*

"Suzanne, will you marry me?"

My mouth hung open. I didn't know what to say. Honestly, I hadn't expected this. I never thought in a million years he would ask me to marry him. I hadn't even said I loved him—but he had to me. He told me he wanted me to say it only when I was ready. And anything before would have been a lie. I didn't know what love felt like—how to compare it. I didn't trust the words, so I felt it was better not to say anything at all. A small part inside of me knew, deep down inside, that I didn't love him. I needed him. I wanted his attention. I craved it. I loved it. But ... I didn't love him.

Sitting there, not answering, must have been awful. But he pressed on.

"I know, you haven't even said you love me, really. You've said yes, when I asked you if you do, but never on your own. But I know you do. You don't have to tell me."

There was buzzing in my ears, and I felt nauseous. I didn't know what to say.

"I ..." I began. "I'm not ready to marry ... I don't want to get married now."

"I don't want to get married now either," he quickly intervened. "I want you to be my fiancée. I want everyone to know you're mine when you go off to college, and you'll look down at your ring and remember you have me here waiting for you. And when you get back, when you graduate, then we can get married." He had such a hopeful look on his face.

"Oh." I got it. It was just another ID bracelet. Like his huge college ring I wore around my neck so everyone would know I was taken. In the beginning, I wanted to show off that I had a boyfriend, so I thought it was cool to wear it. But then once, when I didn't wear it, he completely flipped out. He wanted to know why: Was I trying to meet other guys? Did I not want anyone to know we were together? I tried to explain it was jewelry and it just didn't go with that outfit or the necklace I wanted to wear that day. But he wouldn't listen. He was beet red with anger.

So that's kind of what this is, I thought. He was worried that off on my own at college I would seem available, and this was a way of posting a sign: "No Trespassing."

I wrestled with my answer. *I guess*, I thought, *what's the harm? I mean, it's just an engagement ring. It's a nice ring to wear and to show off and I won't have to wear the stupid college ring anymore.*

"Okay," I said, my stomach feeling better now that I'd resolved the situation. "Sure."

He broke into a big smile, pulled me toward him, and kissed me with relief.

For a minute, I had thought he really wanted me to be his wife. But suddenly I wasn't so sure. He wanted me as his property. But it didn't matter. I pushed the thoughts aside. It was Christmas.

"You do love me after all," he said with satisfaction.

25 | LEGAL WARS
"Jealous Guy," Roxy Music

My mom had been looking for a permanent residence since the fall, knowing that our lease would be up by the end of the year. It was fun going with her to see places, but Joe and I didn't have much say in where or what she would buy. She wanted something easier to maintain and closer to work, not another huge suburban house with lots of land and bedrooms to clean. The house on Georgetown Pike had finally sold, and my parents had split the money, so now she could buy a house and not rent. But we still had to go to court in a few months, and hopefully she would get child support—even though I was eighteen. Maybe she would get some money back. I knew she wouldn't ask for a lot. It was disappointing, but I knew she wouldn't fight my dad hard enough for it. Just the bare minimum, and barely that. She was already back in night school so she could get a better job.

I had refused to speak or see my dad since we left that day, over a year before. Even over Christmas I hadn't called him or taken his calls. I was still angry at him for ruining everything. I didn't know if I ever wanted to see him again.

Except I had to see him, and it would be the first time in months, because my mom's court date was approaching fast, and I promised I would be there for her. Obviously, he would be there too, there was no escaping it. But I needed to be there for my mom. Even though my mom could be stubborn, and finally left him, she wouldn't stand up for herself. She wouldn't ask for money.

I was still intervening, trying to protect her. I intercepted letters he sent, making sure they weren't upsetting. And most were. He accused her of "turning" us against him and even cheating on him.

God, it was frustrating. As if she had to turn us against him. He'd done a nice job of that himself!

My mom worked so hard and was busy taking care of us, while he was gone on all those business trips and late nights at the office. He probably just assumed that what he did, she probably did as well. The accusations were ridiculous and ugly, and I was going to make sure she never had to see one of those letters.

I wrote him a long letter telling him just how I felt. It wasn't very nice and I was sure one day I would regret it, but I needed to let him know.

"Mom did not turn us against you," I wrote. "In fact, that's the opposite. She always defended you. She always said, 'don't talk bad about your dad.' If anyone turned us against you, it was you. You were never around, and when you were, you always yelled and screamed at us—at everyone."

I even brought up the choking incident. I don't know where I got the nerve, but I was not going to let him accuse my mom of trying to set us against him. That was ridiculous.

My mom eventually fell in love with a townhouse just outside of Fairfax, making my drive to school about forty-five minutes to an hour, depending on traffic. But it was nice, and my room had its own bathroom, so I didn't complain.

I hung up all my old posters and filled my shelves with my collection of plastic horses and dolls. My ballet shoes hung from the wall next to the photo of the dance group—now left behind.

I sighed. *Looks almost like my last two rooms.* I didn't hang up my heartthrob collage, and instead layered my closet doors with pictures from fashion magazines. I was obsessed with fashion. Fashion merchandising was turning out to be a great class. I loved doing my book report on Norma Kamali so much, I did another on Perri Ellis for extra credit. I even wrote the designers, explaining what I was doing, and they sent me photos from their shoots.

I was thinking I might become a fashion illustrator. Combine art and fashion. My two favorite things. Or a model. Then I could travel the world doing fashion shoots.

But first, we had to see my dad in court.

My fingers played with the hem of my shirt under the table. But even though I did everything I could to avoid looking at him, I could feel his gaze on me. We were all sitting around a large conference table in a private room at the courthouse. The judge, or whatever he was, sat on one side; a clerk sat next to him, taking notes; my mom was to the left of me, with my brother on her other side, and opposite us was her lame lawyer; and my dad was at the opposite end from the judge—to the right of me, with his lawyer to his right.

The meeting droned on and on ... and we answered questions when asked. I knew he was looking at me, but I continued to ignore his gaze.

"Let's recess and meet back here in fifteen minutes." The judge's voice brought my attention back.

My mom, along with everyone else, quickly stood up and started outside, and I found myself sitting alone with him.

"So, how have you been?" he asked in a quiet voice.

"Fine," I said trying to sound indifferent, but the familiar warmth of my dad's voice sent a pang to my chest.

"I got your letter." His flat, fatherly tone came back, which made me bristle and simultaneously turn red. I felt bad about some of the things I'd said, but I also felt they were true. But I knew what I said must have hurt him, and I felt bad. I didn't respond.

"I've moved back to California," he went on, "and I'm living in Manhattan Beach. I'd love for you to come visit this summer, if you want to?"

I looked up to see if he was serious and saw a sad expression on his face. A desperate, sad look. The familiar glasses were perched low on his nose—head tilted down, eyes peering over, looking at me with concern.

I quickly dropped my head and mumbled, "I don't know."

"I see you have a ring on your finger." He reached over and gently tapped my ring. "Are you engaged to that guy?"

That guy? He wasn't being nasty. He actually sounded more concerned, and I think he was trying to be nice. I knew he didn't want to lose his "little girl," so he was trying really hard not to.

"Yes, I am," I said, my chin up, determined not to let him see any feelings. Thankfully, I didn't need to say anything else, because at that moment the door opened and everyone came back in, sat down, and we continued.

When it was over, I stood up and turned to him and gave him a hug, which caught him off guard, as well as me, and said goodbye. Then I quickly turned to go.

I just didn't want to go without saying goodbye. I felt bad for him, but I didn't want my mom or brother to feel like I was betraying them.

The appalling thing was that my mom didn't ask for anything. She just wanted a percentage from the sale of the house, and some child support for me until I was nineteen, which was less than a year away. He, on the other hand, didn't want her to have anything. And that's why I was so angry with him. But in the end, she got what she asked for. She could have gotten more ... alimony, for example. But she didn't even ask.

On a side note, as far as I knew, nothing was formalized, but he promised to pay college tuition for both me and my brother.

I could tell Steve was angry when he picked me up. His face was set in a dark scowl.

"What's wrong?" I hoped it wasn't something I did.

"Nothing, don't worry about it." He turned out onto the parkway and headed toward the mall. Tysons had two theaters—the one upstairs near where I worked, and one at the other end of the mall that had more theaters in it. That was the one where you could sneak from movie to movie.

"What movie are we seeing? I mean, I know you told me, but I forgot." I tried to play down his mood, hoping if I kept up with my smile and light talk it would pull him out of it.

"*Terminator.*" Right, it had that big bodybuilder, Arnold Schwarzenegger. I loved him in *Conan the Barbarian*. And it was funny because I thought that Steve kind of looked like him. He had the same expression and facial features. Well, kind of.

But it was obvious I wasn't getting any more conversation with him, so I just peered out the window, the lights a blur in my eyes.

When we stepped up to the counter to buy our tickets, the girl behind the window looked at Steve and her mouth dropped open. The bubble she was about to blow fell deflated on her bottom lip. She turned to look up at the movie poster on the wall next to her. It was a huge poster of the Terminator. The guy in dark sunglasses looked all serious with his full, wide jawline set in a frown; he held a big silver gun and wore a leather jacket, unzipped and open to reveal his muscular chest. Then she slowly turned back to us, sucking in her gum, and as she looked at him, she breathed out in an incredulous tone, "You look exactly like that guy."

He just raised his eyebrow and grinned.

I wasn't the only one who thought he had an uncanny resemblance to the actor. Thank god Steve didn't walk around with a leather jacket open without a shirt underneath. But he did sometimes wear V-neck sweaters that, um, showcased his muscular cleavage. He was still stuck in the '70s with the music and clothing he wore. It was a good thing I kind of liked that '70s, Steve McQueen look, although mostly in films.

After the movie, and it was pretty cool, we went to get a soda at Farrell's, the big ice cream parlor near the exit of the mall.

It was extremely lively, with birthday parties and couples having dinner or just dessert. Every now and then, a siren, sort of like a fireman's siren, would go off. Then the silly waiters and waitresses dressed up in their Gibson Girl old-time gear would clammer away on little drums while hustling around the place, trying to get everyone to sing along with them to "Happy Birthday."

Looking over at Steve, I saw that he was lost in his thoughts, with a very grim expression.

"What's wrong?" *Is he mad at me for some reason?*

His scowl turned to me, and I saw his hands clench up into fists on top of the table. He didn't say a word for a minute, just kept looking at me, angry and unable to say anything.

My stomach lurched, and I worried I'd done something bad. Did I look at some guy tonight? No, I remembered, he was angry when we left my house. Did he find out I'd been going down to D.C. with Bambie, or did he find out about Caroline and her crazy friends, the smoking and drinking?

But then he relaxed his fists and let out a long breath. "I didn't get accepted into the police academy." His eyes fell back down to study his hands.

"What? Why didn't they accept you? That doesn't make any sense. You're perfect for the job!" I was sad and disappointed for him.

"I don't know," he said, sad and angry. "They just said something about not fitting all the requirements."

"Well, what about D.C.? Aren't there other places you can apply to? Other departments, other than Fairfax County?" I said, trying to cheer him up. "Maybe they have different requirements?"

"Yeah, I know. I've applied to them all," he said softly. "I haven't heard back." He stood up suddenly. "Come on, let's go."

Leaving my half-finished soda, we left before the next cheery "happy birthday" song started up again.

On the way back to his house, he didn't say a word. I was afraid to say anything to set him off. I wanted to go home instead of spending the night, but I didn't want to upset him more. And I thought he would need to cuddle.

When we got to his room, he immediately started taking his clothes off.

"Get in bed," he ordered, his voice cold and hard.

I quickly shed my coat and my sweater and removed my jeans, folding them neatly on his chair in the corner, and jumped under the covers with my underwear still on.

He turned the light off and climbed in after me. "Turn over," he said, his voice cold, and a distant cousin from the voice of the sad, lost Steve from earlier. I had been sure he would want to cuddle. But now I knew that wasn't going to happen.

As I rolled over on my side and tried to cover my body, he yanked the blanket down.

"What—" I started to say, but a hand was suddenly over my mouth.

"Don't say another word." he snarled.

Shocked by the venom in his voice, I squeezed my eyes shut, trying to keep from crying. I was cold, yet a sweat broke out on my forehead. I was afraid. When he was this upset, he was unpredictable with his games. *Is this a game?*

"Relax." His voice dropped lower, his breath deepening.

I couldn't relax. I was scared, and it didn't feel like a game.

He apologized to me in the morning, telling me he didn't mean to hurt me. Lots of couples had rough sex and enjoyed it.

"Well, not me," I told him. In the daylight I was a bit braver.

"Come on." He pulled me back down into his arms as I started to get up. "Don't be mad," he purred into my ear, hugging me to him in a tight body lock.

Pushing back up, I managed to wrestle free, grabbed my clothes, and hurried to put them on. "Not again."

"Okay, okay," he said sleepily. He turned over onto his back, pulled the sheet down right below his belly button, tried to direct my gaze, and winked. Yes, he *actually* winked. "Drive safely, I'll call you later."

"Argh!" I growled, and huffed out the door, hearing him laugh behind me.

I was learning to say no, although it was much easier over the phone. I had a harder time in person because he was always so convincing, and intimidating. But over the phone, I was practicing "no" more often. But this time, something swelled up in me, and I couldn't stop myself. I was starting to listen to that little voice inside of me.

26 | DANGEROUS GAMES
"Drive," The Cars

Ever since that night at Steve's, I'd tried to make myself busy and unavailable, sending silent messages to let him know I was still angry. That I hadn't forgiven him. And that he owed me big-time.

Payback was only sort of gratifying. I mean, did it count if he never found out about all the excursions to D.C., dancing with other guys, and the occasional drink? Bambie was right. It really didn't.

A few days later, Moe invited me over to her house, and because it was so far from where I lived now, I planned on spending the night.

Moe and I were sitting on her couch in the basement watching a movie on TV. Well, not really watching as we were mostly gossiping about some of our friends, or friends of friends from school. But mainly guys. We talked a lot about guys. Just because I was dating Steve didn't mean I hadn't noticed other guys. And I still had a huge crush on Doug. Apparently, he was on and off with the redhead. Actually, I didn't know the details, but Moe loved to fill me in.

I'd see Doug with my brother or Peter, and we were on friendly terms. There was always a little bit of flirting going on—although never when Steve was around. Actually, most guys completely ignored me when he was around.

I sat on the couch, fiddling with my ring. It didn't matter that we were "engaged." Nothing had changed. The ring was sweet but small, so most people didn't even notice it. Sometimes I told people, but most of the time, I just didn't. I warned Steve not to say anything around my mom. Of course, she knew, but she didn't take it seriously. She rolled her eyes when I showed it to her. She basically said, "You're going to meet so many new people and boys when you go off to college."

Surprisingly, Steve never talked about the engagement. It was almost as if it meant nothing to him. We never talked about our future, let alone a wedding. It was just about now, where I was, where I was going. I was right. The ring was just another way to say he owned me.

My thoughts were tangled when it came to him. We'd been together two years now, and I did care about him. Yet sometimes I felt like pulling away. But I ignored the feeling and shoved it back down inside me.

"I know why!" Moe said, cocking her head to the side, her mouth pushed down in a frown. I was just trying to explain all this to her, hoping for a sympathetic, nonjudgmental shoulder to lean on.

"Oh, stop it. I know you don't like him. That's no big mystery. I know he's not everybody's favorite. But he loves me, Moe. He ... I don't know. I think I love him, but I don't know. I mean, come on, nobody else has ever even asked me out, except those idiot friends of my brother's. I'm a senior now and not a single guy I had a crush on ever even noticed me! Do you remember Anthony? I made a fool of myself following him around in ninth grade, leaving him love letters in his locker."

"Yeah, that was kind of goofy." She laughed. "That and the stupid bells you used to tie to your shoelaces."

"Right!" I cringed. "Adolescent shit. I was such a dork. Steve ... he's different. He's not like those stupid high school boys. You of all people know what I mean, both Rob and Peter are older than you. Steve is mature, acts mature, and sex is fun with him ... most of the time."

"Oh, please!" She drew out the "eeesss" with disgust, stretched her legs across the couch, and plopped them on my lap. "You're finally questioning this relationship! That's normal. He's a control freak, a jerk, and a pervert. And you obviously like freaky sex."

"Shut up. He's my boyfriend, and even though I'm confused ... oh never mind, I don't want to talk about it." I flung her legs off me and put mine on top of hers. "Time for a subject change. So, what about Doug? What's his deal?"

"Yeah, what's up with you and him?" She lifted my legs up, placed them on the coffee table, and strung her legs across mine again, with a determined look that just dared me to move them again. *V* played in the background on the television, but the sound was all the way down. "He's been acting kind of odd when you're around."

"Huh?" I sat up straighter. "What are you talking about?"

I couldn't believe it. Even after all this time, when I heard the name Doug, my heart skipped a beat. There was just something about him, something in his lopsided goofy smile and ... that body! Wiry and lean, not bulky.

"Well," she said, lowering her voice even though we were alone and in the basement, and no one else was around. "The other day in school when we were talking with Peter and Doug walked up, he couldn't keep his eyes off you. I think he has a crush on you."

"What? You're crazy. He does not!" My cheeks and ears felt so hot with embarrassment. But I wasn't so much embarrassed as excited. Could it be true?

"Look, you're blushing! What gives?"

"Really, I think you're seeing things." I stuck my tongue out at her. "You know I've had a major crush on him ever since the beginning of freshman year. But he doesn't even know I exist except through you all. You remember in sophomore year before the ski trip when they had 'buy a senior— for a ... day'!?"

I could barely get that out because we'd both started laughing really hard. "Yes!" she choked out between gasps of laughter. "God, I almost forgot that! How could I? But then you went off and almost got married to Steve!"

During the fall of our sophomore year, the seniors had organized "Buy a Senior for a Day." Moe and I bought Doug. And our idea for him was brilliant: Moe decided we'd dress him up in girls' clothes.

"Oh my god, he made such a cute girl!" Tears of laughter were running down my cheeks. But I sobered up pretty quick. "I don't know if he will ever forgive us for that. And possibly he's planning some sort of revenge."

She pulled her legs up under her and gave me a devious look. "What do you think he's doing right now?"

"Why, what are you thinking?" Knowing Moe, she was up to something sneaky.

"Oh, I don't know." She bounced up on her feet and loomed over me. "Let's call him!"

"What? No way! You've completely lost your mind. We can't call him."

"Why not? It's perfect. And you definitely need a distraction from Steve the Pervert."

"Shut the fuck up! I won't play nice if you do that," I said, crossing my arms and frowning.

"Okay, okay. I'll stop making fun of poor defenseless Steve. But come on, think about it—how much fun would it be to call up Doug and tease him?"

"Hmm. As a matter of fact, I know what would get him—what would get any of those little Langley boys." I gave her my own devious expression, wiggling my eyebrow. I could arch my left eyebrow really high, just like my cool grandma could.

"Yes! I like your thinking. Here, hand me the phone."

I reached over the coffee table, grabbed the phone, stretched out the green cord, and handed it to her.

"Do you know his number?" I asked, feeling a bit nervous about this impromptu plan.

She reached over and grabbed a little book off the side of the couch, which turned out to be her address book. "Here we go!" She pitched the "go" in her extra-high voice.

"Oh god, you're prepared!"

"Mm-hmm." She started dialing, and I laughed at her determination. Oh my god. *What are we getting into!*

She sat there and looked at me with that sideways grin on her face while I imagined the phone ringing. She was a contradiction in her old-fashioned, high-necked cotton nightgown with tiny, pale peach-colored flowers decorating it like butterflies and her dusty blond hair falling around her face. Freckles scattered across her nose and cheeks, giving her a look of innocence. Moe had had long, long hair, and short, short hair. Medium long suited her the best. She was crazy cute. That and her personality were why boys fought over her.

I was wearing my fuzzy pink diamond-print one-piece pajamas. Pj's, as I liked to call them. Neck high, and all the way to the ankles. I looked like an overgrown eight-year-old.

"Hello, Mrs. Sands, this is Moe, can I please speak to Doug?" Moe suddenly said in her sweet, mannerly voice. Everyone liked Moe—all the parents. She was the biggest deceiver. And I mean that in the nicest possible way. She came across as this smart, dependable, responsible young lady to the adults and teachers, which she was. But then she had this crazy wild side. Her first boyfriend was a drug dealer, for god's sake! And even he had her mom fooled.

Moe had the best party freshman year. She just blew away any other parties out there. Her dad unwittingly made flyers for us, and then we wrote on the back that we were serving grain alcohol, and "bring your own." We set up a table on the side of the house, blocking the space to get to the backyard so we could collect money for the band. They played in the backyard surrounded by the woods, with many dark places to hide out in case the police showed up. And they did eventually come to break it up considering there were at least a hundred people there. Yeah, it got way out of control. It was amazing Moe didn't get in trouble with her parents—and they were upstairs the whole time.

But that was all before Steve. I couldn't take him to parties. He didn't drink. And when I did talk him into going to a big party like hers, he just talked down to everyone, constantly asserting his authority, acting like my friends were just little kids, and that he knew better.

"Hi, Doug. What are you up to?" Moe said in a singsong voice. Pause. "Oh, I'm sitting here with Suzanne. She's spending the night with me." Another pause ... a long one. "Well, we were just reminiscing about the old days, when you used to wear a dress," she said in a silky voice, and then burst into a giggle. Damn, I wanted to know what Doug was saying. But she wouldn't give me the phone. And suddenly I wasn't sure I wanted it. Cold feet? Yes!

"Yeah? Well, we're just sitting here in our little nighties giving each other back massages and thinking we could use some company. That's when Suzanne suggested we call you."

I had been leaning far out over the couch intently listening to her. When she said that, I fell off the couch and then jumped to my feet.

"What the fuck, Moe?" I whispered to her.

But her expression was filled with a devilish light. She was ignoring me. Obviously that suggestion went over well.

"Mmm? Really? Yes, that would be lovely." She covered the mouthpiece with her hand, holding back laughter and looking at me with a huge grin. "He is so totally into it. I think he's going to come over!"

My hand flew to my mouth in horror, and I felt sweat break out over my forehead.

"Yeah?" she continued to Doug. "Well ... okay, hold on." She shoved the phone at me so quickly I barely had time to jump away. With no choice, I grabbed the phone and held it to my ear. My heart was pounding in my chest; I could feel the blood rush through me and felt hot all over, almost nauseous. I could hear breathing on the other end. My elbows felt tingly, and the sensation traveled right up my arms to the back of my head. I couldn't bring myself to say anything. Moe sat there grinning at me, nodding her head as if to say, "Go on, say something."

"Hello? Suzanne?" Doug said quietly on the other end. I guess he could hear me breathing too.

"Hi," I squeaked. Then I cleared my throat, barely able to breathe. *I think I'm about to have a heart attack.*

"What are you two up to over there?" His voice was quiet, and only slightly teasing. He sounded ... kind. Suddenly he didn't sound as young as he was. I mean, I guess he wasn't a silly high school boy anymore, being that he graduated two years before.

I still couldn't say anything. I was trying. I was trying to come up with something sharp, witty, or sexy. All this training with Steve, and here I was completely shy. Embarrassed. An idiot.

"Hello—are you still there? Suzanne?" He was luring me out of my frozen state with his sexy voice. The way he pronounced my name was like licking icing off a cake. Yummy.

"Hi, um," I said, clearing my throat again, "yes, I'm here. I'm sorry ... just ... well, how are you? We miss having you in school." I finally was able to talk in a somewhat calm voice. "What have you been up to? I heard you're going to Mason and still working at Clyde's." I was babbling. Not able to stop myself.

He laughed on the other end, and it stopped me short. "So, what are you and Moe up to over there? You didn't just call to see how I'm doing, did you?" Oh, how I loved the sound of his voice. "From the sound of it, it looks like you're doing something fun."

I was so glad he wasn't there to witness my embarrassment. I glared at Moe and took a big, deep breath.

"Well, like Moe said, we"—big gulp—"we need a third to get this party going."

There, I said it. Moe sank into the couch shaking in hysterics as she hid her laughter behind a pillow.

"Really?" he said, laughing now.

"Don't laugh!" I said, feigning outrage. "You might just blow your chances with the two hottest girls left at Langley!"

"Oh? Now that's something I have to see."

Oh jeez. "Yes, well, wouldn't you like to?"

"Are you still going out with that muscle man?" *Oh my god*, I thought, mortified. Of course I knew he knew about Steve. I wasn't sure if I was more embarrassed by his description or the fact that he'd brought him up.

"Well, yes. But does that really matter?" I said, ignoring my discomfort.

"I suppose not. I was just wondering. So, you're sitting there with Moe devising ways of getting me to come over." He was quiet for a moment, then, "Okay, I'm on my way." He hung up the phone with a pronounced *click*.

"What?" Moe looked at me in shock as I hung up the phone. "He's not really coming over, is he? He can't! My mom is upstairs!"

"Errr ... he hung up so fast, I couldn't tell him it was a joke! Besides, you should have thought of that before you invited him over."

Oh man. Now we were in it deep. *Fuck.*

Moe turned and looked at me. I looked at her. Then we started laughing again and fell on each other. I laughed so hard tears ran down my cheeks and my sides ached.

"Okay, seriously now. We need to do something about this," she said, standing up and looking around in a slight panic.

"Well, I'm going to go touch up my makeup." I stood up, wiped the tears from my cheeks, and headed to the bathroom. "Do we put our clothes back on, or stay in these childish pajamas?"

"What are you going on about? Shit, I'm gonna sneak upstairs and make sure my mom and dad are asleep. Do you think he has the sense to park on the street, not in our driveway?"

"He's not dumb. I'm sure he'll figure that out. And he knows to come around to your bedroom on the ground floor. If he's quiet and sneaky, your mom may never even know it."

"Yeah, and it will take him at least twenty minutes to drive here from his house."

Standing in the bathroom, I looked at myself in the mirror. I looked crazy. All tweaked out with excitement, my face flushed pink, and my eyes all bright. Well, I didn't look too bad actually.

I added some lip gloss, Bonnie Bell Lip Smacker—it made my lips look fuller, and it smelled really nice, like candy. Then I headed back out to the room. It was a huge room in the basement with a fireplace in the back. Over the mantel were all these old cast-iron butter molds. Moe's parents had lots of these antique items. It was more rustic down here and a bit fancier upstairs. I imagined an invisible "do not touch" sign on everything upstairs. All old, and probably very valuable. Not like our house, where all of our furniture was pretty much bought after each move, only to be discarded and replaced with new furniture for the next move. Everything seemed replaceable. Every move was like that. I had to keep a sharp eye on my things: toys, clothes, photo albums.

I guess that's why I have a hard time letting go of things. If I looked the other way or was out with friends or playing in the backyard before one of our cross-country moves, when we got to our next destination and I unboxed my stuff, I might find everything gone.

Moe wasn't in the family room when I finally made my way back, so I walked to her bedroom to see if she was there getting ready. It was also empty. She was so lucky to have her bedroom in the basement or ground floor. The back of the house opened up onto the backyard, yet from the front of the house it looked like only one story. Her bedroom was next to the garage. Another useful thing—we always knew when her parents came home.

I headed out to the family room and stood there quietly listening. *Maybe she's upstairs.* But then I heard something outside on the enclosed porch. It was dark out there and I couldn't see if anyone was outside, so I walked over to check it out.

The back of the house had a large, enclosed porch with glass windows. The very same porch where I'd sat with her sisters smoking pot at the infamous freshman party.

As I headed over to the glass door that led outside to it, I could see her sitting in the swing chair with her robe wrapped tightly around her. Great. I didn't have a robe to cover up my crazy getup. But at least my crazy getup covered me.

I opened the door and started to walk over to her and stopped short. Sitting there on the couch across from her was Doug.

Doug, in all his natural, sexy yum-yum: old Levi's and a thin worn gray T-shirt under a brown leather jacket. He was sitting forward with his elbows on his thighs, his chin resting on his hands, listening to whatever Moe had been going on about. As the door closed behind me, making a loud *clank*, those dusty gray-blue eyes turned up to look at me. His head tilted up toward mine and with that lovely grin, he took me in from head to toe.

My breath caught in my chest as I realized right then just how much I liked him. Always had. Painfully so. But I'd never let myself think about it.

"Oh man, I'm gonna see if my parents are up or if they're still watching TV upstairs." Moe popped up out of the chair and headed toward the door. As she opened it, she swung her head around and said, "Don't get too wild down here!"

Doug patted the space next to him.

I found my legs and walked over and sat down next to him. It wasn't a long couch, more of a loveseat. Which meant I was forced to sit close to him. My leg an inch from his, if not closer.

"Hey, love your sexy evening attire." Grinning, he leaned all the way back, placing his arm on the back of the couch behind me, the other resting comfortably on his leg.

Doug. Casual. Almost languid. He reminded me of a cat. I don't know why I was thinking all this. He was different from Steve in so many ways. Not a domineering bone in his body. He always seemed so ... gentle. Young, eager, nice, with no agenda. But now I could see he was more than that. He was a man. Not just a boy in high school anymore. He was in college. But less than two years older than me.

"What are you thinking?" His hand had moved and was resting on my arm, gently nudging me out of my thoughts.

"Oh? Sorry—nothing." I was stumbling over my words. "I mean ... why did you come?"

"You invited me, remember?" He grinned. My eyes were glued to that full mouth of his. *Really lovely lips, wow.* I shook my head violently, trying to shake it off.

"What's wrong?" His brows knit together, and he looked even cuter in his concern for me.

"Oh, Doug." I sat up straighter and shook my head. "You shouldn't have come."

"Why not? Why did you invite me if you didn't want me to come?" A bemused look passed over his face.

"Well, I wanted you to. You know that. Um ... I don't know," I sighed. "It's just—you know."

"Yeah, I know. Steve."

"Yeah." I cleared my throat.

We sat there for what seemed like ages. Just quietly looking at each other. I took a deep breath. He looked at me with a question. But before he could ask it, I leaned over really quick and placed my mouth almost on top of his. But right as we were about to meet, I stopped, just hovering, and slowly closed my eyes. I could feel the heat from his breath against my mouth. He didn't move a bit. He just seemed to wait for me.

And then I leaned the extra two inches and gently, ever so gently felt my lips against his full warm lips. So different ... so nice. And then I felt his hands grip my arms, pulling my body closer to him, and his mouth opening and the warmth of his tongue. Our heads were tilted at opposite angles; our lips fit perfectly. And as I was just starting to lose myself completely in that kiss, the door banged open.

I bolted up and out of the seat so fast Doug almost fell forward. My face flushed and my head felt dizzy. I stood there and looked at him.

"It was so nice to see you, Doug," I said. It was as if I were talking in a tunnel, it was so disconnected from me. "I'm really tired now and I'm going to go to bed." Like a robot.

I turned and bolted and almost ran right into Moe.

"Where are you going?" she started, but I brushed past her fast and let the door close on its own behind me as I found my way back to her bedroom and dove onto her bed. I buried my head in her big soft pillow.

27 | PLANS TAKE HOLD

"Should I Stay of Should I Go," The Clash

"Prom sucked." I sprawled out over Bambie's bed, wiggling my toes to get the polish to dry.

"Well, big surprise. You're dating a dick."

"Oh, fuck off, would you?"

It really did suck. And he really was a dick. I looked like a stupid Southern belle bride all in white with long gloves and satin white shoes. So innocent. Right. A six-foot giant dressed like a little girl. I mean, I couldn't blame him completely, I'd picked it out, but that's because I knew he would like it. I just didn't look like myself.

"When I went to my brother's prom it was so much fun. I don't know … it was easy. Scott was nice and since we weren't dating there wasn't any head drama. It didn't have to be perfect."

"Where did you guys go? We all went to the same restaurant and then headed over to the prom. You would have had more fun if you'd both joined us." She was studying the back cover of this new record she'd bought when we were in Georgetown last time, at Penguin Feathers.

"Oh, the place was nice. It wasn't that. It was really fancy. Steve really did go all out, as far as expenses. I mean, there was no limo; he thinks his new gold Pontiac is so hot. Did I tell you about that? Well, whatever, it's used, but at least he doesn't look like he's driving around in a beat-up Nova anymore." I felt kind of bad complaining. "It's just that he acts so weird around people. He gets so uptight if any guy looks at me, but then he openly flirts with waitresses." I thought he'd stopped doing that, but I guess I hadn't gone out in public with him in a while. He usually just made me meet him at his place, and we spent most of our time in his room.

"He's always done that, that's nothing new."

"Well, I'm tired of it!" I leaned back, closing my eyes. "Did I tell you that Doug is having a party this weekend?"

"Yeah, you mentioned that. But how are you going to go? Steve hates those guys; he would never go."

"Forget that. I don't want to go with him. He'd be a jerk to everyone, like the last time. I'm learning. I do Steve things with Steve, and everything else without him. And he doesn't need to know."

I rolled over to my side and stared intently at my impossible fingernails. I'd bitten them down to nothing again. "It's like I have a separate life. So, I'm going to spend the night with Moe and we're going to go to the party. He'll never know, and he doesn't need to know."

"You're such a weirdo. Now you're sneaking out on your boyfriend!" She stared at me, shaking her head for a minute, and then went back to shuffling through her albums.

"Not like he isn't." I scowled.

"What! Is he still doing that?" She looked up from the album with a frown.

"Oh, never mind." Bambie was the only one I shared Steve's "indiscretion" with. It was just too humiliating. I knew what my other friends would say. Anyhow, they were my problems, and I was dealing with them by myself. Besides, I didn't think he was doing it anymore. He had this job where he worked all the time, and I hadn't found any more pictures. I mean, he did propose to me—that should mean something.

But it also made me feel less guilty about my secret crush on Doug.

"I know what you're thinking. I mean ... but I don't know." Rolling down onto my back again, I stared at the ceiling and groaned. "I'm confused. But, hey I'm young, and I shouldn't have to be committed to one guy. But, yeah, I know he would freak out if I said that."

"Yeah, and that's fucked up because he did that to you."

"Yeah, but he's not doing it anymore."

"Well, which is it? He is or he isn't?

"He told me he wasn't." I lied.

And you believe him?"

I got up, walked over to her vanity table, and sat on the stool, gazing at myself in the mirror.

"Why would he have proposed to me then? I mean, that was like him saying, without saying, that he'd stopped. Besides," I said, more quietly, "what choice do I really have?"

"Listen, I know why you started dating him, but I don't get why you stick with it. You have nothing in common. He's stuck in the seventies listening to classic rock, and what ... Alan Parsons Project? Ick." She made a face as she continued riffling through her records. "You are not into that shit—"

"That's not entirely true," I interrupted, swiveling around and looking at her, but she was avoiding eye contact. "I kind of like them ... and he does like Bowie—"

"And yet he wouldn't take you to see him last August at the Capital Centre for Bowie's '83 tour. I mean, Siouxsie, that was epic."

"Hey, that's not fair, he just took me to see Duran Duran!"

"Oh my god, you said you had the worst time. Everyone was standing and screaming, having fun, and he made you just sit next to him. Sit?!" She had picked up a record at this point and was standing there looking really frustrated. "He doesn't even like Duran Duran. You told me when you raved about the Bauhaus and played him their record, he dismissed them, saying the guy was just imitating Bowie. I mean, come on. And"—she was on a roll now—"he wears these velour V-neck sweaters, tight cords, and a hairstyle from *B. J. and the Bear*! It's so 1979."

"Okay, now you're just being mean." I pouted and turned back to the mirror. Leaning in, I sat there and looked at myself, frowning. Who was this girl? What was wrong with her? Nothing Bambie said was untrue. But I kind of liked Steve's look. I mean, I used to be really into it. It was just now ... I don't know. There were other things I was into. But did that really matter? Don't they say opposites attract?

"What do you two even talk about?"

"Okay—" I started, getting a bit pissed off at this point.

"You know what?" she interrupted, changing the conversation as quickly as it started as she put the needle down on "Ghosts" and The

Jam began to play. "It's going to be great. Two more weeks and then graduation!"

"We are the class of 1984!" we both sang loudly, forgetting the frustration and criticisms from just a moment before.

"Then it's summer break, and you're off to California to see your dad, all by yourself! Then September will be here and before you know it and we're off to VCU."

I turned around and put my hands on my knees to keep them from bouncing up and down. "Oh my god, Bambie, I can't believe it. I just can't wait!"

"I still don't get it."

"What?"

"I mean, he's so controlling of your every move, and you seem ... well, kind of unhappy. Why don't you just break up? Wait—just how did you convince him to let you go to California, and, by the way, VCU?"

"One day you'll just walk right out of his life. And then you'll wonder why you didn't before." Bambie sang, changing the words of the song.

I moaned; this conversation was going downhill quickly. "Listen, I don't know if I want to break up with him. I mean—I don't know. I mean no one's perfect. And he loves me, he really does."

"Ugh, a psycho could love you and you wouldn't turn it away," she groaned.

"No, seriously! He does, really. But listen, I just told him that I need to see my dad. I mean it's been almost a year, except that one brief moment at court. And when he started to protest, I said if he didn't like it, it was too bad."

"Really? You said that?"

"Yeah, I did. And you know what? That was all there was to it. He totally caved. He didn't know quite what to make of it."

"Wow, I'm impressed," she said, turning around stunned.

"The same with college. Well—actually, I lied. I didn't tell him I also got into the Corcoran. I kind of made it seem like VCU was the only school I got accepted into."

I'd had only two choices: Corcoran School of Art, right here in D.C., or Virginia Commonwealth University, an hour and a half away, in Richmond. The Corcoran would artistically be the smart choice;

it was an amazing school. But it would mean I would continue to live with my mom and be near Steve. VCU was a decent art school—in comparison to the Corcoran, not so great—but going there would mean I would have the distance I needed. The chance to get some freedom, to really think about what I wanted. Because I just wasn't sure anymore.

And it didn't hurt that Bambie was going there too.

I'd finally broken down and called my dad a week ago. I hadn't talked to him since that one time at court in over a year. I couldn't bear it. I blamed him for everything.

He hadn't just hurt my mom, emotionally and physically. He'd hurt my brother. He'd hurt us all emotionally. Even though more than a year had passed, and the slamming of doors in the house had stopped, I still jumped when someone came in and shut the door too loudly, especially if the slam was followed by a deep male voice. It left me paralyzed in anticipation of the angry, hateful commands that would follow. But I was starting to jump a little less each day.

Meanwhile, I was beginning to dread the phone calls from Steve. He knew I was getting ready to graduate and go off to college, and he was panicking. I could tell. He wouldn't say anything, but there was an air to him that was different.

He couldn't stop me from going to college. There were some things he knew he couldn't force me to do and going to the college he wanted me to go to was one of them. I'd never even told him that I applied to a school in the area. He would have flipped out if he knew I'd chosen to go to a school more than an hour away, especially after I'd been accepted to the school closest to home.

Sometimes, he was just so controlling. But when he wasn't, he was tender. He was caring. He was fun. He was just very protective. He was ... my cowboy.

"Well, it's going to be great. I hope we can share a dorm together," she said.

"Yeah, and it's so cool your brother is already there!" I laughed. But then her words registered. "What do you mean, 'hope'?"

She was sitting on the floor, going through some albums.

"Bambie, didn't you get your mom to fill out the forms yet?"

"Well ..." she said, drawing out the "l's. "She hasn't sent them in yet, as far as I can tell. I don't know. You know how she is."

"Yeah, I do. She thinks I'm a bad influence because you blamed me for dyeing your hair!" Frowning, I said, "Everybody's parents have always liked me; I'm the good girl. This is crazy that your mom doesn't like me. And for the first time, it actually matters. If we don't get a dorm room together, I'm going to be really bummed out."

"I know. We'll get it worked out," she promised. "But you're right. We're going to have a fantastic time because David will take us to some cool shows. Richmond has the best gigs, next to D.C."

"You know, Bambie, it's like this whole new chapter is about to begin." She had swapped the Jam for Duran Duran, and the sex-infused "The Chauffeur" started up.

I jumped up and met her in the middle of her room. Facing each other, with grins on our faces, we each placed our palms against each other's. Palm to palm. Her left palm flat against my right, my right against her left. And then, to the music, we gracefully, with alternating hands, pushed backward and forward, our shoulders and hips moving to the rhythm of the sleekly melodic tune.

"*The sun drips down getting heavy behind, the front of your dress all shadowy like, and—*"

"SING BLUE SILVER!" we both sang out loudly, then collapsed to the floor on our backs.

"It's going to be brilliant!" We sighed at the same time.

28 | TESTING THE BOUNDARIES

"Hot Love," T. Rex

I found Moe in the kitchen amid a cloud of smoke, waiting for her turn at the keg. She was talking to Peter and some boys who had graduated two years ago.

"Where have you been?" she said, turning to me and grinning. "Out smoking one of those clove cigs?" Bambie and I had picked up these yummy-tasting cigarettes called Djarum when we were in Georgetown last week. They tasted sweet, like cloves, and made your lips tingle. They didn't make you smell like cigarettes either. We were going to shows at the 9:30 Club when we could, usually, to see Eric, Bambie's boyfriend, play with his band, the Meatmen. but we also went to the club on the corner. Steve worked Friday nights, so it was a perfect escape.

"No, and it's not what you think," I said, giving her a warning look. "I can't seem to 'find' what I'm looking for."

"Love your top! It's so cute. Where did you get it?" She felt the fabric with her fingers as she swatted away the cigarette smoke from her face. She didn't smoke because she was allergic to it. I think it gave her asthma or something.

"You know that cute shop at the mall, Georgetown Cotton?" It was a new purchase from my paycheck from the record store. I bought it because it felt soft and silky, and it looked great with my jeans. It was a halter top, so my back was bare, so I couldn't wear a bra with it. But that was okay because it was loose the way it hung on me. It was off-white with geometric patterns of light blue and looked like it was made from a scarf. As long as it wasn't a cold night, it wouldn't be too outrageous. But thank god my dad didn't live with us or he wouldn't have let me out of the house. Oh, and Steve never would have allowed it.

Peter leaned over with his rosy cheeks and red lips. He had the most luscious lips. Lips I would never touch again since that kiss in the cemetery in eighth grade. Moe and Peter were on and off, but now they were on again. Lately she'd been acting just plain weird and jealous whenever Peter and I stood next to each other, and I couldn't figure out why. She'd never acted like that before. I mean, he was cute, but he was like a brother to me.

"What can't you find, Zanny?" he teased.

"Don't call me that! Ugh." I spun around and headed for the bathroom.

Huge line. Typical. Those were the times it would have been most convenient to be a boy. Outside, bushes. Easy.

"Hey."

I whipped around, my stomach in my throat. But it wasn't Doug. Just Peter again.

"What are you doing?" I was relieved and disappointed all at the same time.

"I have to go to the bathroom; what do you think I'm doing?" He looked confused.

"Oh. Okay," I said. *I think I'm getting paranoid.* "Listen, Peter, what's going on with Moe? Why is she acting weird? I mean, like, she gets all pissy and stuff whenever you give me hugs or whatever. She never used to do that. What gives?"

He looked down at his feet and I could see his face turn red.

"What? Tell me!" I reached over and poked him in the shoulder.

"Well, um. She asked me if I thought you were hot."

"What?" I said a bit too loud.

"Shhh. She'll kill me if she knows I told you this."

"I'll kill you if you don't tell me the full story, now!"

"Okay, but take it easy." He ran his hands through his shiny black hair. "She asked if I thought you were hot, and I said, sure." My eyebrows rose, and I started to smile. "Then she asked me if she and I weren't dating, if I'd sleep with you."

"What the fuck? Who asks a guy that question?"

"Yeah," he said and grinned. "Even you know that."

"Shut up! A guy will sleep with anything given the chance. Oh man," I groaned. "What did you say? Please don't tell me ..."

"Well?"

"Well, what? What did you say?!" My smile was gone, and panic had started to set in.

"Well, I told her yeah, you were hot, and sure I'd sleep with you, but only if I'd never met or dated her. By the way, you do look hot in that top."

I could have died right there. What an idiot.

Ignoring his last comment, I snorted, "And somehow you thought that was a smart answer?"

"It was an honest answer," he said defensively.

"By the way, am I supposed to be flattered?"

The door opened and it was my turn for the bathroom.

"I'm outta here. This is your mess. You just fucked up our friendship, Peter. No more hugs! You know we'll never be allowed to be alone together even for a minute, even with her in the other room. Ever." I stuck my tongue out at him, childish I know. I'm sure he thought it was cute. I turned and slammed the door to the bathroom.

So far, no Doug. I had no idea where he was. I guessed he was back with the redhead and off making out with her somewhere. She was hot, so I didn't know why he wouldn't be. He'd probably completely forgotten that little moment at Moe's.

Angry at Peter and starting to give up on ever bumping into Doug, I wandered into the living room where the extremely tall and charismatic Scott Brenner was manning Mr. Sands's bar—never intended for the likes of us. I walked over and over the chorus of "Sweet Home Alabama," which was blaring loudly from the stereo and being echoed by the strains of voices from the surrounding crowd, I shouted, "Have you seen Doug?"

He motioned to his ears, followed by a "hands up in the air" signal for "I can't hear you," then started pouring Jack Daniels followed by ginger ale into a big plastic cup with a Redskins logo and handed it to me.

"Here you go," he yelled over the throng of noise, smiling with his big white teeth.

Looking around the room, I saw mostly older kids from two classes ahead of us. Moe was nowhere in sight, or anyone else I knew. I shifted back and forth on my feet, not sure whether to sit or stand. In a not-quite-graceful way, I took a big gulp of my drink and shuddered. Yuk. But I was really nervous, and I figured it would relax me. So I took another huge gulp.

The house was big, although you couldn't tell from the outside. From the front it looked like a one-story. Like Moe's house it had a basement level that let out to a yard in the back. The whole house was built on a hill, so it was quite big. A large deck shot off from the living room, which is where most everyone was hanging out, and loomed out over the yard.

I walked down the stairs, taking another big gulp of my drink for support, and started to feel a bit wobbly from the mixture. I followed the path of grade school through high school photos of Doug and his sister lining the wall, until I found myself downstairs in quiet solitude. Weaving my way through the hall, I opened a door to the right that led into a room that looked like Doug's. But it was empty.

I was relieved. *What am I thinking? Why am I even here? This is crazy*, I thought. *I hope he doesn't come in towing the redhead.*

I looked around at the trophies, posters, guy stuff really. It didn't look that much different than my brother's room. Different than Steve's, though. Steve's was barren of "things." This room, it seemed ... normal. It felt kind of right. Nice. My room was filled with girlie things, kind of goofy and personal. This room felt like mine: personal. Only masculine. *I really shouldn't be lurking here. I need to go.*

I took another big gulp of the drink and then spun around to leave, and nearly jumped out of my skin, making a choking sound.

Standing quietly by the door studying me with his swoon-worthy gray eyes was Doug. My stomach lurched, sending my pulse racing a mile a minute.

"Yikes," I said out loud.

"Yikes is right," he said, laughing.

I said "yikes" again, but this time to myself, not out loud. God, he had such a great laugh.

"I've been looking for you," he said as he walked over to me, smiling. "And all this time you were in here, waiting for me." He raised his eyebrows up and down in a comical way.

"What? You were—looking? Waiting? Me?" I stammered, "No, I ... I was looking for the bathroom, because the one upstairs had this huge line, and I ended up here."

"This doesn't look like a bathroom." He grinned.

"No, I mean, yeah, I know. I figured that out. I was just looking at the photos on the wall ... and yes of course I knew this was your room." I always just seemed to babble when he was with me.

He was standing right next to me, and I felt so awkward, I turned away toward the wall and pointed at a photo.

"Where are you all in this photo?"

He was still facing me, not even looking at the wall. He was standing so close, it startled me when he spoke into my ear, "Wherever it was, it would have been a whole lot more fun if you'd been there."

"What? Oh, you are so full of shi—"

He interrupted me with the touch of his fingers on my chin. He gently turned my face toward him, and with the sweetest expression, he leaned in and kissed me. Warm, soft lips, and then the world disappeared around me. My mind went blank. I forgot what I was going to say or do. No second-guessing why I was there. Finally, just the two of us, alone. And kissing!

It seemed to last forever, like watching fireworks lying on your back with the hot July night to hug you and dreaming of doing just this. Kissing a boy's warm wet mouth.

His hands found my hands and, backing up, he drew me toward the bed with him. He sat down and pulled me onto his lap so that I was facing him. Straddling him. Thankfully I was wearing jeans, not the skirt I'd originally laid out.

His hands smoothed across my shoulders and down my bare back, sending shivers down my spine, making me light-headed, with a sensation of floating on air. His hands were warm and smooth as he circled my waist, forcing me closer. My arms, with nowhere else to go, clumsily moved up around his shoulders and I clasped my fingers together behind his neck.

Now we were face to face.

"Hey." There was a kindness in his voice that felt so real, and open.

"Hi." My voice sounded nervous and silly in my head.

"So now what?" He grinned again.

"Oh, I don't know." I shook my head in mock seriousness.

"Don't be like that." He mocked me right back. "We don't have to do anything ... if that's what you want."

I shook my head slowly. Oh, how I wanted to kiss him again!

This time, he moved in more passionately, one hand on my lower back, pressing me to him, the other behind my head. My head was spinning, my stomach tight. They were the kind of kisses you waited a lifetime for.

It's funny how different a kiss can be, I thought.

I couldn't tell if it was me, but it felt really hot in the room. My body started to pulse with electricity, the feeling engulfing my senses.

Coming up for air, I mumbled, "Oh hell."

He leaned back, laughing, pulling me with him, his legs sliding between mine, pressing against me, as we twisted over and lay on our sides facing each other. His movement seemed intentional as he rubbed me with his leg, and his lips moved to my neck, a sensitive spot that sent shivers down my spine and made me incapable of saying no ... to anything.

My hand moved over his back, around and down his hips, as he pressed his body harder against mine. Then tentatively, out of curiosity, I moved my hand slowly over his hip and between his legs, as if I knew what I was doing. But as soon as my hand touched him, I froze. He was hard! He groaned.

I don't know if it was the groan or the massive bulge, but all of a sudden, I came to my senses. The spell abruptly vanished even with the overwhelming heat that was spreading across my face and body. I untangled myself from him and jumped off the bed.

He just rolled over on his back, placed both hands behind his head, smiled at me, and sighed. Was he disappointed? Or did it seem like he knew that's exactly what I'd do?

"I can't," I apologized.
"I'll wait."
I bolted.

29 | WHAT'S REAL ANYHOW?

"Sex (I'm A...)," Berlin

I opened my eyes and shook my head violently, trying to shake the image of Doug kissing me in his bed. "Oh," I groaned. "What am I doing?"

I rolled over, swung my legs out of bed, and rested my head in my hands as my elbows dug into my thighs. I couldn't get him out of mind. *Stop it! I'm in a relationship for crying out loud!*

But Steve *is a cheat!* I argued with myself. *He deserves it! Or at the very least,* I continued, *I'm allowed at least one solitary indiscretion.*

Doug's words echoed in my mind constantly: "I'll wait." *What does that mean? Does it mean what I think? Would he? Why!?* Why would anyone want to get tangled up in this mess that I called my life?

I couldn't stop obsessing about that moment and how I could have handled it differently. I was experienced now. I mean, that's what Steve told me, that we did things only adults did, not clumsy high school kids. And yet, in the moment when I had my chance to act cool, collected, and sophisticated, I acted just like that.

I didn't feel experienced. *Oh, but if I had one more chance*, I thought. But guilt crept over me, as if Steve were listening to my thoughts. Like a watchful, controlling eye. Even my subconscious was controlled by him.

The last few days, I had walked around the halls of Langley with my Aiwa cassette player blasting "Sex" by Berlin and imagined being with Doug. I was obsessed with him and the song, and it gave me a thrill that no one knew what I was listening to.

Oh, the impossible dream, I sighed inwardly.

I have to shut it down, just close down that fantasy—at least for now. I shook my head again and forced myself to move on.

Graduation came and went. The best thing about graduation was that it was held at Constitution Hall. That was pretty cool. But sitting in the row with all my classmates, some of whom I'd known since sixth grade, I felt like an outsider. It wasn't really them; it was the overbearing presence of Steve. He loomed over everything and everyone, and by sheer Steve energy, my classmates kept their distance.

I tried to hold my head high and pretend he wasn't there, but he sat on the sidelines watching me like a hawk. My every move. I watched from the corner of my eye as he took the camera from my mom. Another excuse to have control and be there every step I made. He called my name, and I had to look. Smiling big, dimples disguising the mortification I felt by his presence. I quickly turned to see who might have witnessed his attention. Curious or judgmental eyes gazed upon me. Maybe both.

After the ceremony was over, everyone else went off to their own graduation celebrations, dinners, and parties, while we went to my mom's office barbecue.

She invited us all—my brother, myself, and Steve. I just thought it would be the safest thing to do. My mom deserved to be with me on my graduation. Everyone was really nice, but at the same time, it sucked. The food was kind of gross.

All four of us sat at a picnic table together, and it felt so awkward. There I was in a white dress—always with the white. A pretense at innocence. Just knowing Steve liked it. He was wearing a white dress shirt with a tie. It didn't really work on him. He was so bulky now that his shirts were too tight or just sloppy because of the weird fit. What was worse, he just scowled the whole time. My brother looked bored, and Mom just acted like it was all normal.

I didn't know why he had to start taking steroids. He'd started last winter, and it made him so aggressive, and he was getting too big, in my opinion. But he wanted to get bigger and bigger. I think the angry outbursts he had were probably from that dumb drug.

Once again, I longed to be with friends. Yet I knew this was better than bringing him along with me to any school event, no matter how much cooler it would have been.

Later that night, we drove back to his place. As we headed up to his room, I shoved all my misgivings and frustrations down. I was finding it much easier to pretend I was someone else in some other reality. It was so much easier to slip out of my skin, which felt really uncomfortable, like a dirty old prom dress. It was getting easier for me to detach.

"So how are things with you and Steve going?" I couldn't see her expression over the phone, but I could tell by her voice that Moe was hopeful there was an end approaching, because of college and all. "Is he pissed off about you going to see your dad in California? What about school? I mean, what's going to happen when you go off to VCU?"

I sighed, lying on the floor of my bedroom. The sun was streaming in through the window, and it made the floor nice and warm. Thankfully, I had a phone in my bedroom now, so I could conduct these conversations in private instead of in the kitchen like in our old place.

"Nothing's changed with our relationship except that he's pissed off that I'm going to see my dad next week and that I decided to go to VCU, which really isn't that far away. I mean, it's only about an hour and a half ... or maybe a bit longer depending on traffic." I stretched out and continued. "But these are the things he can't control. He can't tell me not to go to college. He knows that would push me away. And he can't forbid me to have a relationship with my dad either. That would seem psychotic, right?"

"Yeah, I guess," she said doubtfully. "I mean, I don't know, isn't he already psychotic?"

"Okay, I have to go." I sat up quickly, annoyed at her comment. She always did that. I mean, I knew she had every right; she was my closest friend, and he'd tried to sabotage our friendship, and he'd done a good job at it. Yet here we were. He couldn't change our bond. But I didn't like the reminder of just how fucked up that was. How fucked up I was for allowing it to happen.

"Zanny, I didn't mean anything by it—"

"It's okay, I love you. But I got to run and get some stuff done." I meant it; I wasn't mad at her. I was mad at myself. "I'll call you later, okay?"

"But hold on, what about Doug? Have you heard from him?"

I sighed. I didn't want to talk about him either. I hadn't seen or talked to Doug since the night of the party. "No, nothing. Listen, I really do have to go."

"Huh? Okay." Her voice perked up. "I just know he'll call."

I hung up the phone, but I didn't do anything except lie down on my bed and think about what she'd said, about what was next, and what I should do.

In the back of my head, I had these little tests that I set up for Steve. If he failed, I would feel more confident about the next step: breaking up. Or that was my plan. But he kept passing the important ones—like college, visiting my dad, dying my hair ... Even if he didn't like them.

I was excited to get away, California and then school. I needed a change. My life with Steve seemed darkly repetitive, and repressive. We went to the movies, then to his house and had sex. We'd play video games and then back to his place to have sex. We'd go to dinner, and then go back to his place. Have sex. Oh, sometimes we would reverse it. But there wasn't a day that went by, when we saw each other, that we didn't have sex. And usually it was at least three times, or more. I'd get there. Then sex. Then snack time. Sex. Listen to music or watch TV. Sex. If I spent the night, I'd wake up to ... sex. Always sex. And most of the time, I didn't want to have sex. It didn't feel good. I never had one of those orgasms that *Cosmopolitan* magazine described. But I did learn to fake it.

My mom handed me a picture she took from graduation, the one where I was sitting next to him at the barbecue.

"You look so sad," she said, just as sad as my expression in the photo.

I did. I looked—well, I looked battered, like a victim.

"Honey." She reached over and pushed my hair behind my ears.

"Stop it, Mom," I said, angry and annoyed. "I'm fine, I wasn't feeling good. The food sucked." And I turned away, hiding my expression. I was minutes away from losing control.

But I was afraid. Afraid of being alone. Of the way it was before. And then I'd have nobody. I wasn't afraid of him. *I don't think. I don't think I am*, I said to myself, reassuring and reaffirming.

30 | AT LAST

"Love Is Like Oxygen," Sweet

When I woke up, I stayed in my bed, keeping the shade down, trying to manage another hour of sleep in the cool air-conditioning. The August heat and humidity were stifling, and there was nothing for me to do. It was only two days left before my trip. I was fully packed and ready to go.

The fresh breezes of the Pacific Ocean called to me. Dad's place sounded really cool. He lived a few short blocks from the beach. It would be a little weird at first, but I had a lot of friends from childhood to visit to keep me busy.

As long as we didn't talk about Mom, it would be fine. I'd already told him that on the phone. She was off-limits.

I pulled the covers over my head to block out the demanding light that the shade couldn't seem to hold back. The summer had spread out, flat and boring. The soothing air-conditioning was my only escape.

Mom was at work. Joe was at work. Steve was at work. Besides, he was being a total dick. He wasn't happy with me headed off to California, and even less with my leaving for college.

Moe was away on vacation with her parents. Bambie too. Nobody was around. Nothing to do. *Maybe I'll go to the mall and look for a new bathing suit*, I thought.

I couldn't sleep, so I tossed my legs over the side of the bed and stood up to go brush my teeth, knocking something onto the floor. Looking down, I saw the book I was reading the night before, *Portrait of a Lady*. I picked it up, putting it back on the nightstand. *No wonder I feel depressed*, I thought.

I washed my face first and then ran a brush through my hair. I had just stuck the toothbrush in my mouth when I heard the doorbell ring.

"Ack." I spit the toothpaste out, rinsed my mouth out with water, and flung the toothbrush down. Quickly, I looked closer in the mirror to make sure I didn't still have sleep goo in my eyes, or worse. All good.

I grabbed my favorite pair of faded jean shorts off the chair, pulled them on, and ran out my door, tripping on the laundry piled up in the hallway. I was wearing my light gray Mickey Mouse T-shirt I'd gotten from Disneyland about five years before. It was small, and it fit tight, and was a little short, so my belly button showed. It didn't really look like pajamas, so I was presentable.

I bounded down the stairs, wondering who was stopping by. Or maybe it was just the postman.

Right before I reached to open the door, I remembered I should look out the window to make sure it wasn't some crazy person. I had been raised in California during the Manson aftermath and grew up with paranoid parents. I peered out through the small window in the door and almost fell flat on my ass.

It was Peter ... and Doug!

Oh shit, I thought, panic building inside of me. My heart raced. *I'm not ready for this*. I looked down again, making sure I was dressed. *Yes, I'm dressed. That's dumb. Okay.* My elbows were weak, and my knees too. *Deep breath. I can do this. Shit.*

Big breath.

I opened the door ... slowly.

I peered around it, only showing my head.

"Hey Zanny!" Peter said with this massive grin on his face. "We decided to stop by for a visit! I think you're the only one left in town."

I couldn't say anything. I just glared at him, but with more panic than anger in my eyes. My indignation was marred by my anxiety at the situation. My eyes darted toward Doug, who was leaning against the side of the door frame with his hands shoved deep in his pockets, looking at me with that lopsided smile, a bit of mischief playing on his lips.

Oh shit. What the hell are these two up to?

"Um, usually people call ..." I started.

"We just happened to be in the neighborhood, really. Just thought we'd stop by to say hi," Doug said, smiling.

"Well"—I was thinking fast—"why don't you guys go across the street to the playground? See it over there?" I leaned out around the crack of the door and pointed. "I'll meet you there, okay?"

"Sure," they both responded at the same time.

I slammed the door and ran into the living room, then back to the kitchen, then back down the hall to the bathroom. My heart was racing a mile a minute.

"What am I going to do? What am I going to do?" I said out loud, over and over again. "Oh my god, oh my god ..."

I went back into the bathroom, looked in the mirror. "Yikes."

I ran back upstairs to my room, into my bathroom, quickly washed my face again, and put on some mascara, blush, and lip gloss.

"Okay, I need to calm down."

But I was too excited. Peter had teased he'd stop by sometime with Doug. But I hadn't believed him. Not one bit.

"Okay, so here's what I need to do. I need to get a grip on myself. This is no big deal. Just act cool." Talking to myself out loud was pretty much the normal for me these days.

"It's broad daylight, and Peter is here," I reasoned as I looked at myself again in the long mirror. I looked fine in my shorts and top. Kind of sexy, kind of cute. *Okay. Just go for it.*

I ran back down the stairs, grabbed the keys off the hook, slipped my flip-flops on, and slammed out the door, stopping on the top step to shield my eyes from the harsh sun and see if they were still there waiting for me.

Yep, they were still there. Sitting on the kiddie swings in the otherwise deserted playground.

Peter looked up and waved, his expression saying, "Come on, don't be shy."

I shook off my fear and headed across the street. It was much different seeing Doug in the light of day. Especially after our last encounter. I was happy Peter was there. I wasn't sure I would know what to do if I was alone with him. It was one thing after gulping down a Jack and Ginger. But clean sober? I shivered, as if cold all of a sudden.

I stepped over the cement wall and walked across the grass to where they were still sitting on the swings. One empty swing swayed between them. Doug reached over and grabbed the rope that held it and swung it to me.

"Sit down?" he said, not commanding, but asking. *That's different*, I thought.

"Cute outfit." Peter grinned.

Self-consciously I pulled at the bottom of my shirt, trying to cover my stomach; as I sat down on the swing, I briefly looked at Peter and grinned, and simultaneously put my finger to my mouth to shush him.

"So, what's going on?" I said gingerly as I swung back in the swing, looking back and forth between the two, pretending that it was kind of normal that they were there.

"I don't know, you tell us," Peter said, still grinning.

"Hey, I'm not the one popping in unannounced, you goon. What are you both doing here?" I repeated.

"Hey, I'm hurt," Peter mock-whined. "I'm starting to feel unwanted."

I swiveled toward him, pointedly looking at him. "What are you talking about? You are always wanted."

"Yeah," he laughed, leaning back, "but not as much as ..." He pointed his head in the direction of Doug.

I turned around the other way and looked at Doug. I could see where this could go. And the fact that they were there spoke volumes to me. I decided I could be brave ... I just needed to pretend I was confident. Sexy. Alluring. I could do this.

I leaned back in the swing, held the ropes, extended my arms long, and kicked my legs forward so my back dipped down. Noting that my shorts were pretty short, and my top was sliding up, exposing my stomach, I grinned back at Doug, and finished Peter's sentence.

"Doug."

He held my eyes ... and I had to muster up all my willpower to hold that gaze. Intense.

It finally broke when Peter asked about my upcoming trip to California.

"Isn't it going to be weird seeing your dad after all that went down?" he asked.

"Yeah, a bit. But we've been talking on and off, and ... it'll be fine." God, everyone knew about what went on in my family.

Our conversation turned to their summer plans. They were both home on their college breaks, killing time doing odd jobs of painting, cutting grass—typical college break stuff. They sounded bored with school already.

I, on the other hand, went on and on about going down to Richmond and getting away from there. Having a bit of freedom.

"What kind of freedom?" The sound of Doug's voice made my elbows weak.

"Well, the kind of freedom that you can't have with your boyfriend looming around watching your every move," I said, holding back a laugh.

"Oh yeah? And what kind of moves are you planning to make?" He had turned completely to the side with the swing so that it was twisted, and the top ropes made a triangle. His feet were rooted in the dirt, legs spread wide, and his arms wrapped around the outside of the ropes, meeting in the middle, right hand grasping his left wrist.

"Aren't you hot in those jeans?" I pointed out, ignoring his question.

"Yes." His eyes grazed my legs. "But you look hot, even with just shorts on."

"Uh ..." I had just started feeling a bit like I could control this situation, but that threw me off.

"Uh, hmm." Peter cleared his throat. He'd gotten up and was standing behind me. "I don't mean to break this up but, I gotta get going. I have to meet my parents for lunch." He playfully pushed my swing forward as Doug stood up to join him. When the swing moved forward the second time, I jumped off, landing with a bounce right next to Doug.

"Hey." He smiled with surprise in his eyes. "You around later?"

"Yes." I cleared my throat to cover the possibly squeaky response.

"Maybe I'll come back?" he asked.

I turned to see if Peter had heard, but he had already taken off across the street, leaving us alone.

"Yeah, sure. That would be nice," I said as I felt tingling in my ears.

He bit the bottom of his lip, smiled, reached out and touched my chin, and then turned and headed over to Peter.

The inside of my chest felt like it was burning as I stood there watching them both get into Peter's car, and back out. My fingers gently lingered on the spot on my chin where his fingers had brushed. As they slowly began to drive off, Doug turned toward me and winked. They drove out of the road and onto the main street, and as they left, Peter swung his head my way and blew me a kiss.

What a goon, I thought.

I stood there a moment longer, and then slowly headed back into the house.

He smelled so good, fresh like apricots. Not the salty, sweaty smell, of … Steve. Steve was all salt and sweat, rough skin, scarred flesh. Calloused hands.

Doug's lips were soft and wet, and his skin so smooth. A man, but with the traces of boy lingering all over his gentle and, at times, awkward touches.

Two hours after they drove off, I found myself in bed with Doug. My walls surrounded us with ballet posters of graceful dancers swathed in pink, photos of models ripped from fashion magazines, plastic horses and dolls standing alert on the shelves, all staring down at me with their vacant expressions.

How we got to this point was a blur. It all happened so fast. He showed up, smiling. Maybe "grinning" is a better word. Next thing I knew we were in my room, undressing feverishly, excited to finally be alone. Our clothes just fell to the floor, and we hopped onto the bed and under the sheets, not leaving any time or room to think.

Just do it, I thought. *Don't think.*

This was no dance, no artistic setup, no make-believe fantasy. This was just the two of us. The fantasy was the reality. It was all I needed, and all he wanted.

We lay naked under the sheets, his hard sinewy body pressed up against mine, arms to the side of me, propping himself up so he hovered over me, leaning down to kiss me as he entered me. And as he did, the tears betrayed me.

He felt so good inside me, and with me. But suddenly, gripped with emotion, I couldn't continue. It was as if someone had poured a bucket of guilt over me. One minute it wasn't there; the next I was consumed in it. Guilt, shame, fear. It didn't matter if Steve had cheated on me. It just didn't. This was me. And I wanted to be with Doug without that guilt.

Doug must have seen the tears on my face, the sadness in my eyes, the stillness of my body, because he looked down at me, lowered himself and wrapped his arms around me.

"I'm so sorry," I whispered. He answered by rolling off me and onto his back. Then he reached over and pulled me to him so that I lay on my side with my head on his chest and his other arm wrapped around me, holding me close. With a gentle squeeze, he answered me. The room quiet, our breathing slowed.

Standing in the doorway, I watched him walk down the stairs toward his car. I sighed as I took in his casual, sexy swagger. He still took my breath away.

As if he could sense my eyes on him, or just knew I would be watching, he turned around and grinned at me.

I stood there, rooted, and watched as he pulled out and drove off down the street. *There goes the boy I longed for.* For four years. And I finally had him, for a moment.

31 | FRESH ON A DREAM

"Learning to Fly," Tom Petty

Everything was packed in my little yellow Karmann Ghia, which defied its size, allowing for all the important treasures I needed to make me feel at home in a strange dorm with a strange dorm-mate. Bambie's mother, predictably, refused to let me and Bambie room together. So, I was headed toward the unknown. Completely. But at this point, I didn't care anymore. Excitement replaced any feelings of fear.

The previous night I had been grilled, over and over. The rules. When to call. When to visit. To drive to his place first when I came home on the weekends. Study don't socialize. Every single rule completely expected. It was nothing new.

I was listening, but while he was listing out all his "rules," I was already checked out, imagining what I'd be doing, and it was exactly the opposite.

He couldn't just show up; I'd be an hour and a half's drive south. The dorms had security, and you needed to sign people in. This wouldn't be like high school where he could just appear, always checking in on me. Always hovering. He couldn't call every night because it was long distance and the dorm floor had only one pay phone, so even that would be an interesting experiment.

"What are you thinking?" He took his strong, unforgiving hands, grabbed my chin roughly, and turned me to face him.

"Ow, that hurts," I whined. My chin smarted with his tight grip.

"I'm sorry," he said, softening his voice and his hold on me and looking into my eyes. "I'm sorry, but you're not here. You're thinking of something else." His eyes went from dark clouds to open portals of worry. "You've already left." I noticed a sense of panic, demand, and something else. "You're mine. You will always be mine and you need to listen to me. Are you listening?" Shifting back into the darkness.

"Yes," I squeaked under his glare, trying to pull away, but his grip was too firm.

"You can't trust those college boys. I know. So just, just ... don't forget what I'm saying to you."

"Okay," I whispered, closing my eyes as he leaned in to kiss me.

I said my goodbye to him later that night and drove back home. I felt the heat of his anger with that last physical exchange he demanded. I still hurt this morning, but my excitement for my new adventure that awaited me pushed all that out of my head.

I was learning to separate, to section off what hurt from what didn't. To just stick that bit of pain in my pocket and let it be. Just focus on what was good.

I was still humming from my trip to California. Which turned out be awesome. My dad was really happy to see me and share his new life with me and he was happy that I was going to art school.

We drove down the coast, ate Mexican food, and drank beer together. I introduced him to *Thriller*; he couldn't believe how amazing each song was. He had always been very open to music. When I came home with a Led Zeppelin album from the neighbors, who I babysat for, and asked him to tape it, he'd happily agreed. He said they were "quite talented for a bunch of long-haired hippies." He was a big opera and classical fan so it really surprised me. He just didn't like Bob Dylan. He'd said, "That wasn't singing."

I met up with my old friends from grade school, and we went to Disneyland just like old times. The same friends I kept writing to over the years. I never stopped. Penning those letters was one of my anchors to California.

I sighed with excitement and joy. At last, the car was packed, like an overstuffed sofa. My mother walked over from where she was sitting on the stoop of our townhouse to give me a hug. The smell of love, warmth, and strength—of Mom—engulfed me, and I felt a tightness in my chest.

"Wait," she said, holding up the camera she had been hiding. "Let me get a picture of my baby girl headed off to college." Her grin was an older version of mine, with her deep dimples. Our smiles were so much alike, but the eyes ... my eyebrows were sharp and expressive, like my grandma's. There was no one I adored more than my Grams. She was my symbol of strength and attitude, where mom was my warmth, my constant. Soft eyes that were always there to comfort you.

I could lie and say I groaned when she lifted the camera, but I actually loved having my picture taken. It's probably because I wanted so badly to be a model or a dancer, and when that dream was squashed, I decided hamming it up in front of the camera whenever I could would work just as well.

"Okay," she said after she took the picture. "Come here and give me a hug."

"Oh, Mom." She would carry this on forever if I didn't get going.

I towered over her as I leaned down to hug her. "It's okay, Mom, I'm not that far and I'll come visit. And you should come down and visit me too sometimes."

I kissed her goodbye and crouched down to get into my little but roomy car. My brother had just installed this awesome cassette player as a graduation gift, so I was all set with tunes for the road. I had just created a great mix that I called "My Great Unknown Journey."

"I love you, Mom," I said as I leaned out the window. Then I shifted into first gear and drove off.

As I headed south on 95, I imagined being a bird, flying above. Looking down on myself as I drove off into my future. This was only one step in some unknown direction. A taste of independence. I reached over and turned up the song that I queued to start my journey: "Learning to Fly" by Tom Petty. I let it fill me up and lift me along as I drove.

"*But I ain't got wings* ... Mmmm," I sang along.

School didn't start till Monday, and as it was only Friday, I had the whole weekend to settle in. Bambie was being "moved in" by her parents, so I probably wouldn't see her till Sunday. But I lucked out because one of my co-workers, Margaret, from the record store, had a twin sister named Mary who was also going to VCU. She was driving down to see her, and I was going to meet them and their roommate, Jamie. We were going to Hard Times, a club in the heart of VCU, on Harrison and Cary Street. My first night out, in a new city with new friends. This was just the beginning.

32 | GIRL ON CAMPUS
"Eighties," Killing Joke

The first few weeks of school flew by so fast between figuring out my classes and where they were, as they were spread out around Richmond. The art school was off to the side, in an old pre-war-type building. Conveniently, there was a Burger King behind it, which I made my routine stop before class. The walks were accompanied by my trusty Aiwa tape deck with some new tunes I had blaring. I had to giggle when I was in the bubble of bad-boy ridiculous lyrics circulating through my body. No one had any idea what was blasting into my ears. Even with the unforgiving heat and relentless sun, made worse by dirty city streets, empty lots, warehouses, and homeless people, the music allowed me to soar beyond the experience.

Even though I wasn't sharing a room with Bambie, I ended up really liking my new roomie. I had no idea who she was going to be. The afternoon I arrived, I walked down the hall toward our room, which was at the very end of the hallway. Our names were written on the outside of the door in marker on little cutout paper clouds and inside posters were plastered along the far end of the room, indicating that my roommate loved Prince. Tons of photos of Prince. She wasn't there. Maybe she had gone off to explore.

After I unpacked, I went out to explore myself and see where Bambie's room was. Along the way, I met a lot of the girls on my floor. They all had such musical or French-sounding names. I loved French names. I insisted that everyone pronounce my name the French way: Sue-ZAN. Not Sue-SUN. My name had a Z. I don't know why that was so hard for some guys. They loved to call me Sue. Or Susan.

There was Lakisha, Latasha, Sunshine, and Charissa. I introduced myself and asked if they had seen or met my roommate, Charmaine, yet? No one had, so I took off looking for Bambie's room.

When I found Bambie, she was hanging her He-Man posters (yes, we loved He-Man, Master of the Universe) and her Duran Duran posters. Bambie was all decked out in black, with her new paste-white makeup she'd bought over the summer when she was in London with her brother. She even had these really cool Day-Glo tights and a Siouxsie and the Banshees T-shirt, black, with more Day-Glo for the letters. We had nothing like that here in the U.S. Maybe New York City had it, but that was a long way from Richmond. She'd brought me back a three-inch silver cross with blue stones in it.

After we caught up and made plans for later, I returned to my room. As I walked in the door, I met my new roommate. She was tiny, with short brown hair and a funny accent. She was from New Jersey. I had never met anyone from New Jersey before.

I didn't know what to expect. I guess by the sound of her name and the Prince photos, I just assumed she was Black. It was kind of strange they'd paired the two White girls together. Was that a coincidence? But I was in the South now. Northern Virginia was not the South.

As I crawled into bed that first night, I thought about Doug. There was a small tightness in my chest. I missed him. Our experience together didn't exactly leave us with a "relationship." I only received word about him through Peter that he was back in school.

Doug and I never really had a chance. We'd never hung out before, or got to know each other, so it wasn't like just because we had that one hot summer encounter we were going to suddenly have more contact than before.

But he had been sweet to me. Something that could have turned out to be a humiliating experience ended up being a comforting memory. He planted this little seed within me: I was desirable. And guys could be kind.

I questioned that before I met Steve. And then desirability became a game with him. It was something he seemed to dangle on a string in front of me. He said I was desirable, but it came with so many conditions and contradictions.

He said I was cute, but then I was too tall with small breasts. I had sexy long legs, but I was knock-kneed. I had cute dimples in my cheeks, but the crinkle in my chin looked funny when I pouted. I had flaws that I could never change. And he reminded me of them, as if to say ... I love you anyway. See? No one else would.

I shook the thoughts of both Steve and Doug out of my head, and as I fell asleep, in my new bed in Richmond with the unfamiliar sounds from all around me, a smile spread out across my face. This was going to be awesome.

Charmaine was turning out to be a great roommate. We didn't exactly go out together a lot, but we got along great. We went to the cafeteria for dinner and did our homework together in the room and popped popcorn in the bubble machine.

The first few weeks just flew by. I made friends with the girls in the hall, and on nights when I came home after clubbing with Bambie and my new friend Jamie, the one I met through my co-workers at Variety Records, I would fill them in on what bands played, or what club we danced at. Sunshine even braided my hair one night because she thought I'd make a good Bo Derek. But it hurt so bad, not to mention it looked ridiculous on me, so it only lasted a day before we took it out, and then magically I had some serious Studio 54 hair.

It turns out that Jamie was in almost all my art classes, so we bonded immediately. So now I had two good friends in school: Jamie and Bambie. Jamie and I were already dreaming about our sophomore year, getting an apartment together, and where we would live. I really wanted to live with Bambie, but I knew her parents wouldn't let her, so she would end up moving in with her brother off campus. But first we had to pay our dues in the dorms our first year.

33 | SHADOWS

"Words," Missing Persons

I lay on my bed, trying to think up an idea for my installation project. All my ideas were lame. I was constantly trying to mix fashion into my art. But the teacher kept kicking out each idea as predictable, uninspired, or just bad. My eyes were just starting to close when ...

"Sue-zaaan?" Followed by a knock. Then the door opened before I could answer, and Sunshine's head popped though. "Girl, that crazy-ass boyfriend of yours is calling again!" She had a big frown on her face. "He called last night too when you were out."

No one liked Steve, and they hadn't even met him yet. There was only one pay phone on our floor, and we all had specific times for our calls. He originally wanted to call me every other night, but between the expense, and the outrage of my floormates, we worked it down to three times a week: two during the week, and one on the weekend, if I wasn't going home.

"I'm so sorry, Sunshine," I said, sliding off the bed, "I told him not to call all the time. I was supposed to call him last night at ten, but, well, I forgot."

"You didn't forget." Her Southern accent elongated the syllables in the sweetest way. It was so easy to parrot the accents and sounds around me. I was a sponge when it came to language. I had to try hard not to sound like I was just imitating her, or my roommate's New Jersey accent. "You *was* out with your girlfriends at one of those crazy punk shows you go to," she reprimanded me. "And you were drunk last night when you rolled your sorry ass down the hallway."

I couldn't contain my laughter, and as she turned away, she burst out in laughter too, calling over her shoulder, "He's still on the phone, you know. Waiting for you."

"Oh, shit," I said, rushing toward the door. "Wait, what did you tell him last night?"

"Don't worry," she said as she kept walking, "I just said you were sound asleep, and I refused to wake you for his sorry ass."

I hurried down the hall and picked up the receiver. "Hi, Steve," I said, trying to sound normal, and rushed on so he couldn't even try to cross-examine me. "Sorry about last night, I was just so tired from studying damn history. It's a killer. I don't know how I'll survive the term."

He was quiet on the other end of the buzzing line.

"Steve?" I said, slower, quieter. "You there?"

"Yeah, I'm here." He didn't sound mad. "Are you coming home this weekend?"

"Oh, well I came home last weekend," I said weakly. "I have a lot of schoolwork and studying to do. You know it's only a little over a month before winter break and I have a lot of projects to do before then." This was not a lie. Although it wasn't what I had planned that weekend. There were a few shows happening down in Shockoe Slip, and I wanted to go. And not with Steve.

"Okay, I'll come down to see you," he said in his firm, end-of-story kind of way.

"Huh? You want to drive down for the day?" I stammered, "Because—because you know you can't spend the night? It's not allowed, plus I have a room—"

"Yes, I know," he interrupted. "It's not that far. I'll come up in the morning, take you to lunch. You can show me your dorm room and then walk me around the campus. And later we can go to dinner somewhere, before I drive back."

"Oh." I was completely taken off guard. I mean, I knew at some point I would have to let him come visit. He'd want to see what my life looked like. So far, he was satisfied with me driving home to his place every other weekend. And just like he planned, I would drive straight to his place, and only stop by my mom's after I visited with him. Every time. And each time, all we did was stay in his room. I felt like a prisoner the whole time I was there. It just kept getting worse. I mean, I was becoming more and more detached. And the more detached I was from what he was doing, the more he tried to take from me. As if he was trying to wake me up. But I couldn't stop. I couldn't fight him. But I couldn't pretend.

He grilled me about every detail. School, where I went, what I did with my free time. He didn't like what I was doing to my hair either. I had trimmed the left side shorter. Just the part that went around the ear, so it looked like a half Mohawk. But I didn't shave it. And then I started painting my hair with Jolene Creme bleach. The stuff you use to dye your mustache. My roommate did that. So, I borrowed it once. It worked really well. I'd just paint a bit on, let it sit, and the hair would lighten up so fast. Then I'd paint on different colors of food dye. Pretty harmless, as it washed out. But some of the girls in the dorm were starting to call me Calico.

All these things he pointed out, but I easily deflected, jutting my chin out and saying I was expressing my creative side. I was an artist.

I begged Charmaine to stay in the room when Steve came to visit, even though it was going to be a nice sunny day. I just, well, I didn't want to violate the sanctity of our space with his predatory schemes. Yeah, I'd picked up that term in psych 101. The teacher described a relationship between a guy and his girlfriend, and well, it sounded like she was talking about us. A little. The girl had just been drawn further and further into his world, while he fed her all these lies about her, making her feel more and more dependent on him. So, she would eventually lose all contact with her friends, and become his slave, pretty much. Like, all the twisted stuff he made her do became acceptable because he was taking care of her and loved her. Something like that.

But that wasn't me. I mean, some of it, yeah. But he couldn't control me. And I didn't want him coming up here to my dorm, my school, and making it his as well.

My plan was to go to lunch, then walk him around campus, and later show him my dorm room. Hopefully Charmaine would be there, as planned.

Lunch was fine. I took him to a place where nobody I knew would be. A Chinese place on Grace Street. Afterward I gave him the tour, walking down Grace and back over to Franklin Street where most of my art classes were in this beautiful old historic building called Franklin Terrace. Then I led him over to the Pollack building on Harrison Street. I loved how the building hung over the sidewalk. We wove our way through the campus while I pointed out various things, and the whole time he forced my arm in his or held fast to my hand.

He looked happy to see me, but also agitated. Anytime I saw anyone I recognized from class, I pointed him in the opposite direction. It was easy to do because the buildings were so spread out around the campus.

We eventually, and reluctantly, made it back to Johnston Hall, my dorm. I stopped and pointed up at the tall red brick building. "See the eighth floor, corner window?"

"Mm-hmm." He looked up, shading his eyes. *When did he get so big?* I thought. I mean he was always muscular, but he wasn't cut anymore. He looked puffier. Maybe it was just the other guys I'd been around and saw at the clubs; they were all so skinny, it made him look ... weird to me. Like out of a comic book.

"That's our room." Trying to sound cheerful, even though my stomach was tightening from the dread building up in me because I had to bring him in and show him our place. While Charmaine had her Prince posters all over, I had my whole side of the room plastered with Billy Idol, Cyndy Lauper, Bowie, Blondie, U2, Madness, Thomas Dolby, all mixed in with spreads from fashion magazines, band flyers I'd saved, and of course, on my desk, a framed collage of pictures of Steve, all centered around my favorite postcard of Grace Jones. Funny how she was the center of that. Her strong-ass feminine self.

"Show me." He didn't really ask. It was finally time. I'd killed enough of it. I just crossed my fingers on my free hand as I led him in the front, and signed him in.

As we got off the elevator, I saw Sunshine and Lakisha sitting on the floor outside their adjoining rooms with their nail polish spread out around them. They always did that. They didn't want to stink up their room.

"Hey." I smiled, and rolled my eyes toward Steve, with a nod. "This is Steve, my boyfriend." I tried to keep walking, pulling on Steve's hand. But he stopped.

"Hey, ladies. How are you?" He was being the gentleman. Or he was about to try to get some info.

"Hi there," they both said at the same time. Their eyes scanned him from top to bottom, eyebrows raised.

"Well, you sure are big," Lakisha said, not too quiet. "Mm-hmm." And then she abruptly looked back at her nails. I could see her smile. I had to ask her later about that. Sunshine said nothing, just looked at me knowingly.

I yanked on Steve's hand. "Come on, it's down here."

When I opened the door, I could have died with relief to see Charmaine sitting at her desk, looking like she was deep in study. She was actually going to MCV, the medical division of VCU. So, where I got to make ridiculous art pieces, she was actually studying biology, chemistry, math ... I don't know. Stuff I always failed at.

"And this is Charmaine," I dramatically announced. I hoped he didn't notice my relief. "And this is our amazing room, not at all cluttered." I laughed, because it was just that.

Charmaine just looked up politely and said, "Hey," and then stuck her nose back in her work.

"What are you studying?" Steve tried to engage with her, but she just mumbled unintelligibly, something I couldn't make out.

"She's got a test tomorrow," I whispered. But he had already turned away from her and was inspecting my "area." I watched him as his eyes went from one wall to the next. I was hoping he wouldn't open my desk drawer and find my stash of Djarum cigs. Looking satisfied with my collage of him, he turned toward me and then glanced down at Charmaine, and a frown passed over his face.

"Walk me to my car?" He reached over and grabbed my hand, but he was only being polite in front of Charmaine, I could tell because his look was intense. "Nice to meet you, Charmaine." But he didn't wait for a response as he turned towards the door.

"I thought you were going to stay, and we were going to dinner," I said, being led abruptly out. I could hear Charmaine behind me as the door was closing: "Byeee."

She was not impressed.

"Yeah, well I have stuff I have to do," he said blankly, hand still gripping mine tight.

Thankfully the girls were gone, and we didn't pass anyone in the halls. And even a bigger relief that the bathroom had lots of activity inside. It was a huge communal bathroom with multiple showers and stalls. But I knew if it had been quiet, he would have dragged me in there.

As we walked to his car, I kept distracting myself by pointing out things: a monument here, a building there, trying to fill my quiet dread with some joy.

He led me to his gold Pontiac, opened the side door, and simply said, "Get in." I bowed my head and slinked in, trying to sit low. We were a few blocks off from school, so no real sidewalk traffic here. Absolutely empty. *Great*, I thought. I knew what was going to happen next, but at least I also knew it would be quick, and then he'd be on his way home.

34 | NUMBER ONE FAN

"I Don't Want to Hear It," Minor Threat

Bambie's brother took us out at least once a week, if not more, to all these great clubs that either had live bands or a DJ. Far from Steve's watchful eyes and his threats, I allowed myself to flirt. And the guys there, well, they wouldn't have known if I'd had a boyfriend. Although, I wouldn't lie if asked, but I wouldn't announce it either.

Every Friday night, live bands played in Shaffer's Court, an outdoor space in the dead center of the university. It wasn't the first time I'd experienced Richmond's infamous band Death Piggy; they were already on my latest mixed tape. The first time I saw them play was at the 9:30 Club. Bambie and I often jumped in my little "no way can that car go 90 mph" and sped up 95 to D.C. for a show, only to return late that night. Oh yes it can!

You could find the Death Piggy logo everywhere—a perturbed pig sticking his tongue out with evil-looking eyebrows—throughout the mishmash of VCU, including the Fan—an area west of the campus that spreads out like ... a Fan—drawn on jeans and arms, in bathroom stalls, and on buildings alike. The swine stared out from the bus stops at the passengers along the route from Richmond to D.C., although most of them "knew not the hostile hog."

I don't know why Death Piggy appealed to me so much. The silly lyrics of Fatman: "Products on TV, they are buying me, eating all I see, I will eat TV ... We love you, Fatman!" And the equally ridiculous Bathtub in Space: "I'm way up in space, I'm giving up hope, when I got out, I slipped on the soap."

Well, it just felt like the most genuinely free music I'd ever heard. So much out there in the hardcore punk scene was uptight and angry. Or sexist. I mean, I was into a lot of different sounds besides punk and new wave, but with my headphones on, walking to art classes, my soundtrack was the Meatmen, Death Piggy, Government Issue, Minor Threat, The Clash, Violent Femmes, TSOL, Flipper, Berlin, and the Missing Persons. And Pretenders. Girls also had strong voices and attitude.

On stage, Death Piggy had a really silly and stupid act, ending in ridiculous stunts, like pouring mayonnaise down their pants, throwing banana peels into the mosh pit where all the guys were slamming about, or distributing pies and paper airplanes to the crowd. They invited viewers to be part of the act, in a way. It was free of all rules. They thrashed, but were also silly, more of a performance act. It was a mix of inventiveness with absurdity on top. When they weren't playing, they'd be down in the pit dancing with the rest of us. And this was like dancing I'd never done. A freestyle, borderline aggressive stomp. But it depended on the show you were at, how aggressive the dance—or, in this case, slam—would be. Black Flag was rough. But Death Piggy—it was just tongue and cheek.

It was the voice of the singer that really got me. I had never talked to him but was enthralled watching him perform and listening to his deep, seductive voice. His name, Dave Brockie, seemed to fit his personality perfectly. On stage he was a mix of serious, yelling at the audience, and then silly. And he was handsome. Really cute.

Bambie and I got our wrist bands then grabbed our beers and made our way to the front, where we found a nice step to sit on, not far from the stage. Lucky for Bambie she was grandfathered in and could legally drink at eighteen, even though the age limit was nineteen now. I had just turned nineteen on October fifth, which passed very uneventfully because it was during a school week. Even my dad forgot. I finally received a sorrowful note and care package of art supplies a week later.

It was a Friday and early afternoon, so everyone was relaxed, just taking in the warm October sun. There was such a great eclectic mix of kids. The new-wave kids, the jocks or fraternity boys, the faculty, and of course the punks. The punk scene was big here. I mean, I'm sure compared to D.C. and New York it was small, but for this city, it was big.

We only had one kid in our high school who was punk, and that was Bambie's Brother, David. Not to be confused with Dave Brockie! There were so many Daves and Davids in our school, surnames were added or replaced their given name. Her brother was skinny and wore green fatigues, black combat boots, and a black T-shirt with a black leather jacket. His hair was dyed black too. His expression was always serious, and this was his everyday look. Not just on Punk Fridays. The rest of the kids who thought they were punk were pseudo-punk, or what you would call new wave. And even then, not every day. Friday posers.

This here was commitment. I saw new haircuts and dyed hair I'd only seen when Bambie and I went to Georgetown to see the Meatmen. But not in our school. Not anywhere in Northern Virginia.

The sound poured out of them, comical, absurd, and ridiculous, as expected. Not really singing, but a mix of singsong shouting and narration. *Sigh.* Dave Brockie. He pranced around in his pants with no shirt and his semi-shaved head. His deep, deep voice was completely unexpected each time I heard it. I was smitten. I had to meet him. I was truly his number one fan.

After the show broke up, Bambie and I made our way to the Village, a cafe not far from the square where we sat and drank beer out of large, chilled glasses and smoked cigarettes. I wasn't really a smoker, but cigarettes went well with beer, so I always had some on me, just in case. My favorite, besides cloves, were Benson and Hedges, Ultra-Light Deluxe. A long tongue twister you had to try saying without sounding completely idiotic at the 7-Eleven checkout.

"I saw you lusting after the singer." She blew out little smoke rings, and then took a nice long gulp of the cold beer. "You know he's probably going to be at that party later tonight."

"What are you talking about? I wasn't lusting," I denied. "I was admiring." I tried to downplay it, hiding my giveaway cheeks behind the mug of beer.

She ignored my denial. "My brother said he'd swing by the dorm and pick us up at ten."

"Yeah, that sounds fun." I was trying to sound casual about it, but my heart was pounding so hard with excitement, like an eager child ready to burst free. Or maybe I was going to have a heart attack.

My outfit was premeditated. Look cute, look punk, but not too much. And definitely original. Knowing how the singer just wore jeans and T-shirts, I just wore my skinny black skirt, the one that flared out at the bottom, like a bell. Over that, I put on a white T-shirt that I'd drawn the image of Bill the Cat on, a character from the comic strip *Bloom County*, which I read religiously every Sunday in *The Washington Post*. It hadn't gotten past me that Dave was an artist and published a comic strip called *Mr. Donut*. I was collecting them.

On top of all that, I just had on a long, black, droopy V-neck sweater and my army jacket. I'd have to strip down if I wanted to pull out my comic beacon. I teased my hair over to the side and gave it a spritz from the huge pink can of Aquanet, carefully arranging it so you could see the fresh cut on the left side my head. A half Mohawk? Not really. I was always slicking it back on one side with gel so I just thought cutting it would make it easier. And it ended up looking better than I thought. I still had the black underneath, but I'd added more lightener around the frame of my face. *Yep*, I thought, *definitely the calico look prevails*.

Bambie's brother picked us up just like she said. Even though he'd graduated two years ahead of us with my brother's class in '82, they weren't friends. Joe was more of a Rush fan, whereas David was a Clash fan. I didn't really know him at school either, and what I remembered was that he never smiled.

But now, even though he still treated me like his kid sister's friend, he was really nice. The fact that he brought us with him and his friends to a party, and on other nights to dance clubs, spoke volumes to me about who he really was. Under that tough punk exterior was a very nice guy.

We ended up at an old townhouse in the financial district on Main Street. I think it was a townhouse, or a row house, or a brownstone. I don't know, but it was old. Built in the 1800s or something, and four stories high. The bottom was a frame shop, so it was quiet and closed at night. A band called Absence of Malice lived in the upstairs portion of the building.

Most of the old places were empty above the storefronts. So rent was cheap because it really wasn't a safe place. It was very dark around the area at night, and no one was on the streets—except prostitutes, male prostitutes. You could see their shadows passing silently from sidewalk to the cars that cruised up, stopping, windows rolled down, some exchange, and then they would slip through the door and the car would take off.

But this place—I looked up at the building, noting the address, 18 East Main Street—was busting at the seams with life as music poured out of the widows from above.

Bambie slapped me on the ass. "Come on, what are you waiting for?"

The stairs up were steep and straight. Posters, or I should say flyers from past shows, were plastered all over the place: Absence of Malice, Unseen Force, Bad Brains, Scream, Prevaricators, White Cross, and many more I didn't recognize. I smiled when I saw the Black Sabbath poster.

The kitchen was packed, but we stood in line and grabbed a beer from the keg and soon lost sight of her brother in the crowd.

I immediately spotted Dave over in the corner laughing and talking with some extra-punk-looking guys. They had short, spiked hair, ripped jeans, torn shirts, and leather jackets with silver spikes and band names painted all over them. They also looked really young, like junior high young. I'd heard the house took in runaways.

As I predicted, Dave wasn't dressed in black. He was just dressed in jeans and a T-shirt. But he still had this edge to him. My heart sped up as I stood there taking him in.

"Come on, let's go find my brother," Bambie said, leading me through the thick crowd under an archway into another room. He was standing in the corner talking to two tall guys, one of which was like the other two in dress, but over six five, and definitely not younger than me. He had lots of thick dark curly hair, and, like the other guys, he wore a heavy leather motorcycle jacket with band names stenciled on it and silver studs.

"Hey, welcome to the Crew House," the taller of the two said with a big smile. He looked so tough, but he was the sweetest guy. "My name is Graves; this moron is Andy."

"This is my sister Barbara, and her friend Suzanne," David said, sounding bored. I don't think he really wanted us tailing him around.

"Hey," we both said simultaneously. Graves couldn't take his eyes off Bambie.

The smoke and the noise were so loud, and Bambie had immediately fallen deep into conversation about music with Graves, so I decided to wander out to the roof. You could crawl out the back window and walk right onto it. Other kids were out there smoking, so I thought I'd join them. There was no way I was just going to stand there looking like an idiot.

I climbed through the window, and at the same moment, they all got up and climbed up the ladder that was leaning against the side, which led to the top-floor rooftop. Curious, I followed them, and after I pulled myself up onto the roof, and yanked my skirt down, flattening it out, I made my way over to the edge. I sat looking down on the city below and lit a Clove. Sure enough, I saw a car pull up right below me, and the passenger window rolled down. From the tree's shadow out walked a young guy. He leaned into the window, and it seemed like they were talking, but then he opened the door and popped in. But the car didn't drive off.

"That shit will kill you," a deep, husky voice said.

I nearly jumped right off the ledge. "What the fu—" I turned with an angry look, looked up, and almost had a heart attack. There, right before me, talking to me, was Dave. There was never a guy that seemed so sure of himself, and yet with so much natural ease.

"Oops, sorry, I didn't mean to scare the shit out of you." He wore a mischievous grin.

"Um, it's okay." *Shit, that's all I can come up with? Here he is, right before me, and I have nothing. Not one thought. My mind is a super blank hole of dead space ...*

"I haven't seen you here before." He sat down next to me on the ledge. I couldn't believe it. I mean, here he was, sitting next to me. I still had nothing. I had to try.

"That's because I haven't been here before," I started. "I mean, I just moved to Richmond this fall. I'm going to VCU, and I came here with my friend and her brother, David. David C. Do you know him?"

He bellowed out a deep, throaty laugh. I guess I was hysterical.

"Yeah of course I know David."

"Hey Brockie," somebody yelled from the edge of the roof, their head just visible over the ladder top. Dave looked over at them.

"Yeah?"

"You gotta come here, we need your help."

He turned to me. "Well, sorry, I gotta run. Nice meeting you, um ..."

"Suzanne."

"Suzanne. Nice. I'm Dave." He stood up.

"Yeah, I know."

His eyebrow raised.

"Oh. Well, come to our next show." He handed me a flyer, and then winked, and turned and walked off.

"Okay," I said softly. "Okay."

35 | HOLIDAY OBLIGATION
"Love Is Pain," Joan Jett & the Blackhearts

I was so frustrated that I had to miss their next show, but it was my weekend to visit Steve. I only had less than a month before Christmas break and I wanted to keep going to shows, and meeting people, and I didn't want to visit Steve. I was so worried he would just show up, like he did in high school, or when I was at a friend's house. I'd turn around and he'd be there. Always trying to catch me up to "something." Even away at college, I could feel his grip on me.

I started hating him so much in these moments, but I also felt guilty and wrong about what I was doing.

I wasn't *really* doing anything. But to be honest, I was thinking about it.

If I felt like this about Steve, why couldn't I just break up with him? Something was holding me back. Plus, he wouldn't just let me break up with him that easily. I was his. He'd made it very clear.

Like the dutiful girlfriend, I packed up my overnight bag and jumped into my little yellow Ghia, popped my mixed tape of tunes into my tape deck, and sang along loud and furious, demonstrating my independence. At least I felt independent when I was in my car and screaming along to my music at the top of my lungs. Punk was fun, but punk hardcore was the antidote to my pent-up frustration. It's moments like this when I played T.S.O.L. or Bad Brains, veering away from anything too soft.

I drove directly to his house, tearing up the long gravel drive, and pulled in front of the old house, with its angles and peaks, like it had extra dark rooms that hid secrets. My mood changed. A moment before, it was happiness, and now some shadow passed over me. The last of the fall leaves scattered across the yard, and the barren trees, with the loss of adornment, gave me no comfort. The gloomy gray skies reflected a sort of premonition that was confirmed each time I walked through the doors to that house.

I was already anticipating the evening. Steve would come out, and be happy, but angry at something I did. I was late. I took too long. I drove too fast. My outfits were getting stranger, my hair was getting weirder. What was I doing down there in college, studying or partying? Nothing. Nothing, I would try to explain. Just having fun, but nothing to worry about.

Yet all I could think about was getting back to school: Cool punk guys and Dave. But here I was with Steve. But I wasn't really. My body was, but my heart wasn't in it. I was just going through the motions. Pretending it was all fine. Trying to convince him and myself.

He didn't care about my experiences. The music. My art. All he wanted was my body. He wanted to possess me. To own me. It'd taken me a long time to realize this. And maybe because ... well, because I wanted to be possessed. I wanted to be owned. Because it felt like love. But now I wasn't sure it was love.

I sat there, just staring at the house. Unable to move.

The door opened, and he came out. There was no smile to greet me. Storm clouds circled above him. I knew I better move, or he would get angrier.

He barely said hi to me as I walked toward him. He just grabbed my hand and abruptly took me straight upstairs.

I lay there under him looking past him, out the window, at those trees stripped of joy and the darkening sky.

The rest of the month flashed by, a whirl of shows, classes, and dancing at the Bus Stop, our favorite place because it had the best DJ who knew all the perfect songs to dance to. He had the nicest smile and twinkly eyes. But he also seemed impossibly untouchable with his black Robert Smith hair and skinny black pants. And it didn't help that the DJ booth was in a bus! It was toward the back of the room, and you could see him sitting behind the windshield. Anybody who wanted to make a request had to go to the door on the side, like when you get on a school bus.

There were several venues that played live music, but not many that had good dance music, like in D.C. The Bus Stop was the place. The floor looked like a chess set, and the tiles lit up alternately, while a TV screen showed music videos.

We'd kick out our legs to the beat of "Love Will Tear Us Apart" and step from one lit-up tile to the other, trying not to accidentally knock into our neighbors. When we did, we'd inevitably laugh and giggle.

I didn't spot Dave again, although everywhere I went, I looked.

The semester ended, and with it my escape. It was time to go home for the holidays. I signed up for as many shifts as I could at the record store to avoid having to be with Steve. He worked too, so I made sure I worked a lot of opposite days so we wouldn't have to spend as much time together.

John Senior raised his eyebrows at my hair, and the other John just laughed. Caroline thought I looked cool and couldn't wait to take me out to meet her new boyfriend and show off her "punk college girlfriend."

That was my escape: work. And of course, going out with Bambie. Being around the old crew, laughing it up, playing music and sharing stories of my Richmond experience took the edge off what was otherwise a very uncomfortable time.

Steve was becoming more and more of this ... other person who didn't fit in with my life. I didn't have answers to my mom when she asked me why I hadn't broken up with him when I went off to school. She never said anything about how she felt about him, or what she thought. I could guess. But she acted like it was perfectly normal to go off to school and break up with your high school boyfriend. But I reminded her that he wasn't in high school. It wasn't the same.

Steve had been the only one who ever really showed me how much he cared about me, and the fact that he was so jealous and didn't want me to go away just proved to me that he wouldn't abandon me. But I didn't feel like myself when I was with him anymore, even though I was good at pretending I was okay with everything he demanded from me. I had almost started to convince myself it was true—that I was okay. Slowly, I began to feel like I was losing myself. Pretending made it easier. But now, I didn't think I could keep it up much longer.

36 | DID I DREAM LAST NIGHT?

"Never Say Never," Romeo Void

I watched Bambie touch up her makeup in the dirty bathroom mirror while I ungraciously hovered over the toilet seat, relieving myself of the beer I had just inhaled. I was stressed out and frustrated after the holidays. I knew deep down I had to break up with Steve.

"What's wrong?" She looked at me through her cleopatra eye makeup. There were a lot of girls who tried to pull off the Siouxsie look, but Bambie really nailed it and at the same time made it her own thing. With her starkly drawn-on black brows, thick, smudged black eyeliner, pale face, glossy lips, and crimped black hair, she looked fucking cool. I just looked, well ... sweet. Even with my half Mohawk. It wasn't even shaved, just cut short. There was no way to hide my dimples. I wanted to look as mad as I felt. But I hadn't quite mastered the snarl.

I stood up and pulled my skirt down right as the door opened and a triumph of loud angry music forced its way in. Absence of Malice was up, and I knew Bambie would want to go check out the guitarist.

"Hey, Maggie." I completely ignored Bambie's question. Maggie was dating the drummer, but we weren't close.

"Hi, y'all." She said in her high, childlike voice. Unabashedly, Maggie pulled up her little black miniskirt, yanked down already ripped fishnets, and did her own version of the toilet squat.

"Guess what?" Bambie put her makeup away and gave me a pointed look as I washed my hands in the filthy sink.

"Hmm?" I grunted, not very interested.

"Guess who's playing Thursday night on Valentine's Day at Goin' Bananas?" she said with a look of mischief about her.

"I don't know."

"Near East."

"Who? Oh ... them." Unimpressed.

"There's nothing wrong with them ... What about the Landlords?"

"Huh?" I dried my hands on the very last paper towel hanging halfway out of the dispenser and turned to her. "Who?"

She stuck her face in mine, her eyes nice and wide. "How about your favorite band, Death Piggy!" She took me by the shoulders; even with her small frame she commanded my attention. "Now, does that mean something?"

The color must have drained from my face.

"I thought so," she said triumphantly. "I knew that would make you happy and forget about you-know-who."

I smiled so big my mouth hurt.

"You have a crush on Dave Brockie!" Maggie's sudden interjection was loud and unexpected. We had both forgotten she was sitting there. I nearly jumped out of my skirt.

"Oh my god, Maggie!" I laughed. "Who doesn't?"

We all laughed at that, and the door opened again, the music pouring through with all its loud, aggressive guitar banging and pounding drums, reminding us it was time to join in the fun.

Not often, but sometimes, we'd all cram into my Ghia. Usually, we caught a ride with Bambie's brother or sometimes Jamie. Jamie, Mary, and Margaret lived off campus in school housing, but it didn't look like housing. It just looked like an apartment complex. We would take school transport over there and then grab her car. But she also let me park my car there because it was a nightmare to park around campus on the side streets. It was a sure thing to get a ticket, if not towed.

Tonight, we decided to take my car to the show. The four of us all squeezed into my itty-bitty car, and as usual I drove at a high speed that defied the little machine's reputation. As I pulled a right onto the main road, a siren went off behind me.

"Oh fuck!" I groaned. "Was I speeding?"

Bambie was wedged in the back with Mary, and Jamie was up front. It was hard to believe, but you could actually fit two small people in the back.

"Um, I don't know," Jamie said, as I pulled over to the side and we waited for the officer. I rolled down my window and asked Jamie to get out my registration from the glove compartment.

"Good evening, miss?" A question was left in the air as the officer leaned down and stopped, seeing four cute but punked-out girls, obviously on their way to a party—or something. "How do you even fit in that thing?"

We all laughed. "Determination," I said with a grin. I knew from my experience with cops that you just had to smile a lot.

"Do you know why I pulled you over?"

"Um, I was speeding?" I didn't even try to deny it. Why would I argue? People always did that, and I knew it annoyed them. Besides, I *had* been speeding.

"Oh, um, yes, you were." He cleared his throat. "Anything else?"

"I don't think so?"

"Yes, well, you didn't stop at that stop sign."

"Oh. Gosh, I didn't realize it." I looked shocked. Even though, honestly? There was no one around, the streets were completely dark. *Really?*

"Yes. Well. I'll let you off with a verbal warning for speeding, but I'll write a written warning for the stop sign. If you don't do anything else in the next six months, it will go away."

"Oh, thank you so much," I said as sweetly as I could.

As we drove off, all the girls at once went, "Oohhh-oo, aren't you sweet with the po-lease!"

"Yes, sirree." I winked.

The show was at Goin' Bananas in Shockoe Slip. My favorite venue for live shows. I just loved the location. Cobblestone streets on a slow incline, or decline? It was very cool. I felt like I was in old England or something.

After we found a spot, we headed in.

The place was packed, and the energy was high. We bumped, we slammed, we danced, we drank. I might have had too many drinks. I didn't like beer from the cans, so I always ended up with pints. Which did seem like a bit more than in a can. But it was nice and cold and tasted so good.

As the night went on, time jumped from one thing to another. A condition of drinking. Piggy was finally playing, and I stood front and center with Bambie by my side. Some asshole threw a glass on the ground, right in the middle of where everyone was dancing—if you could call it that. And I told him he should clean it up, someone might fall on it. He looked at me with venom with his skinny punk (and not rock) mask that defined him as jerk.

"Fuckin' West End bitch." He sprayed his drunk fumes in my direction.

Bambie and I just burst out laughing. I turned to her and said, "What an idiot." She rolled her eyes at him, and we both turned back to listen to the band.

When the show ended, we went back upstairs. The bands played in the lower space with a high, tiny window that looked out at the sidewalk. Upstairs was a bar and tables. That's where we stood, drinking the remainder of our beers while everyone started spilling out from below and onto the streets.

"Hey," said a deep voice next to me. Turning, I saw Dave Brockie there, and he reached out and handed me a flyer. "We're having a party at our place," he said. "Bring your friends." He grinned and walked off.

I felt light-headed as the sudden pounding of my heart took my breath away. *Did he remember me?* I turned to say something to Bambie and Jamie, but Bambie was gone. Jamie didn't seem pleased.

"No," she said. "I don't think you should go."

"What?" *She knows I have a boyfriend and she probably thinks it's cheating.* "I'll be fine, and if you're thinking about Steve, forget it."

"I don't want to go, I have class tomorrow, and so do you," she said with her arms crossed in front of her chest. The disapproving mom.

"Come on, Jamie, I want to go. You don't have to come. You can take my car. Besides, I've had way too much to drink anyhow." And I handed her my keys. "I'll be fine. And I'll be closer to the dorm."

"Humph." Just like in the movies. That's what it sounded like. Total disapproval and disbelief.

He stood toward the back of the smoke-filled kitchen next to the keg surrounded by friends or maybe fans. He seemed to command attention just by his presence. I gazed at him from the doorway nervously.

Through the window I could see that the snow had started coming down with its white softness and had begun sticking to the windowsill.

The smell of the beer was overwhelming and slightly nauseating, and yet I was thirsty again. I was the contrast to his completely relaxed and casual stance. Shaking from nervousness, I slowly made my way through the crowd.

"Hey, I didn't know you were coming tonight," Jimmy said as he stepped in front of me, blocking my path to the keg and my real destination, Dave. Jimmy was a skate kid who was in my art class with Jamie.

The party from the after-show concert had grown larger—it was Valentine's Day, after all—and it was the perfect time to just get drunk and, well, forget it was Valentine's Day.

The kitchen light was so bright and unflattering that everything stood out starkly. As I moved past Jimmy, I stepped into something sticky on the floor and looked down. I'd stepped on something gooey ... maybe gum?

I grabbed a plastic cup off the table and made my way over to the keg, trying to avoid Dave as I passed next to him, even though every fiber of my being just wanted to stare at him.

I leaned down to pump the spout and felt breath on my neck as someone whispered, "Hey," in that deep, throaty, fucking sexy voice. "You came."

I woke up with this intense desire to just laugh out loud. And I did. I felt so happy. *Did I dream last night?*

I rolled over, and there, next to me, was Dave. His eyes opened, and he grinned, that one eyebrow arched high, with an expectant question. What a smile! I just couldn't do anything else but jump right on top of him. Straddling him from above, smiling miles of gratitude for the feeling of joy that swept over me. A wave that just kept crashing.

He grabbed me by the waist and pulled me over, laughing as he rolled on top of me, and then looked down at me. "Wow," he said in that deep, husky voice. That same voice that bellowed off the stage over the heads of the interested and uninterested, posers and players, the expectant and the bored. "This is a great way to wake up." He leaned down and kissed me.

We furiously picked up where we'd left off in the wee hours of the morning. I would say "the previous night," but it was only a few hours before. He had so much energy. He was wiry and fit. I mean, he had nice, normal-sized muscles, but not obscene. Not like Steve. I shook my head, getting his unwanted image and name out of my head.

He nipped at my ear, kissed my face, and pulled me in tight. He was fun, full of light, and sexy all at once. I was soon lost in his intoxicating scent, as waves of pleasure rippled over my body like nothing I had experienced before with you-know-who.

After a flurry of loud moans from him, and joyous "oh, oh, ohs" from me, he collapsed next to me in a sweat and turned to look at me, again with that big grin, and smiling eyes. "Wow," he said. "You're kind of a howler. No, no I mean that in the best way possible," he backtracked, seeing my full and utter embarrassment as I buried my face in the pillow. "Some girls don't make any sound, and just lay there like a dead fish. I have no idea if they're having a good time." He pulled me toward him and lay on top of me, his sticky body pressed against mine. "I love that I know you enjoyed it as much as I did." He kissed my nose, and then he rolled off, hopping out of bed.

Hmmm. I smiled to myself. *I don't think I ever made that noise with Steve, what with his family always downstairs. And. This feels different.* I was very good at faking what I thought was an orgasm so it would end faster. Steve never wanted to finish unless he knew he had given me one. Was that kind, or was it just that he wanted to prove something? I shook the image of him out of my head again.

I knew right then and there it wouldn't last; it wouldn't go anywhere. I mean, I wanted it to. But right now, right in this moment, I was filled with complete and utter happiness. Something had shifted inside me. I wasn't going to ruin it with my expectations. But I knew it deep inside.

I bounced out of bed and joyfully pulled on my clothes from the night before as he grabbed a banana from the kitchen for me. I was starved and yet didn't have time to sit around. He didn't either; we both had class. Well, to be honest, I didn't hear what he said he had, I was so busy just being overwhelmed with any attention he directed at me. I just knew he was studying art.

Leaning up against the door frame, he grinned at me once more with that memorable smile that seemed to say, "I will never forget you," and I walked out into the new day, not even sure where I was.

How is it that having sex with a guy five years older than me for three years never felt that good? Steve always told me he was more skilled, more knowledgeable, more mature than guys my age, even the ones two years above me. He lied. He didn't know how to have sex or make love. He hurt me, he forced me, he shoved, manipulated, and brainwashed me! I gave up everything, and for what?

As I walked out into the gray morning light, I recognized where I was—not far from school. I must have looked like a wreck. I headed back across campus padding through the delicate layer of snow, just enough to be white but only as much as powdered sugar on a cake, keeping my head lowered to avoid the few students who passed on the way to their classes.

I had a faint headache from all the beer, but the whole night was pretty foggy. I ran my hand through my messy hair and looked down at my outfit as I tried to piece back together the evening before and wondered where my car was parked.

Oh, I thought. *That's where my car is. Jamie took it.*

37 | IT'S MY TURN

"Dear Prudence," Siouxsie and The Banshees

Several weeks had passed and I hadn't heard from Dave. Not that I expected it. His band wasn't playing anytime soon, which was actually a good thing. The last thing I wanted was to look like a stalker.

That was the last time I'll do that, I told myself. *I'm not sleeping with guys on the first date anymore. If you call that a date. They have to chase me!*

I didn't have any guilt about cheating on Steve, because honestly, I was pretty sure he was still cheating on me. Nope, I didn't have any guilt. It was just ... it still hurt. I didn't want to be an object.

Steve had proved his point without even knowing it. Guys just wanted sex from me. Not a relationship.

"Your boyfriend called looking for you."

"Mm-hmm ... thanks." I smiled at the girls as I passed and rolled my eyes, indicating what a nuisance he was, and trudged back to my room. I was trying to play it cool, like I was the one in charge, but really, I was worried he was going to be mad. But I wasn't going to call him back now, it was too late. Besides, it was two o'clock in the morning, and I was drunk. It was better for him to think I just forgot.

Charmaine was sound asleep as I crept in. I sat down on the edge of the bed and pulled off my combat boots that I'd bought from my mom's friend who had been in the ROTC. They were the real deal, and thankfully already broken in.

I struggled out of my clothes, tossing my skirt and sweater on the ground, and collapsed on the bed in a delirious bubble of joy from just having spent the night listening to loud and furious hardcore at P.B. Kelly's in Shockoe Bottom.

Hardcore had really taken over the punk scene in Richmond. It was invigorating. When I stood there in the crowd among everyone else, being pushed and shoved, thrashing my head to the frantic rhythm ... well, it was like all the anger you had built up in you, all *my* anger toward my dad and Steve, it just got pummeled away.

And this night was no exception. Bambie and I were so excited because one of our favorite bands from D.C., Government Issue, was playing with two of our local bands: Absence of Malice and Unseen Force. We had met the singer and guitarist from Absence of Malice at their party in the fall. Graves, the guitar player. He had this huge head of hair that he spiked with egg whites and Jell-O when he played on stage. Thanks to Bambie's brother we were meeting a lot of these cool artists and musicians.

My head was spinning from all the beer, but I kept playing the evening over in my head. There was nothing terribly important that happened to me. But I could tell Bambie had taken an interest in Graves, and he never stopped looking at her.

During the show as I was being jostled about and enjoying it, the next thing I knew, Bambie was singing at the mic with Stabb, the lead singer of Government Issue, in some kind of rock star moment.

Did that really happen? I thought. I couldn't wait to ask her tomorrow.

Unseen Force was a force to be reckoned with; the violence of their music was intoxicating. And even though the lead singer was a hot wiry guy with long dreads, to me the star of the show was the kick-ass bass player, a girl named Greta with short blond hair who wore a tartan kilt-style miniskirt and tank top. She was the epitome of cool. More woman than girl. It was just the way she held herself. Confident.

And then there was Scott, the guitarist. He was terribly cute with his black teased hair and black shirt buttoned all the way up to the neck with an Iron Cross necklace. And he wore skull earrings.

My head was ringing a bit from the music, but not bad. I lay there awake for a while, looking out the window, the distant streetlights casting an alternating green, then red glow on the street. I thought about what I wanted to do. Images, music, and thoughts filtered in and out of my head. But one thought kept coming back to me. I forced myself to focus on it a bit harder. And then finally, I came to a decision.

I decided right there, in that moment, I was going to tell Steve I wanted to see other guys. *Yes*, I thought, *the next time we talk* ...

I was in my room working on a project when Sunshine poked her head in the door and told me he was on the phone.

I looked up at her, then slowly peeled myself off the floor. Reluctantly, I trudged down the hall to the pay phone.

Tonight, I had plans with Bambie. We were all going to Goin' Bananas to hang out and hear some bands. Bambie, her brother, his friends, and her new boyfriend, Graves. Yep. The night after the G.I. show, we were back at P.B. Kelly's because ... why not? More bands and more fun. Graves was spinning records between bands, and it was his birthday. And that's kind of how it started. With a birthday kiss.

I didn't know if they were officially dating. But they liked each other for sure.

Graves was friends with Scott, that cute guitar player from Unseen Force. I was really hoping to meet him.

All this was going through my head as I picked up the pay phone. I was nervous, but with just a little bit more confidence than usual.

"Hello?" I inquired, as if I weren't sure who was calling.

"Hello?" He immediately caught this, and his tone sounded pissed. "Who else is calling you?"

I sighed deep. I shouldn't have started it out that way. But I really wanted to pick a fight.

"What are you talking about? That's how people answer phones. And you're not the only one who calls. I have friends, and my mom or dad could be calling," I said breathlessly.

"Fine," he said, then more softly, "Why haven't you been there when I call? I called you at ten and you weren't in the dorm. I told you I would call you at ten. Where were you last night?"

"I was out with friends." I lifted my chin in defiance. "I can't always be here at ten, that's when we're going out."

"What friends? Who are these friends you're always out with and who's calling you?" I could hear the anger in his voice.

"Listen, Steve, we have to talk," I said, and my heartbeat started to race. My arms felt all shaky.

"What? Talk about what?" He sounded cautious, with an underscore of menace.

"Well," I started, then stopped and cleared my throat, and then just said it. "I want to see other people." I quickly rushed on so he couldn't interrupt me. "I'm in college now and … well, I'm going to see other people," I repeated, firmly. "And you have to stop just showing up."

I could hear the crackle of the pay phone … and a long silence.

"No," he growled. "Absolutely not. I don't want you to see other people." I could hear the anger in his voice, but something else was there.

"No," I said calmly, "you can't say no. It's my turn, and I want to see other people, and if you have a problem with it, then we should break up."

"So that's what you want. You want to break up?" he said with a low threatening voice.

"No, that's not what I said." I started to panic and yet I felt excited by this idea. "I said I want to see other people, and if you don't like it, then you can break up with me."

"Do you want to break up with me?"

"No, it's just my turn!" I heard myself saying. "I just want to see other people."

"Fine."

"Fine?"

"Yes, fine." And he slammed the phone down.

I sat there listening to the dial tone for a full minute.

I got up slowly. And then, suddenly, I began jumping up and down and shouting, "Yes! *Yes!!*"

Back in my room, I opened up the lid to the new stereo my grandma gave me for Christmas and carefully placed the needle on my Siouxsie and the Banshees record, planning out in my mind my outfit for the night.

There was a knock on the door, and Bambie stuck her head in. "Why aren't you ready?"

"Bambie! I did it! I fucking told Steve I wanted to see other people!"

"Oh my god, finally! Now we can celebrate." She came over and gave me a squeeze and then pulled back and looked at me. "Are you okay?"

"Yes, I am. I really am." I was, I really was. This was a huge step.

"Okay, so hurry and get ready." She turned toward the door. "My brother will be here in, like, fifteen minutes."

"Ack, okay, I'll meet you in your room in fifteen."

I quickly tore through my closet, grabbed what I was looking for, tossed the clothes on my bed, and hurried over to our makeshift vanity. Basically, a mirror over a dresser. Looking at myself in the mirror, all I could see was this excited face looking back between the band and unicorn stickers, concert flyers, random postcards, and Prince photos littering the mirrored surface. The top of the dresser was covered with makeup, hair supplies, and pretty much junk.

I really didn't see any of it; it was peripheral to the open excitement that was expanding inside me. Was it because of the loosening of the reins, or was it just about the possibility of meeting this boy?

When we walked in the club, we were greeted by a group of very tall guys in studded leather jackets, ripped jeans, safety pins, band shirts, jean jackets with graffiti of bands painted or drawn all over, and girls in kilts, black skirts, T-shirts, leather, and military-style jackets. Hair teased, dyed, stiffened, shaved, dreaded, girls and boys alike. I was wearing a black sweater over my lucky white Bill the Cat T-shirt, with a black skirt. It fit snugly down the hips and flared out over the knees. Not so much a ruffle, but more of a tulip shape. I'd paired that with my black combat boots over ripped tights. I didn't have a leather jacket yet, so I wore my short wool Eisenhower jacket I'd picked up at the Army Navy Store. Over that I wore the silver cross necklace Bambie had given me. My hair was brushed over to the side to enhance my haircut and my growing number of earrings up the ear—mostly bats and skulls.

Bambie wore a black sweater under a pin-striped olive blazer, with a GBH button—an English punk band. Quite minimal, except she also wore her amazing collection of silver necklaces that looked like fringe. Very Egyptian looking, which went well with her makeup.

David, her brother, went straight back to the bar, saying hi to Graves as he walked past him. Graves said hi and looked over David's shoulder at Bambie, his whole face lit up. He immediately came over and gave Bambie a hug. He was so tall that she only came up to just under his arm. He grinned at me, then turned and called over to Scott, who was standing off to the side.

"Hey, grab that table," he yelled over the noise, and at the same time directed us toward it, while Scott sat down.

Even though they were both tall and wore leather jackets, they had their own unique style. Graves wore ripped-up jeans over black long johns (it was freezing out) with a white T-shirt that had a hand-drawn image, most likely a band logo. Over that he wore a leather jacket with his Absence of Malice Iron Cross on one shoulder and GBH on the front of the right side, accessorized with studs on the collar. His hair, which hadn't been teased or stiffened into spikes with Jell-O, was thick, loose, and wavy.

Scott wore black jeans, less ripped, and a Slayer concert T-shirt. His leather jacket had neat rows of studs on the epaulets and band buttons on the front. I sat to his right and Bambie sat on my right. Graves went off to grab beers for us. No introductions. This was on me.

"Hi," I said quite shyly, "I'm Suzanne." I really needed a beer.

"Hi, I'm Scott." He seemed just as shy as me.

The table was immediately swarmed with people. Graves placed some beers in the middle of the table, and we all reached out and grabbed one at the same time.

It seemed like the whole crew from AOM was there. Besides Graves, there was Tim, the singer, who had his own look: at once casual, not punk, and yet absolutely cool. His ripped jeans were inked with band names, like Black Sabbath, and he wore a yellow O.P. T-shirt. Over that, a jean jacket.

Vicky was the bass player; I'd met her several times already through David, Bambie's brother. She was beyond cool. She had a full-on Mohawk. She hadn't dyed her hair like most of the girls, but shaved it on both sides, making her look like a Roman centurion. Tonight, she wore a black turtleneck sweater with an army-green vest. It was a very minimal look. When I met her the first time, at her apartment, when we were tagging along with Dave, she introduced me to her rat—a big fat rat named Watty. I was definitely going to get myself a pet rat.

David and Margaret were there too. Margaret was David's friend, and I'd met her the week before at an art opening or something, and we'd discovered we were in the same art class.

The conversation was hard to follow over the loud room and the music pounding from down below, but I was in heaven. There I was, sitting at a table surrounded by new friends. I felt like it took forever in high school to fit in or make friends. But here we were, surrounded by the coolest people who just wanted to express themselves differently. People I could relate to.

When I turned to talk to Scott, he was watching me. My pale makeup couldn't possibly hide the blush spreading across my face. Thankfully Bambie drew his attention away and saved me by asking where he was from.

I pulled my camera off from around my neck and laid it on the table. It was a Christmas present from my mom. Although it was a cheap Sears Nikon knockoff, it still took good pictures. I was taking a photography class, learning to develop the negatives and make my own prints. My teacher, Mr Stover—although he let us call him by his first name, David—played in the Prevaricators, and he'd been really helpful and nice, giving me advice on how to set up the aperture and ISO for night and club shoots.

It was getting a bit confusing with the number of Davids I kept meeting. Actually, Scotts, Davids and Margarets.

I started bringing my camera with me everywhere; it was much easier to interact with the crowd when you hid behind the lens. I took a lot of photos of all the bands, and the ones I knew were really encouraging and let me up on stage with them.

I couldn't decide what my favorite part of photography was—bringing to life the ghostly images with special chemicals in the pitch black and watching them reveal a story, or the supercharged rush I felt when I was in the crowd or up on the stage taking pictures. One part was so solitary, so personal. The other made me feel like I was part of the show.

Bambie picked up the camera and snapped one of me and Scott, who then grabbed it and took one of us. Then from out of nowhere a guy with a much nicer camera shot some photos of all of us, individually.

I stood up, grabbed my camera, and started shooting pictures as everyone goofed around, and then we all headed downstairs to listen to the band.

Sweat beaded on my forehead as the small room swarmed with bodies, flailing here and there, in a kind of spastic rhythm to the music that machine-gunned off the stage. I laughed, bumping into Scott, and he laughed back as I continued on, mostly dancing with Bambie, in our club-meets-hardcore style of movement.

We departed the club, cigarettes dangling from lips, clomping combat boots and sheets of laughter, Bambie and I cramming into the back of David's car, with Graves between us, and Scott in the front. Their place was on the way, so we dropped them off, and waved goodbye as we headed back toward the dorm. David dropped us off and headed on his way.

"Well," Bambie said, as she opened the front door and we nodded our hellos to the night watch, then headed back toward the elevators, "what's going on with you and Scott? Anything?"

"I don't know." I pushed the elevator button. It could take a while; these things were old, and sometimes a bit scary. "I mean, he seemed to like me. I think he's super cute!" We stepped in as it opened up. "But he also seems a bit shy, so I doubt he'll call."

"Don't worry, I have an idea." The elevator stopped at our floor, and we got off.

"What?" I was curious and excited. Bambie always had good ideas and great advice. She was probably the smartest and most level-headed of my friends.

"Well, I told Graves I was free Saturday. So, maybe we can make a double date of it." She grinned as she opened the door to her room. "Just let me handle it."

I left her at her room and continued on to my own.

Oh my god, this was so cool. Steve would be pissed and jealous if he found out, I thought. *Wait, did I tell Scott I had a boyfriend? I feel like I might have mentioned it. But maybe not. Well, I have to be honest. I'll tell him next time.*

Thankfully the nightlight was on as I entered the otherwise dark room. Charmaine's heavy breathing let me know she was sleeping, deeply burrowed in her comforter. I creeped over and began quietly taking off my boots, my sweater, slipping my necklaces off, then my silver rings, and then stopped. I looked at my small, sweet engagement ring.

A clock ticked from somewhere in the room.

I slid the ring off and tucked it into my jewelry box. I did not put it next to my other rings that sat waiting for tomorrow's adventures.

38 | SICK GIRL

"Thin Line Between Love and Hate," Pretenders

The next week seemed to go by really slowly as I tried hard to focus on my classes and homework, with only one exciting interruption when I ran into Vicky. She mentioned that GBH was playing in a couple weeks, somewhere near Norfolk. And GBH was huge. There was a reason everyone had either a button or their logo painted on their jacket, or both. They were from England, formed in 1978. They were basically pioneers of English street punk. I was definitely going to see them with her.

On Friday, as I was trying to study for this insanely boring art history quiz, someone knocked on my door. I jumped up and opened it to find Bambie, Graves, and Vicky.

"Hey, Zanny," Bambie grinned. "Thought we would stop by and say hi."

"Come on in," I laughed. "Our room is a disaster, but yeah, come in."

"Dude, your tastes are all over the place," Vicky said, as she came in and picked up my white plastic horse. I reached over and picked up my camera and began snapping photos of her. "You have a U2 poster, Thomas Dolby, Eurythmics, Billy Idol." She made an incredulous gasp. "Billy Idol? Yuk! He's a sellout." Then she laughed, all while posing for me. Then Bambie and Graves joined in and I snapped a few more photos.

"So, what's up?" I sat down in my chair, and they sat on the floor.

"Yeah, we're gonna go out tomorrow night. Do you want me to invite Scott, hmm?" Graves said with a grin, and then winked at me.

"Date night!" Vicky shouted out and laughed.

"Okay, stop." I was mortified. Vicky was already like an older sister who seemed to want to look out for my well-being around all the guys.

"Okay," she said in a singing voice, "have fun with that. I gotta bolt. Things to do you know." And with that she skipped out of the room.

I rolled my eyes as I turned back to Graves. "Yes, please!" I said with a smile.

Graves and Scott picked us up in Scott's yellow station wagon that night, and we headed to this disco drag bar where they had fifty-cent beer till ten.

We danced, shouted over the music, laughed, and talked. I got drunk pretty fast. The next thing I remembered we were all sitting on the roof of the Crew House—the same place where I met Dave Brockie the first time, and also where Grave's band lived, among others—with Bambie, Scott and Graves drinking Thunderbird from the bottle while the rain drizzled down on us. I'd always wanted to feel like one of the boys and to keep up with their drinking, so I didn't know when to stop.

I was cold, and so tired I could barely walk. I guess they decided it would be best for me to spend the night there, because next thing I knew I was in bed with Scott. Fully dressed, lying in his arms. Then I passed out.

I woke up freezing cold and shivering uncontrollably.

Where the fuck am I? All of a sudden there was a face in my face. Scott.

"Are you okay?" he asked, rubbing the sleep out of his eyes, smearing his eyeliner even more. He looked pretty concerned.

"I'm ... ffff-rrrr-eeee-zing," I said, my teeth clattering.

He put his hand up against my forehead. "Wow, you're hot. Lemme go ask Greta, maybe she has something for you. You definitely have a fever." He got up and opened the door and walked out.

Oh, I'm at Scott's place. I could hear people in the kitchen, so I pulled my coat on over my sweater, which I had worn to bed, and slowly started down the hall to the kitchen. My head hurt so bad. Greta was there, and Dewey too. They were like the parents of the house. They all lived right next door to the Crew House. I guess it was the Unseen Force house, but I'm not sure if they officially called it that.

Greta turned to me when she saw me come in.

"Here, sit down," she said, and handed me a pill and some orange juice, and felt my forehead. "Yea, you have a fever. Scott, you need to take her home. She needs to sleep, and she's not going to get any sleep here with the band practicing in a couple of hours."

The rest of the day passed in a blur. I remember Scott driving me home. I remember sleeping. Then waking up, throwing up, falling back to sleep. And it kept going on like that. When I woke up in the morning, I was so thirsty. I drank so much water. But I just kept throwing it up.

Girls knocked on my door. Jamie was waiting for me. We walked to school every day. But I told them I was sick. I knew she didn't believe me. I played sick a lot.

Later that day, Bambie stopped by. She saw me and immediately went out and bought me Gatorade.

More time went by, and then I found myself in the communal bathrooms throwing up. A lot. The Gatorade wouldn't stay down. My attempts were either just water or dry heaving. *It just won't stop.*

Bambie came back the next morning and somehow was able to walk me to the clinic, which was about five blocks away. The doctor wasn't very helpful; he just told me to get some sleep and take aspirin.

More pain, more throwing up. Nothing stayed down. The next morning Bambie was back. This time, she had help. Charmaine helped her walk me to the clinic again. This time a different doctor was there, and he seemed more concerned. Something about never taking aspirin when you have pneumonia and a viral infection. Or was it bacterial?

Next thing I knew I was in a cop car. I guess they didn't have an ambulance. It was only a few blocks from the dorm, but finally I was taken to a hospital.

I was lying on a cot in a hallway. People came by and poked at me. Then someone stopped and yelled, "Why isn't she in a room?"

The next time my eyes opened, I was in a room and more people kept coming in, asking the same questions and taking blood.

It seemed like I was in this room forever when finally, a doctor who seemed like he knew what he was doing shouted at the attending doctors.

"Bring her to ICU, now!"

And then everything went black again.

I woke up and felt things all over me. Wires with pads were stuck all over my chest. A bag or mask or something loosely covered my mouth, and something was sticking up my nose. I felt air flowing up my nostrils, which tickled. There was an IV in my arm, which is what actually woke me up in the first place, as a nurse was removing it and switching it to my left arm.

What is she doing? I wondered. *She's stabbing me relentlessly.*

"What are you doing?" I heard this from the other side of the room. "You're not doing it right." Irritation laced her voice. "You're going to mess up her veins and leave terrible bruises."

Then I felt the needle going into the top of my right hand.

I hated needles so much as a kid. I would run and hide in the doctor's office if I even heard or suspected a needle was on its way to me. But now, I just lay there in a dazed stupor watching this going on—as if I were watching a movie play out in front of me. They had been prodding me with needles all day, or was it yesterday? *What day is this?*

Then it went black again.

I remembered my mother. Her concerned face.

I remembered her saying my father was there.

He lives in California, why is he here?

And then I was sitting up. They were helping me sit up. They wanted to see how my heart was when I sat up. I looked to the left at the TV screen with lines and numbers. The numbers climbed higher.

So they pushed me back down.

I fell back asleep.

I was sitting up again. The numbers seemed stable. "High," someone said, "but stable."

I don't have the bag on my face anymore, I thought. *But I have those things in my nose, a needle in my arm, and these pads stuck all over me, with wires attached.* I wondered how long I had been there.

The nurse gave me something to sip. *Is this soup?*

The door opened and the nurse stuck her head in and told me I had a visitor.

I really couldn't make out what she was saying, but then Steve walked in. I'd never seen that expression. Concern? His eyebrows knit together, not in anger but worry. His mouth parted as if he was going to say something but didn't know what or how. It irritated me that he was there. Then he said something, but I couldn't make it out. Weakly, but firmly, I said, "Please go. I don't want you here." I felt cold all over looking at him.

That took a lot of effort. To talk. I had no breath left in me. I was exhausted. The nurse helped me lie back down, and I closed my eyes.

When I opened my eyes next, I was in a different room and my mom was sitting there. She was happy when she saw me wake up. I felt so much better. I could breathe again.

They thought I wasn't going to make it. They called my father, she told me. They said my right lung was filled with fluid, and if it had started in on the left, I would have been in serious danger.

When I opened my eyes again, it was Easter Sunday. My dad was there. He stood there telling me about my campus, my art, what I should be doing.

I should have a sketch pad with me always and be drawing nonstop. Why was I not doing that? It was great to meet Jamie, and she'd been showing him around campus. Boy did I have a bunch of fun-looking friends. On and on he went.

This dad seemed very different from the "before" dad. He was still dictating what I should or shouldn't be doing, but he seemed ... different.

Later, Bambie was with me. I was so happy to see her. My dad had really exhausted me. She had just come back from spending the weekend with her parents, because it was Easter. Jamie would be back soon too, she told me.

"It was so funny; I wish you could have seen it. Everyone was there." She pulled the chair up closer to my bed. "Everyone was there, in the ICU waiting room. Tim, Graves, Vicky, Scott ... all these spiky-haired, leather-jacket-clad punk rockers."

I smiled. "That's so sweet, they came to see me?" I tried to scoot up a bit. Bambie reached out and propped the pillow up for me.

"Well, yeah, I mean they weren't allowed to come in, but they were worried. Did you see? Vicky left some cards for you." She pointed to the side table, picked one up, and handed it to me.

"Oh my god, this is so sweet," I said, overwhelmed. "She drew a horse on it. She knows how much I love horses."

"Let me finish telling you. That's not all." She seemed like she had a bunch of things to get out.

"Okay, go on." I put the card down.

"So, then your dad walked in."

"Yeah, I know he's here, or was here. He left today now that I'm out of danger."

"Yes, but your dad walks into the room, with all these punk rockers, and he looks, well, amused. I mean, he didn't get mad, wasn't rude. He was really nice and introduced himself. Everyone did. It was surreal," she said with a look of wonder. "I mean, I know he can be strict, but I think he thought these were a bunch of cool artists."

"Yeah, he really wants me to be an artist." I sighed. "He likes to tell me how to be an artist." I rolled my eyes. "He would much rather have them in my life than Steve."

"So ... they call him, and he goes into the ICU room to see you. Your mom wasn't there, so thankfully they didn't have to see each other." She put her hand on me. "But listen, he goes in, and in walks Steve."

"What?" I groaned. "Oh, yeah, I vaguely remember he came in." It was coming back to me now.

"Yes, but listen," she continued. "He walked in, and he was really uncomfortable around everyone. I don't think he knew what to make of them." She nodded. "Right? I mean, this look is not anywhere he hangs out. We don't have a lot of punks, if any, hanging out in Fairfax. You have to go to D.C."

"With all their leather, and spiked hair, he was probably scared." I laughed. "The big tough bodybuilder was scared!"

"Well, he asked me about you, and I said your dad was in with you, so he went outside to wait!" She brushed her hair out of her eyes. Her bangs were getting long. "He wouldn't wait in the waiting room with all of them. He asked me to let him know when he could go in."

"You know it's funny, I don't remember seeing my dad in the ICU. He came yesterday, and this morning to say goodbye. I don't even know what day it is—"

"Tuesday," she interjected.

"But I do remember Steve. I was groggy as hell and out of breath with that oxygen mask over my face and IV stuck in my arm. All over my body there were a dozen little electrode pads connecting me to a machine. The nurse popped her head in and said I had a visitor, and then he walked in behind her. I just looked at him and told him to go home. I didn't want to see him."

"What? You broke up with him?"

"No, I didn't break up with him, I just told him to go home. I said something about being too tired and sick." I looked at her straight on. "Bambie, he made me feel sicker. He doesn't even look the same. I mean, from when I first met him. All those testosterone injections just made him bigger and angrier. I don't recognize him. And I ... I just didn't want him to be there. I mean, I kind of feel bad now. He looked hurt. Maybe shocked. But I didn't care. I was too tired to care about his feelings at the time. I just wanted my family. And my friends."

"Well, that explains him coming out and not saying goodbye. He just stormed out."

We just looked at each other. I squinched the side of my mouth, raising my eyebrows, indicating an expression of "oh well."

There they all sat, surrounding my bed with their ripped jeans, Iron Crosses and pins, earrings and spiked hair. Graves, Scott, Tim, Vicky, Bambie, and Jamie. They were all so worried about me, and happy to see I was better. They laughed about my dad when he came to visit—walking into the waiting room to see this scraggly bunch of kids all there waiting to hear how I was.

"And that guy, the muscle man, was that your boyfriend?" Graves asked. "Man, he looked scary."

I looked up at Scott and did a sort of sheepish smile. I had wanted to tell him about Steve, but not this way.

"Yeah, I guess so. He's kind of an asshole, but I'm ending it." I tried to shrug it off, like nothing. "Besides, I think you all scared the shit out of him. You're not the kind of people he's used to bullying."

They told me the doctors thought I wouldn't make it. *Wouldn't make it? What does that mean? Die. Really? And all that time I just felt like I was floating, sleepy and tired.*

A nurse came in and told them they weren't supposed to be there, there were too many people in the room, and it was after visiting hours, but then she winked, and asked if anyone wanted a soda.

The rest of my time in the hospital seemed endless. They wouldn't release me till Thursday. I was so bummed because most of my friends were headed off to see GBH in Hampton, a bit south of Richmond. Not that I could have gone if they'd released me. I could barely stand I was so weak.

When I was released, I felt like an escaped patient. It took so long for the "release" forms that I just got dressed and left. I skirted the whole wheelchair-to-the-curb rule and just walked out. I stood there on the sidewalk, by myself, and looked up at the bright blue sky. I breathed in deeply, relieved to be able to take a deep breath of fresh air. *I'm changing. I can feel it in every part of my being. This didn't kill me. It made me stronger.*

Class tomorrow, then off to Kelly's for a show. I was excited to get back to life.

39 | IT'S A NEW WORLD

"I Heard it Through the Grapevine," The Slits

I was so excited when I was finally released from the hospital that I went out the next night, despite the doctor's orders. I had already missed out on too many shows! Black Flag, GBH, and Death Piggy. Plus, I wanted to get to know Scott better.

When I walked into Life Drawing Friday morning, my teacher looked at me with furrowed brows.

"Suzanne"—he cleared his gravelly throat—"you've missed a lot of classes this semester, but this really takes the cake." He crossed his arms in front of his chest, trying to appear authoritative. But he was just a short, skinny guy. He barely came up to my shoulders. He was hardly threatening, although he did have the power to fail me.

I walked up to his desk without a word and put my doctor's note on the table. It said I was excused from school, or recommended it, until the following week. It spelled out in great detail where I'd been and what had happened to me. I asked the doctor for this note knowing full well my teachers wouldn't believe me because I'd already set a pattern with them. They didn't trust my excuses. During senior year of high school, I'd started some bad habits, and they stuck with me.

"Oh my god," he said, looking at me sincerely. "Well, honestly, maybe you needed this to help you realize you need to slow down." His eyes scanned me from top to bottom. "You lost a lot of weight."

"Bonus from eating only liquids for ten days." I grinned and sat down by the easel in the corner. He rolled his eyes and turned back to what he was doing.

I had a lot of catching up to do. I didn't listen to my teacher, or the doctor. Bands, clubs, dancing, drinking. Repeat. Bands, clubs, dancing, drinking. Repeat. And so on.

Graves was now a good friend, more like an older brother looking out for me. He was always telling me to slow down. They made such a cute couple, him and Bambie. But I knew it was hard for her because she had just broken up with Eric. I knew deep down I needed to do the same with Steve. I was just avoiding the confrontation. Just like I avoided his phone calls. I swore I'd be down to visit soon; I just had a lot of makeup work to do before term was over. Which was only about a month away!

One day, Graves and Scott surprised us at my dorm. Bambie and I had been working on our art projects together in my room with papers and paint spread out on the floor, while also discussing our planned trip to California after school let out, when one of the girls said we had a call from downstairs. "Somebody's here to see you," she said in a singsong voice.

We had to go let them in and escort them up. Raised eyebrows and smiles followed us along the hall. I was definitely entertaining my dorm-mates without even trying.

So, there we were, all four of us sprawled out on the floor, and they joined in with paper and paint. It was so cute. These two tall guys clad in leather and studs, earrings and tattoos hanging out in my room.

After that, I started to see Scott more often. I'd go see him play with his band, or hang out at his place, in his room, and watch TV. His room looked like a living room, but with his bed in the corner. We were rarely alone though; people were always hanging out there too. We would listen to his eclectic music collection. He had the hugest collection of albums I'd ever seen—they filled two walls. We talked comics and art. He was a really good artist. He was quiet, shy, and very nice. We kissed, but no further than that. I kept waiting. But he never made one move on me. Which comforted me and yet confused me.

Bambie and I drove down to Shockoe Bottom one night, the car making a racket as it struggled over the cobblestones. P.B.Kelly's, which we just called Kelly's, was our go-to club destination. Bananas was good, and so was Rockitz, but Kelly's had a lot of shows where our friends were playing and hanging out. It was under the highway and amid the farmers' market, which I'd never seen in action because I was never awake that early.

We headed in, grabbed a couple of beers, and elbowed our way through the crowded room to watch Scott's band play.

"Hey, did you get your rat?" Vicky popped up next to me. Her hair was freshly shaved at the sides, all fluffed up into a Trojan horse Mohawk. Her single upside-down cross earring played an extreme contrast to her sweet cherub face. She used to intimidate me so much, but now, well she still did, but she was so sweet, and kind of like the older sister I never had.

"Yeah, I did." I had fallen in love with Vicky's rat, so I'd decided to get my own. She was much smaller, and I named her Tara. She was adorable. I pretty much carried her everywhere with me around campus. She would stay up on my shoulders or on my neck and hide under my hair. If I wore my sweatshirt with the single front pocket, she would hide in the pouch.

"Cool, dude!" She smiled. "Let's have a playdate!" she shouted over the music.

I had to go to the bathroom, so I caught Bambie's eye. She followed me through the crowd, shielded by my tall frame as I wove a path for us.

"What's going on?" she asked as we entered the small space—very dirty, plastered with flyers and graffiti.

"Nothing. I don't know. Well, Scott never tries anything. He just, I don't know. He smokes pot and I don't like to get stoned anymore." I leaned against the wall, then moved away quickly. "I did it so much in high school, I just don't. And it's not so fun to be around people who are high when you're not." I moaned. "But I really like him."

"Well, maybe you should break up with Steve. Maybe that's why he doesn't try anything. By the way, Graves and I are taking it slow too." She leaned in toward the mirror and touched up her very white nose. The makeup she'd picked up in London was great, but you had to keep checking it or it would slide right off when we were all sweaty at the clubs.

"Yeah, you're right. I mean it, I do like him. He's so nice." I squeezed in beside her and applied some Chapstick. The look was pale everywhere except the eyes. Even though Bambie called me Siouxsie as a nickname, I didn't paint my eyes like her. That was Bambie's look. "Hey, pierce my nose!"

"What? You're crazy, are you drunk already?" She looked at me like I was nuts.

"What? We've pierced each other's ears before. What's the difference?" Bambie and I both pierced each other's ears often. I now had six in my left ear and two on my right. I liked the asymmetrical look.

The door to the stall opened up and Maggie stepped out. "I'll pierce your nose!"

"Really?"

"Hell ya." She started to leave. "I'll go get an ice cube and a safety pin!"

We sat out on the curb, me leaning against Bambie while she looked a bit worse for wear. I was pretty drunk too and my nose throbbed, but the ice really helped, and it looked cool. It's amazing you could pierce a nose with a safety pin. Pulling it out and then shoving a stud earring in it was far worse and made my eye water.

I stretched out my legs, which looked skinny in my washed-out Guess jeans with the tight zippered ankles. I loved my little black boots that I'd studded by hand. I was studding everything. I couldn't wait to get a leather jacket and put studs all over it too.

"Don't you love my little boots?" I slurred to Bambie, who perked up next to me at the sound of my voice. I wiggled them for her.

"Mm-hmm." She was wearing all black with those long silver fringe necklaces. I didn't wear all black usually. I always liked to toss in color. Tonight, I was wearing my orange-striped shirt, all buttoned up to the neck, with my silver Isis pendant (O Mighty Isis!), and my hair pulled to the side under my fisherman's cap.

"Want me to pierce your nose?"

"No!"

"Hey ladies, we're headed to a V-Tex party, you wanna come?" Graves interrupted our babbling nonsense conversation, appearing before us with Scott at his side. Scott was swaying a little bit too.

"Sure," we both said at the same time.

We headed to Church Hill, just up the way from the Bottom. Maybe a five-minute drive. It was right off Broad Street, one of those old houses with a porch. Like Graves said, the party was being thrown for or by some of the people Graves worked with at V-Tex, Virginia Textiles. A textile printing company that did shirts. Or something. A lot of them worked there: Tim, Graves, Bob, and his girlfriend, Joy.

I found Scott outside on the porch and sat down next to him. Bambie sat down next to me and started telling me about the recording session from the night before. Graves had filled her in, and she was giving me the update. I was half listening as I scanned the place.

A tall boy walked out the front door with bleached blond hair. Not as tall as Graves, who walked out with him, talking as they stood off to the side, and the boy lit a cigarette. He wore jeans, Converse sneakers, and a plaid button-up shirt.

"Who's that?" I interrupted Bambie. "He's cute."

She quickly looked toward Scott, but was looking the other way.

"I don't know. He came with them to the recording studio. I think Graves said he's from Charleston. That's how they all know each other. They all lived down there before heading here."

"Oh." He was really cute. I loved the dyed blond hair with the dark roots. And he had these great lips. Immediately I thought of Frank Langella from *Dracula*. I mean, just the mouth. It was the way his lips curled and were so full. And the way he talked, and then laughed with Graves. His laughter came from his whole body.

He looked toward me, and we made eye contact. I smiled, and he smiled back, and raised his eyebrows toward Scott. I shrugged and turned toward Scott, who looked like he was nodding off. I shook him and he popped his head back up and smiled.

Oh man. I looked over toward the boy, who grinned back at me, tilting his head back as he laughed, and then he turned around and walked back inside.

As I drove back toward our dorms, Bambie squeezed in the back, while Scott sat dazed in the passenger seat, I couldn't stop thinking about the curious boy at the party.

After that night I kept seeing him. Everywhere.

Each time I talked to Steve, he'd ask me to come home to see him. I hadn't been home since before I was in the hospital. I'd gotten out only two weeks before and he'd seen me there. But I didn't mention that. I felt bad about being rude. But I'd been sick and told him I had just been in pain. It wasn't actually a lie. I was. But still ... I felt bad, especially because he told me his parents had driven him up. He was too worried about me to drive himself. Ouch.

When I said I couldn't come home for one reason or another, he suggested coming to see me. My excuses were creative: Charmaine's parents were visiting, or I was going to her aunt and uncle's that weekend. All true.

He was finally resigned to seeing me when I came down the first weekend of May. I had to go home so I could switch cars with my mom. There was no way all my stuff would fit in my little Karmann Ghia. Thankfully, she was going to let me take her Honda Civic wagon to move all my stuff out of the dorm. It was hard to believe I'd moved in everything with my little Ghia, but I'd accumulated a lot of stuff, like the stereo my grandmother gave me for Christmas.

Ever since I'd been in the hospital, I could feel myself physically and mentally pulling further and further away from Steve. Even though he'd been sweet to me on the phone, it just felt ... fake. It felt like a trap. I knew he didn't like seeing all those boys hanging out in the ICU waiting room. I knew he probably thought I was sleeping with all of them. He was just waiting. Biding his time so he could punish me for my ... behavior. I couldn't risk being alone with him ever again.

I was so good at burying my feelings, my thoughts, the pain, that I created a fog around us. To make it feel less. To make me see what I wanted to. But shards of memory were piercing me like glass, poking me to remove them. To do something. To stop it. Completely. And there was only one way.

But then, how was I going to end it? I couldn't bring myself to do it over the phone.

40 | TAKING THE LEAD
"Love Song," The Damned

He found me sitting on the curb outside of Kelly's with Bambie and Graves singing at the top of our lungs.

Scott's band was playing inside, along with Dr. Know. I liked them and all, but I needed fresh air because my head was spinning, and I wasn't sure if I was going to lose it or not. I was such a lightweight now, probably from losing so much weight. But now, I was feeling much better; the fresh air had washed away the stale smells of Red Stripe and sweat, and the three of us were belting out ridiculous show tunes, starting with "Green Acres."

And then from out of nowhere, *he* sat down next to me and started talking to me. Just like that.

"And that's why you don't drive on the highway with a guy who is fucking high," he ended. Then he smiled, tilted his head to the side. "I'm Chris."

He was hard to figure. He seemed kind of shy, but then it was so easy to talk with him. He didn't act shy at all around his friends—he had leaned over and punched Graves in the shoulder by means of a greeting.

"Hi." All of a sudden, I felt shy. "I'm Suzanne. This is Barbara, my bestest friend in the whole world."

Inside, Scott's band banged away, while outside, despite the cold, we sat, drinking our beers, laughing, and talking about the bands playing that night.

During the next week, I looked for him everywhere I went. I was still with Scott, but I was getting tired of the way the relationship was turning out. There was just so much spark, so much energy between me and Chris. I felt drawn to him in a way that I couldn't ignore.

I finally happened to stumble upon him over the weekend at Schaefer's Court. He was sitting on the steps with Vicky while some kids were skateboarding, jumping on and then sliding off the steps. I casually went up to sit down next to Vicky, but as I sat down, she popped up to go talk to someone she just saw.

"Back in a sec, Suz," she called over her shoulder.

It was broad daylight and I hadn't had a single bit of alcohol to help calm my nerves to talk to him. But I wasn't going to let him think I was intimidated.

Trying not to stumble over my words, and trying for a super-casual attitude, I leaned back on my hands and turned to look at him. "Hey."

"Hey, yourself," he said with that smile. "I like your shirt. Did you make it?" He indicated with his cigarette my Bill the Cat T-shirt.

"Uh, yeah."

He asked about what I was studying, where I was from, and I asked him the same questions. He wasn't studying anything. He was just "crashing" at the Crew House between jobs. He had no intention of going to college, he said. At least not yet. He wanted to just write. Maybe even direct films. One day he was going to California. Which was great, as I told him that was my plan as well once I graduated.

We ended up talking for a while before Vicky came back over, grabbed his hand, and hauled him off.

If I didn't know before, I knew for sure the next night at Bananas that I needed to end it with Scott. My flirtation with Chris was getting a bit obvious. There we were, Scott and me, standing in the crowd, listening to a band—it was a huge lineup—and Scott was slightly in front of me, his head moving with the music, to that *thump, thump, thump* hardcore beat. I was a bit bored. I turned to the side, and there was Chris. Looking sideways at me. I stuck my tongue out at him and made a face. I know, real mature. He laughed and made a face back.

When I looked over at Vicky, she had her eyebrow up and head cocked to the side, watching us. I wasn't sure what she was thinking, but I knew she and Graves were always looking out for me at the clubs when someone shoved or got too "physical." *But she's friends with him*, I thought. *He must be fine.*

He turned to her and said something, I couldn't quite make it out, but she laughed so hard, I felt a flood of relief. She did like him.

Oh yeah, I thought. *She probably thinks I'm two-timing Scott. And she knows about Steve. So, I'm three-timing?* I shrugged. *I'll explain it later.*

This was the second time that someone had liked me outside of just sex. There was definitely more chemistry with Chris than I shared with Scott. I wasn't sure Scott knew me, the real me, even after almost a month. In less than a few hours, Chris and I had talked more than Scott and I had in three weeks. Maybe it was because Scott and I were never alone together.

I just had this deep, familiar feeling with Chris. Like I knew he and I were meant to be together. I'd never had this feeling before. Sure—desire, longing, dreams. Whatever. But this was different. This was like looking at yourself in the mirror. Like you'd found a part of yourself that you were missing.

As Scott and I drove back from the show that night, I decided I needed to make a decision. It wasn't fair to him or to me.

We sat in my car outside the building where he lived with the band. His building, an old white brick townhouse, was right next to the Crew House, a similar-looking townhouse where Graves and his band lived. Chris was staying with them. There were always people crashing at the Crew House, from friends to kids coming through town to see a show or just passing through. A lot of the younger kids hanging around were runaways. It was a crash pad.

Whereas Scott's building had rooms with couches, beds, and some furnishings, the Crew House basically had nothing cozy going for it. Walls decorated in graffiti, with obscene drawings and crude effigies, like cartoon drawings in black marker. Rooms barren of bed frames, mattresses on the floor, and clothes in duffle bags. The main feature was an old TV set, and a beloved stereo. A wall of records stacked in crates.

As I sat there talking to Scott about the show, and, I don't know, stuff, I was distracted by the sight of Chris sitting in the second-floor window, peering down at me with a silly grin. I broke into a smile, and Scott— who had been slumped low, leaning lazily in his leather jacket, hands interlaced behind his neck, blending into the leather passenger seat—sat up and twisted around to see what had made me smile.

"That guy's obnoxious," he said, turning around and slumping back down with his round mirrored sunglasses and bandana headband. It was kind of a Nicky Sixx from Mötley Crüe look.

"No, he's not. He's kind of funny." I looked the other way so he couldn't see my expression. "Listen, Scott, I've been meaning to talk to you about this ..." I started.

I tried to do it nicely, or delicately, but I'd never done it before. I just said something like: "You know, I'm not ready ... my boyfriend up north ... I need to break it off with him before I get serious with anyone in the future ... I think maybe we're better off friends." I mean, it was all true. But the real reason?

I wanted to pursue Chris. And I didn't want to do it while I was with someone else. Er, I mean, with two other people. I needed to also break up with Steve ... but that would be harder.

He seemed a bit stunned by my long and flawed breakup speech. Like he couldn't believe I was breaking up with him. I didn't say any of the other things I thought: *You get stoned too much. You haven't even tried to have sex with me, not once.* Of course, I did respect him for that, considering I had a boyfriend, and I'd told him early on I wanted to take it slow. But this slow? We had to face it. The chemistry had left the building.

"Okay." He shrugged and opened the car door. He didn't argue. He didn't try to fight for the "relationship." He just looked kind of ambivalent in the end. Maybe he was equally bored with me.

I got out of the car as he climbed out. He turned to walk away toward his place, and I sneaked a peek to see if Chris was still there. Yep. Leaning against the windowsill, he seemed confident, arrogant, and amused. *He's watched the whole thing. I mean, he couldn't have heard us. But he knew what just happened, I guess by our body language.*

He gave me the biggest grin, winked, and disappeared into the house.

I didn't think it was cool to hop out and visit Chris, so I drove off, unexpectedly excited.

That was nothing, I thought to myself. *The hardest part is next*. At least that was what I knew I should do: settle things with Steve before I got into another relationship. *I wish it were going to be as easy as it was with Scott.*

As the weekend passed without any Chris sightings—he wasn't at Kelly's on Saturday—I decided to take matters into my own hands. I couldn't just go from club to club looking for him. Tuesday night, Death Piggy and the Butthole Surfers were playing, so I was going to be brave and go to the Crew House.

After running out of my last class, I hurried back to the dorm to change because I was covered in paint. I grabbed my little bathroom caddy, headed to the communal bathroom, jumped in and out of the shower, then raced back to the room to do my makeup. After carefully lining my eyes, I threw on my favorite skinny gray jeans and my orange striped shirt, which I buttoned all the way up, and then swapped my Oh Mighty Isis pendant for my Iron Cross one. Then I put my large blue studded cross over that and zipped up my black studded boots. They looked better than my combat boots with my skinny jeans and were more comfortable. My hair was freshly bleached in the front, and teased out to the side, newly shaved on the left. It was getting lighter each time, with the strands underneath dyed black. I put on my fisherman's cap and stood back and looked at myself. Ready.

I pulled up in front of the building and parked. I got out of the car and stared up at the house. It was dark now, and all lit up. Music blared out of one of the top-floor windows, competing with music blaring out of the second-floor window.

Walking up to the front door, I double-checked my outfit. I thought I looked okay, but my hands were shaking.

I took a deep, encouraging breath and let myself in. Nobody knocked … nobody would hear it. But I called from the bottom of the stairs up toward the main level.

"Hello? Anyone here?" I called.

"Hello?" Graves said as his head popped over the banister. "Hey Suzanne, to what do we owe the pleasure of your company?" he teased, knowing full well why I was lurking in the hallway. I had already shared with him and Bambie my pathetic breakup with Scott and crush on Chris.

I walked up the stairs toward him, grinning back.

"Shut up, you," I said as I gave him a big hug, standing on my tippy toes.

Graves was the tallest guy I had ever met. And it was hysterical because Bambie was so short! It seemed kind of unfair that short people matched up with tall people. Especially when the guy was tall. Tall guys were scarce.

I reached up and tousled his thick, dark, wavy hair.

"You have the best hair."

"Thanks, sexy lady. Your hair is pretty cool too." He grinned and slid his fingers across the freshly shorn side of my head. "Let me go tell Chris you're here. Trust me, you don't ever want to surprise anyone around here." He turned and went up the next set of stairs to the other bedrooms.

These houses were huge. The bottom was a business of some sort, so you came straight up to the main floor, which was kind of the second floor, where there was a living room, if you could call it that, two other bedrooms, and a kitchen. Upstairs, on the third floor, there were two other bedrooms and a walk-in closet, which was swapped in and out as a guest room or storage space. Whatever or whoever needed it the most.

I followed Graves up, giving him plenty of lead so he could give Chris enough warning of my arrival. I thought it would be funny to surprise him, but I think Graves had a point. I wouldn't want to walk in on him and somebody else. Ugh. That would suck.

I stood outside trying to listen but the music in the room was loud and I could only hear some mumbles. Then Graves stomped out, trailing with, "You're a dick, Chris." Then he looked at me and said, "He's all yours, honey."

It's hard to believe that a six-foot, six-inch punk rocker who played in a band called Absence of Malice and had spiked hair and ripped jeans could be so adorably sweet. But that's exactly what Graves was.

"Thanks," I said with a shrug and hopeful smile.

I pushed open the door and walked in, and there was Chris sitting on the floor in front of a record player listening to music with his eyes closed.

"Um, hey. How's it going?" I tried to cover up how nervous I was. I didn't know if it was the new look, the hair and all, but I was feeling much more confident lately.

"Hey there." His voice was low and deep. There was no urgency in it. And even though I knew he was from South Carolina, he didn't have a strong accent, yet he had that lazy mannerism. There was a smile in his eyes and a twitch to his lips the way they curled up, but otherwise his body language was so casual. Almost like he was teasing me. "What's up?"

"Oh, I just stopped by to see if you were going to the show tonight. Death Piggy and the Butthole Surfers are playing at P.B. Kelly's." I sat down on Tim's bed.

"Is that tonight? I thought it was April thirtieth." His head tilted in thought.

"It *is* April thirtieth."

"Huh, I thought it was February still." He grinned, took a swig of his beer, and asked me if I wanted one.

"What year is it?" I opened the can, even though I hated canned beer ... it made my tongue tingle. Just the thought of it makes me shiver.

"You got me. I stopped checking in '81."

"1985." I took a long swig. "This is the year when everything changes."

"How do you mean?" He looked up at me with interest.

"Oh, you'll have to get to know me better before I divulge that juicy information. But let's just say, I'm going to make some changes." I tilted my head to the side and pushed my hair over to the right, running my fingers through it. I noticed how his eyes followed the movement of my hands. I wanted to tell him about Scott, but I wasn't sure how to say it without it being obvious why I was telling him.

"Well?" I asked again. "Do you want to come with me to the show?"

In answer, he leaned over and swapped records on the little turntable. A song started up and he started singing along with it while looking at me and grinning.

"Ooh oooh ooh oooh jet boy, jet girl ..."

"I like that, who is it?"

"The Damned." He turned it down. "You know them, right?"

He didn't say it in a way to make me feel stupid if I didn't know them, but in a curious way. Like he cared, and he wanted me to know them.

"Actually, I do. I mean, I think, yeah, I'm pretty sure they were the first punk record I bought in D.C. *The Black Album*. 'Let's wait for the black out, wait for the night ...'" I sang, rather poorly. I had a terrible voice, despite my years in choir.

He tilted his head back and gave a deep laugh. "I love your impression of an English punk rock singer."

I reached out and kicked him in the shoulder, fake pouting as I did.

"Hey." He reached out and grabbed my ankle and pulled, sending me down to the floor with a hard thump on my ass. "Ouch," I complained.

Laughing, he took out a cigarette and offered me one. "To soothe your anger."

"No thanks, I have to get going. So ...?"

"Naw, I'm not going." My heart fell. "I went with those goofballs ... you know, Tim and Graves, and the rest of those clowns, to D.C. yesterday to see the Dead Kennedys. The Butthole Surfers and Rites of Spring played too. I don't care to see them again, plus I'm burnt out." He put the cigarette in his mouth, lit it, and took a drag. Then he leaned his head back while slowly exhaling a cloud of smoke. I was mesmerized by the elegance of this gesture, while at the same time I was crestfallen.

He must have noticed, because he immediately said, "But I'm going to Rockitz tomorrow to the Subhumans and Scream show. You going?"

"Yep." I stood up, trying to seem nonchalant about it all. "I'm going. It's going to be a big lineup. AOM, Unseen Force, and Judge Dredd ..." I started to turn to leave, but then turned back. "This is the same Subhumans from England, right?"

"Yep." His right leg crossed over his left, and I realized he was wearing the same or similar plaid shirt from the first night I saw him. He mashed his cigarette out in the ash tray. "Yeah, they're good. And they're playing with Scream in L.A. in a few weeks."

"Oh, cool. I didn't know that. Barbara and I are going to L.A. to stay with my dad for a week. Maybe we can go see them there."

"Hey, that's cool."

I really couldn't tell if he was interested or not. I mean, he sort of sent out those vibes, but then he acted, so, well ... so laid back. It was hard to figure out.

I turned back toward the door. But then I made the decision. *I'll just do it.* I slowly turned back, after taking a deep breath.

"Um. So. Just to say ... I broke up with Scott." And before he could say anything, I turned and disappeared out the door.

41 | MICKY MOUSE EYES
"Too Drunk to Fuck," Dead Kennedys

Wednesday, May first, 1985. I'll remember this day forever. This is the day I fell truly in love. This was going through my head as I lay on the floor of the practice space, staring into those dark and dreamy eyes. Then finally, they closed, and I fell into the warm frothy waters of my beer-soaked dreams.

I woke up startled, the echo of a dream—Steve's ruthless words from not long ago still lingering: "Don't kid yourself, Suzanne," he'd growled. "You're lucky to have me. These guys just want to fuck, they don't want a commitment." His laughter was harsh. " I give you both. I give you what you need."

It was dark and in the windowless room it took my eyes a moment to adjust. I shook off the ugly words as dark shapes loomed around me. I pushed myself up, trying to make them out. I was surrounded by instruments, and there on the floor was Chris, sound asleep next to me. I breathed a sigh of relief; we were both fully dressed. I didn't want to fuck this up with sex. Steve was wrong about that. He was wrong.

I ran my hand through my tangled hair and thought back through the previous evening's events. It was a little bit fuzzy; there was a lot of drinking. But I remembered.

My ass hurt from sitting on the hard narrow curb. Bambie and I sat outside Rockitz planning our trip to California. Only one more week of classes, then exams, then summer break. Somehow, I had to drive to my mom's, switch cars, pack up all my stuff, then drive it all back to her place. And we wanted to see GBH at the Wilson Center in D.C. before our trip to L.A., which was the week after! And I had to break up with Steve.

"Do you know how you're going to do it?" she asked in a soft voice. "I mean, do you know what you're going to say?"

"I don't know." I picked a long string off my jean jacket. "I haven't really planned it out." I flicked it off to the side. "I mean, I'm just going to drive down ... I mean up ... this weekend." I turned and looked into her eyes. I know my worry mirrored hers. "I can't see him. I can't do it in person. I know it's shitty, but I don't know how. I just don't know what he'll do. If ... if I'm in person, he'll dismiss it, and then ... well, he'll try to convince me. He'll threaten me." I shuddered.

I really didn't know what he'd do. He'd never been violent. Not in a traditional way. He didn't hit me. He hurt me in other ways. Ways that didn't leave bruises. He manipulated me in a way I couldn't explain. I didn't know how to process it. I couldn't even talk about it. I never shared any of the stuff that made me uncomfortable with my friends. I shut them out. It was too painful to share. To see expressions of helpless concern. No advice they could give would help or be received. I made it pretty clear not to interfere. Even if it left me feeling alone within my own castle. My prince, long gone. Ha! Beauty and the Beast. Although in this scenario, the Beast would always be the Beast, and Beauty would be trapped forever in the palace.

But it was becoming clear to me that this wasn't true. Being here, in Richmond, hanging out in this scene, was somehow empowering me. It gave me strength.

Bambie leaned in and squeezed me, right as we heard the squeal of tires and looked up to see the van make an abrupt stop and out poured Graves, Tim, Shane, basically the whole band, and Chris. Bambie grinned at me, stood up, and walked over to Graves, while I watched Chris turn and look at me, and then a huge grin appeared on his face.

He looked damn happy to see me, and it sent a shiver of excitement down my whole being. I stayed where I was and made him come to me. He was wearing a T-shirt, ripped jeans, and those Converse sneakers. As he sat down next to me, we easily fell into conversation and then eventually made our way into the club to see the show. He grabbed two beers and handed me one, and we stood next to each other, shoulder to shoulder, as we watched the bands play. At some point, he draped his arm around my shoulder, pulling me closer to him. Between sets, and even songs, we walked outside, under the pretense of smoking, but really just to talk more.

Our talking was innocent, like two schoolchildren. We teased, poked, joked, and punched each other. I think it was a way of being physical without actually being physical. I remember doing that with a boy in third grade. It was just this intense feeling of really liking the person, but not wanting to ruin it with some sort of sexual thing that might take away from the deeper level of the relationship. I felt it. I just knew it was more than sex. Sex seemed like it would break the spell.

When the show ended, or maybe even before, we left, walking side-by-side, kicking stones all the way to the park. This was the park I would normally never go to at night. Not the safest place for a girl alone. But it was just the two of us, and we sat down on a bench and continued talking. It was like we were the only two people in the world. The streetlight shown down on us, like a spotlight on a stage. But the audience was just the trees, and the darkness outside the circle.

He told me about his dad, his relationship with him. He was like an only child, but not. He had an older brother, maybe twelve years older. I would like his dad, he told me.

I stared into those dark eyes. Dark pools of brown. I said something like, "Your eyes are like Mickey Mouse. Dark and big." It was silly. Not that romantic. But it was intoxicating. I knew he'd had a lot to drink, but he wasn't acting like a falling-down drunk or slurring his words. In fact, he seemed quite alert.

I was also running on the same energy—adrenaline beyond description. It felt as if electricity was running through my nerves and pumping a bright light into my heart and brain. How could I be falling for someone I barely knew? And falling hard.

His dark eyes conveyed curiosity and sincerity, and in an offhand kind of way, he told me I was cute and that he'd never gone out with a six-foot-tall girl before. He was usually with these cute little five two "new wavers." His warm and deep voice resonated deeply within me like never before.

Steve had a cold charm about him that I mistook for that swarthy romantic type. That fantasy I had grown up with. The man who would rescue me. But instead, I had just replaced one domineering male figure with another. And the charm had turned into something much darker.

But Chris ... Chris exuded an aloof magnetism. Sweet, mysterious, boyish, and yet still mature. He didn't try for that romantic stuff. He didn't try to be charming. He didn't try to win me over. We just laughed, joked, talked about our families, our dreams, the bands, the bars, how drunk we got, where was the funniest place we'd woken up drunk. Well, I didn't exactly tell him all the details—I still hadn't mentioned Steve. But I was pretty sure Graves already told him. I'd have to make sure I did.

Eventually, and reluctantly, we stood up, and hand in hand, we walked all the way to the Crew House on the other side of town.

The orange glow from the east was slowly spreading its warmth into the wee hours of the spring morning. I couldn't believe we'd spent all that time talking. He led me up the steep stairs and pulled me into the practice room where he was sleeping temporarily, and we lay down on our sides facing each other. Face-to-face, staring into each other's eyes. I could feel the shyness between us. We talked quietly, giggled, and he reached out and pulled me in toward him. His arm draped around me, our foreheads touching. So close.

"I like you." His eyes bore into mine like he could see all the things I was hiding. "You have this irresistible awkward grace about you."

My eyes closed as the corners of my mouth turned up involuntarily.

42 | ENDINGS...

"Love and Romance," The Slits

The next night crawled by. I had work to do—one final art piece to turn in that was due the next week. The first year of art foundation was boring: gray scales, color wheels, basic drawing, and some stupid ready-made projects. I couldn't wait for next year when I could focus on fashion illustration courses. I'd have to retake art history because I already knew I was failing. The teacher was beyond boring.

It was hard to focus on my final piece and all the other things I needed to do with Chris on my mind: turning in finals, going to my mom's, switching cars, cleaning and packing up the dorm room, then packing for California ... oh, and breaking up with Steve. I was trying not to think about it. I focused on meeting Chris later that night. I found him in the middle of the crowd at this performing art space downtown, where I was supposed to meet him. I was late and wasn't in the mood for it. Some guy in the center of the room opening cans of peas, spilling them everywhere, and smearing them on himself, screaming about shit and stuff. *This is art?*

I pushed my way through the crowd toward Chris and tapped him on the shoulder. When he spun around, I crooked my finger, indicating for him to follow me. He raised his eyebrows and smiled, but as he saw my serious expression, his changed, and he followed me out to the car.

We sat outside the performance space in my car. I was turned toward him, facing him straight on, and I just let it spill out of me. I told him all about Steve. Well, not everything. There were some things I could never share. I wouldn't even know how.

"The thing is, he gave me a lot of attention. I know in the beginning he thought the world of me. Like I was a prize. It was like I came from a different world than him. There was just so much chaos at home, and somehow, he seemed steady and stable. It was ... seductive? But then it changed, and he became really controlling about everything. My weight, my clothing, who I could see ... and, well, he's never hit me, but it's like ... he fucks with my head."

He was still holding his beer, and I reached over and grabbed it from him and took a gulp and handed it back.

"I'm like, yeah, but he loves me, and I make excuses for him," I said bitterly. "It concerned me, but he loved me so much. I was pathetic. Weak."

Chris's dark eyes just watched me and let me spill it all. So much that I had wanted to say out loud for so long.

"Everything he told me about the outside world ... he tried to keep me from—tried to get me to be fearful." I was angry now. "But it didn't work. I see it now. I mean, I've seen it for a while." I licked my lips and straightened up.

Chris's eyes glowed in the darkness. I could see he was listening—he was hearing me. And he wasn't happy. Not about me, but about Steve. I think up to this point, Steve was just some joke. Now he saw that he was more than a joke.

"I've been planning on breaking up with him for a long time." I wanted to stop talking about him. "But to be honest, I was scared. Scared of being alone, scared of what he would do. But I'm not scared anymore." I smiled weakly.

As he looked at me, I had this sudden urge, and I just leaned over towards him and kissed him. His right hand came behind my neck, and he pulled me deeper into that kiss. Long and deep. That kiss filled me with a kind of determination that was going to help me get the job done.

Once again, we talked all night and lay face-to-face talking on the floor of the practice space, but this time there was a lot of kissing. No sex. Just kissing. Not even groping. This was all so new and refreshing.

In the morning, he walked me to my dorm, came up, and watched as I packed a small overnight bag. I walked him to the elevator, and as he stood there in his white pinstriped shirt, over his jeans, and that dyed blond hair, I took a picture of him. I wanted to document that moment.

It was the same route home, but this time it was different. Yes, the overnight bag was in the back. The mixed tape in the deck. Stereo turned up as loud as it could go without blowing the speakers. Windows down, fresh air flowing through the car. All the same, except ... I didn't drive straight to Steve's house, as I usually did on my weekend visits. I went directly to my mom's.

I knew this would really piss him off. I wanted to make him angry. That would make this easier.

I walked into my mom's townhouse, put my stuff down in the hallway, grabbed a lemonade, and sat down with her.

"Hey, Mom." I was nervous and excited.

"Hey, honey, how'd you do on your finals?" We chatted for a little bit, about school. About California. But my mind was elsewhere. I couldn't sit still.

Finally, I excused myself and walked back into the kitchen and picked the yellow phone up off the wall with its long spiraling cord and dialed his number.

He picked up immediately.

"Where are you?" Sinister and unforgiving.

"I'm at my mom's," I said, trying for no emotion.

"What? Why? Why did you go to your mom's first?" He was pissed.

"Because I haven't seen my mom in a long time." I was surprised at how flat, how calm I was. Or sounded, at least.

"I don't believe you. You've been acting different lately. You don't call me; you don't answer the phone. You said you would come this weekend, and now you're at your mom's!" His voice started to rise, but then, in a carefully controlled, low tone, he said, "I don't think you love me anymore."

Holding my breath, then letting it out slowly, I tried very hard to control the shaking that was building up in my body so it wouldn't show in my voice.

"I guess not," I said quietly.

I could tell by the silence that he was shocked. He was shocked I'd said this. He expected me to deny it. That's what I always did.

"Then maybe we should stop seeing each other," he said angrily, as if he was threatening me.

"I guess so," I agreed quietly. The shaking had taken over my whole body, and I struggled to keep my teeth from rattling.

Then the phone slammed in my ear.

I stood there startled. So many things just rushed through my body. Relief. Euphoria. Excitement. Terror. Butterflies everywhere. Like a weight lifted from my shoulders. I didn't believe it. Trust it. I stared at the phone in my hand, the dial tone starting to drone. I placed it back on the receiver and turned and walked out of the kitchen, back into the living room where my mother was still sitting on the couch, and plopped down next to her.

I turned to her and smiled. "I just broke up with Steve."

The relief and joy that washed over her face told me so much that she had held back out of respect for me for so long. With tears on her cheek, she leaned in and hugged me. A mother's comforting hug of support, relief, and joy. And I melted in her arms. I wanted to cry, but I was numb. Numb with relief.

I vowed I would never allow myself to feel trapped in a relationship again. Never again.

I was finally free.

43 | THE SUMMER OF '85
"Dancing Barefoot," Patti Smith

The whole day I was riding high on the adrenaline from being free of Steve. It was over. Finally, over. I didn't have to look over my shoulder anymore to see if he was there. I was finally free.

When I got in, I called Chris from the dorm pay phone, and we arranged to meet at Rockitz. Some band was playing, but it didn't even matter. I couldn't wait to be with Chris. To tell him.

But there were so many people there, and he was way up front, right in front of the stage, beer in one hand, head tilted back. That serious gaze, his Adam's apple silhouetted in the light, the outline of his lips. Oh boy, he was cute.

I pushed and shoved my way through the crowd and stood right next to him, my shoulder almost touching, and pretended to care about the band playing.

"Hey," I heard his surprised voice. "I almost thought you weren't going to make it." He draped his arm around my shoulder and leaned in. I liked the way he did that. He didn't put his arm around my waist, but on my shoulder. It was ... more respectable. No, that wasn't it. But it wasn't about claiming someone. It was about needing to connect.

"I had to help my roommate dismantle some stuff for our move," I shouted over the music. "We're moving out this week."

He spun his head back toward me, and I noticed his eyebrows knit together briefly. Was that worry?

"Well then let's get the fuck out of here." He grinned. "I'd rather talk to you than listen to this shit."

I looked up at the band, which I didn't know, didn't care, didn't hear, and grinned back. "Yeah, let's go!"

We walked all the way back to the Crew House and sprawled on the couch in the front room. It was gross, filled with cigarette burns and stuff that was either from food, beer, or worse. But I didn't really care. It was empty, everyone was still at the show.

"You gonna live in their practice space long?" I asked, poking him.

He poked me right back. "Hell no." Then he grabbed me by the upper arms and pulled me down on top of him, so I was crushing him onto the couch, and then he leaned up and kissed me. It was an epic, yummy kiss, but ... "Wait, I don't want to do this here, on this nasty couch."

"No way, I don't either. Let's go up to the roof."

He grinned and pulled me up and off the couch with him, then grabbed my hand and started to lead me out of the room. "I'm going to move into the closet."

"What?" I laughed. "The closet?"

"Yeah, let me show you." We headed up the next flight of stairs. All the rest of the bedrooms were upstairs, and the access to the roof. He held my hand the whole time and led me to the front of the house again, and sure enough there was a small walk-in closet, filled with junk.

"They're going to empty it out by next week, and then I'm going to move into it after I get back from Charleston." He had mentioned he was going to Charleston to see his dad, and maybe get a job, before he moved back to Richmond. After my trip to California, I would stay in Northern Virginia at my mom's and also get a job.

"So, if you want to write to me while you're gone"—he turned toward me and drew me close— "you can send it to this address. I'm sure these bozos wouldn't have the nerve to open my mail."

"I'll do that," I whispered, and he leaned down and kissed me. As abruptly as he kissed me, he stopped and led me back down the hallway to the window. He climbed out, and I followed. We then climbed up the ladder to the top of the roof and made our way over to the middle.

"Oh, hold on, I forgot the beer. I'll be right back."

"Okay." I walked over to the edge and sat down on the ledge, looking down on the sparkly lights of Richmond.

To think that less than five months ago, I was sitting here, crushing on Dave Brockie, dating Steve, and feeling as alone as a person stranded on an island, I thought. *And now look at me, I'm with Chris.*

Chris returned with not only two beers, but two blankets. He spread them out on the roof and then came and sat down next to me.

"You like heights?" He handed me my beer.

"Not really. But something about here just feels safe." My eyes focused again on the deep, dark pools of his eyes. I could drown myself in them. They held wonder, mystery and so much depth.

"I wanna kiss you some more, but I don't want it to be the last kiss we ever have, so let's go over to my makeshift picnic blanket." He winked. And when he winked, it wasn't smarmy, it was funny.

We sat down, and of course now I felt shy all over again.

"When are you driving to your mom's? 'Cause you know there's this GBH show in D.C. on Thursday night."

"Yeah, actually, I'm planning to leave Thursday, and um, yeah go to the show." I tried not to look too eager. "Do you want to drive with me? You could help me unpack and then we could go to the show ... and then you could spend the night. I know my mom would be really cool about it."

He raised his eyebrows. "Really?"

"Yes, to all of it."

"Yes, to all of it." Then he reached out, put his right hand behind my neck in that way that he did, and leaned in to meet me as he pulled me in to meet him.

The way Chris and I made love was just that. It was the first time I'd made love with someone. That expression had always baffled me because I never seemed to feel that romantic intimacy with anyone. What did I have to compare it to? Steve? That was never making love, and Dave was a passionate act of drunken glee. Again, not making love. What Chris and I did, well, that was tender, sweet, and deeply connected.

I woke up with the sun beating down on me. I slowly opened my eyes and realized we had fallen asleep on the roof. Chris was passed out heavily next to me. I gently poked him, but he didn't move. Then I turned to the sound of distant voices and saw that across two houses there were construction workers on one of the roofs.

"Shit," I muttered. Before they could look my way and notice me, I grabbed the top blanket and wrapped it around my naked body, using my half of the bottom blanket to cover Chris's naked butt as I quickly grabbed my clothes and made my way down the ladder into the darkness of the house, looking for the bathroom so I could change.

When I stepped out of the bathroom, he was standing there with his jeans on, shirt off, hands on hips, eyebrows raised. *Fucking adorable.*

"Really?"

"Well," I whined, "I couldn't let them see me naked!"

School ended, and Charmaine and I cleared out the dorm room. We pulled the posters down and cleaned the walls. I stashed all my photos of Steve into an envelope and absentmindedly stuffed them away in a box. After I packed up my mom's car, I picked up Chris and we headed to Northern Virginia.

As planned, we saw GBH in D.C., he met my mom, who adored him, and then I packed up for my trip to California with Bambie.

Even though I hadn't known Chris very long, I lent him my Karmann Ghia to use while Bambie and I were in California. It felt like the most natural thing to do.

California was just what I needed. I missed Chris immediately, but at the same time, I needed to see my homeland. I vowed to move back one day.

Bambie and I had so much fun in California; I built a handmade tent for her on the beach so her fair skin wouldn't burn, we took the RTD bus all over the place (an unheard-of activity)—from Manhattan Beach to Westwood and Hollywood to downtown.

We went to the Subhumans and Scream show at the coliseum downtown. My dad's girlfriend dropped us off, and he was supposed to pick us up after. But we couldn't find him or his car when it was over. We walked around and around looking for him in his Mercedes but didn't see it anywhere. I called on the pay phone to his house, but his girlfriend said he had left a long time ago and must be there. So we kept walking around the Olympic auditorium, and finally we worked our way through this mass of punks outside the front entrance. There, surrounded by tall, lanky, leather-clad Mohawks and shaved heads, was Dad, sitting calmly and patiently in the front seat as they leaned against his fancy car. We hurried to his rescue. But they were harmless. No one was really fucking with him. It was just a place to lean. He thought it was funny. I think he was just taken with us, and thought we were artistic, or creative. And mainly, he was relieved to hear that I had broken up with Steve. Although we never talked about it.

Dad seemed to have changed. Or, at least the nice parts of Dad showed more for me. He was still really tight when it came to money. Didn't help at all with my tuition. His temper was still there. But I was learning how to maneuver around him. And honestly, I think California made him happier. Maybe it was the job. Of course, he probably had a big scare when I was in the hospital. So maybe I could take advantage of that for a while.

After the trip to California, the plan was for me to stay in Northern Virginia for a while at my mom's and try to get some work, while Chris did the same from Charleston, South Carolina, before he headed back to Richmond.

First, I had to pick up my car from Chris, so Bambie and I drove up in her car the first week after I arrived home from my trip. The plan was to meet, hang out, see a show at Rockitz that night, and then I'd go back the next day with my car.

When she drove me over to the Crew House where he was staying, he was sitting on the steps outside the front door.

All of a sudden, I felt incredibly nervous. I mean, I could count on one hand how many times we had hung out together, even though in other ways it felt like I'd known him a long time. But we'd only had sex twice. I turned to Bambie and smiled. "See you tonight."

"Go get him, tiger," she laughed.

As I walked up to him, he grinned and said, "Hey." But he didn't get up. The way he just sat there and didn't move to greet me after not seeing me for over a week, well, I immediately felt insecure. *Maybe he doesn't like me anymore?* But I pressed on, and just sat down next to him and said "hey" back.

But before I knew it, he started with the teasing and poking, and then out of nowhere, he took his left hand, put it behind my neck, and pulled me toward those luscious lips, giving me the biggest kiss.

I sighed inside with happiness.

On my return to my mom's, I continued my hunt for a job, eventually working a few days a week at the record store. My pierced nose and hair weren't helping my efforts to expand into the restaurant business as a waitress in Northern Virginia where you could make good money on tips. Plus, I didn't have experience, which made it harder. A country club manager looked at me like I was a freak when I tried to apply there. Even though he knew my mother, it didn't help me land a position. The punk scene was only in cities, not in the suburbs. You just didn't see anyone on the streets or malls with nose rings and shaved heads.

Chris ended up staying in Richmond to look for a job and filled me in on all the details about his search, the bands he saw, and the parties he went to through the letters he wrote me. They were funny and romantic; he hadn't said it to my face yet, but he signed it, "I love you," underlined.

I really miss you a lot and can't wait to see you again!

And then he confessed to how shy he felt around me.

I have been having so much fun with you. Sometimes in the past I have been pretty shy but please try to understand I'm not going to be anymore! Please take care of yourself! Till we meet again, I love you!

Chris, June, '85

I held the letter to my heart, closed my eyes, and sighed deeply. Then I placed it carefully in a little wooden box and stored it beside my bed.

44 | NOT YOURS ANYMORE
"Suzanne," Journey

In July, Chris traveled up to D.C. with the gang to meet up with me for the Fourth of July events. Our destination was not to hang out on the South Lawn and hear the Beach Boys; instead, we headed to the Rock Against Reagan rally. Hundreds of thousands of people from the suburbs came each year to watch the fireworks, and right there in the middle of it, in front of the Lincoln Memorial, was a punk concert headlining the Dead Kennedys, Crucifucks, Reagan Youth, and more.

When a reggae band played, the atmosphere was peaceful, and at other moments, when the hardcore bands played, on the edges of the crowds, police on horses loomed with their hands gripped tight on their batons. It was exciting, and scary. I knew in the moment that I was part of something big, but with the loud music, the excitement of seeing Chris again, and being alone with him later, my attention was elsewhere.

Lying on my tiny bed the next day, we fell easily into our teasing, playful dialogue. Updating each other on what we'd been up to. I had bleached out the black that I had taken so long to get just right, and he wanted to know why I had done such a silly thing like that. The job search. Trying to fit in a bit, I told him. It didn't work.

As we lay there, the phone rang, and I reached over him to pick it up.

"Hello?" My voice was light and airy, and I smiled at Chris as he put his hands behind his neck, crossed his ankles, and smiled back. We were fully dressed and had been up for a while. We just liked to lounge and talk.

"Suzanne." I sucked in my breath as I felt my skin prickle with fear and my stomach contract. My face must have shown all of this, because Chris lifted his hand and just placed it on my knee. Like an anchor.

"Yes?" I didn't want to give Steve anything, any emotion to let him know he affected me in any way.

"How are you?" His voice carried the memories of every drop of pain he'd inflicted on me. I turned quickly to look out the window. It was like he was there watching me. Like he did in high school. I'd never forgotten that. I just couldn't shake the feeling that he was always there, ready to surprise me with his looming, intimidating presence.

"Um, I'm good." I had tried so hard to convince myself I wouldn't ever see or hear from him again, and here he was. And Chris was right by my side.

"I want to see you," he said. "Just once more."

My throat felt dry, and my heart seemed to be beating right inside my throat.

"Why?" I blurted.

"I just want to say goodbye in person." His voice carried a trace of the person I met on that fateful ski trip—a softness I rarely saw during the time that unfolded into our relationship.

I inhaled deeply. "I don't know." My eyes slid over to Chris who gave me an encouraging smile. "I can't talk right now. I have to go."

"Okay, I'll call you later," he said in a careful voice with no trace of his usual irritation. "I was thinking I'd come by, meet you out back." He paused. "I promise, just to see you one more time, and say goodbye."

"Okay." I hung up and sprawled on the bed next to Chris. "Fuck."

"Was that the Muscle Man?" Every one of my male friends from Richmond, even Chris, called Steve the Muscle Man.

"Yeah," I sighed.

"What did he want?" He pulled himself up and leaned on his elbows, looking at me. Chris looked like he had a temper. Although I'd never seen it. But those eyes definitely looked like they belonged to a fighter. I felt like he'd protect me.

"Well, he wants to see me one more time." I stared at the ceiling, avoiding his eyes. "Ugh."

"You get to choose what you want to do," he said, and then he leaned over, laying his body over mine, blanketing me with his warmth. I immediately felt calm, and safe.

"Thank you," I whispered.

Steve called back a few days later, after Chris had left. I can't explain why I said I would meet him. I just felt like I needed to. Maybe I was curious. Maybe I wanted to show off how happy I was, how different I was. Maybe I felt guilty for breaking up with him.

I told him to pull up on the back road behind the townhouses that night and I'd come out and meet him.

Sweat trickled down the curve of my back, making its way into my jean shorts, and my skin prickled when the warm breeze slid over my shoulders. The tank top I'd bought on a trip to Nags Head when I was fourteen still fit. The iron-on sticker that said "Touch of Class" had faded. The thin straps with the lace edging ticked my skin in the heat.

I stepped carefully off my mom's back porch, my bare feet sinking into the grass, and I opened the gate and looked through the thin grouping of pines that shielded us from the road. There, on the opposite curb, I could see his gold Pontiac, and even though it was dark, and the lights were off in the car, I could see him looking right at me.

My heart pounded as I made my way through the old, dried leaves and pine needles, emerging on the other side. I ran across the street, knowing he was watching my every move. It was quiet this time of night. Not a lot of cars came this way. I just hoped the Neighborhood Watch wouldn't come by and bother us.

I slowed down as I passed in front of the car, and something made me look toward the swings. In their solitary stillness, they glowed surreal in the moonlight, a gentle reminder of a hot summer day that felt like it was so long ago. A day that held the promise of something forbidden, tested and lost. A soft pang tugged at my heart.

I opened his door and slid into the passenger seat, relieved the engine was off. I was worried that if it was on, he would just take off and kidnap me. But instead, he looked at me and asked how I'd been.

"I see you've gone completely punk now, with the shaved hair and pierced nose," he stated, as his eyes slowly lowered and slid over my skin, then my chest, and along my legs. I stiffened with his inspection. His look, while discerning, was also hungry.

Shit, I thought. *What was I thinking?* I was trying to be defiant and dress how sexy I wanted, because now he had no right to tell me my top was too low, or my shorts were too high. But the consequence of that was attracting too much attention I didn't want. I wasn't going to give him anything. My body, or my story.

"Whatever," I said, trying to ignore it. "Why did you want to see me?"

"Because I wanted to see if you were okay. I haven't even seen you since you were in the hospital, and then you came down and broke up with me over the phone," he growled.

"Well, first, as you can see, I'm okay. Never been better." I swept my hair over to the right to emphasize the freshly shaved side of my head, noting his eyebrows rise. I also noted that the look of his pants implied he had a hard-on. *What a creep*, I thought. "And second"—I was trying to ignore the hard-on, and my instinct to fucking get the hell out of there—"I didn't technically break up with you. You walked us into it."

Again, the eyebrow raised. But he didn't say anything, just took a deep breath.

"Are you seeing anyone?" His eyes squinted.

Fuck. I didn't want to talk about Chis or tell him anything.

"If I am, it's none of your business." I decided that was the best way to go.

"Okay, okay," he said putting up his hands in surrender. "You don't have to get all defensive. I don't want anything from you, except one thing."

Oh, that nauseous feeling came up really fast from my stomach to my throat. "What?" I asked quietly.

"I want a goodbye kiss."

There were so many things I thought he would ask from me. Sex was at the top of the list. A kiss was near the bottom. Why would he want to kiss me? He only did that in the beginning, and then later, only in public to claim me in front of whoever was there to witness that I was his property.

"What?"

"A goodbye kiss. You owe me that."

"Okay, first of all, I don't owe you anything, and secondly, I don't think that's a thing." But I knew if I wanted to get out of the car and out of his life, and never see him again, I'd have to kiss him. At least that's what I told myself.

"I promise," he said, reading my thoughts. "One kiss, then goodbye."

I took a deep breath in and then released it as I said, "Okay."

I really wanted to get this over with, so I leaned into him and closed my eyes tight. I felt him take a hand and slide it over my waist, flattening it against my lower back. The other hand slipped behind my head as he pulled me closer towards him. Then his mouth was on mine. I focused on Chris. *Chris, Chris, Chris* I chanted in my head.

I don't know what that kiss felt like. I wasn't there. I don't know what happened next, or where the hands went. I just remember stepping out of the car like in a movie, watching myself. Walking back across the street, through the bramble, opening my mom's gate, and quietly opening the sliding door, making my way upstairs into my room, where I threw myself on my bed, buried my head in the pillow, and cried.

45 | MOVING IN

"Kids in America," Kim Wilde

I decided not to tell Chris about my last meeting with Steve. I didn't want to talk about him ever again. It was time to move on.

Chris kept writing me his letters, and we made plans for me to come back down and stay with him in his new little room. He'd finally gotten a job in Richmond, so he was staying, which made me happy. But I worried about all the drinking he was doing.

> *Recently I have been feeling really weird and kind of depressed. I hope last week was fun for you, I think I acted like a jerk most of the time. But I like you so much it just drives me crazy. So, I've been stomping around the house scaring people. I guess I don't realize what I look like to other people. I mean I'm pretty big, and I must look mean as hell sometimes.*

He went on to tell me how he held back because he was worried about losing me.

> *But listen I can't tell you enough how much I love you, please don't think that I don't! I'm just afraid to tell you sometimes because then I think something fucked up will happen and we will break up or something. I wish you were here right now!*
>
> *Please come down next weekend ...*

And then:
I haven't had time yet to look for an apartment, but I will.

We were going to move in together! I mean, I had already planned to move in with Jamie, but Chris and I would share a room, and this way our rent would be even cheaper.

I really wish you were here. I miss you more than anything I could ever think of missing. I mean it! I love you a lot.
From the insane asylum (crew house),
<u>*Love,*</u> *Chris*

August sauntered in, hot and sticky. The wettest month, even though there was no rain. Jamie, Chris, and I hunted for apartments in Richmond on one of my weekend visits. While we waited for appointments, and landlords, I tried to pull my wet T-shirt away from my body and whined, "Ice cubie," unable to find shade from the exasperating, hot sun. I was not meant for this weather. I longed for the cool breezes of California.

I shared the little closet with Chris on those weekend visits, rising to the hot sun as it beamed harshly through the little window onto our sardined bodies wedged between his record collection and books on one side and clothes on the other.

On one occasion, we drove out in the country to a huge party on the Chesapeake where bands played all day and late into the night. The only other time I had been to a music festival was with Steve, and I hadn't been allowed to move from his side. I strained to remember that occasion, but I had already successfully buried it away. So many of those malignant memories were being sealed off from me.

But here, we roamed together and separately. I was allowed to be me and do what I wanted.

We finally rented a two-bedroom apartment off of the Boulevard. A beautiful, spacious place for $450 a month. It was a lot of money, but my dad had promised to help.

School started up again, and I tried to focus on my classes, juggling that with going out with Chris and our friends. I started to feel more relaxed and less anxious. I didn't even know I was, until I was no longer.

It had been four months since I'd broken up with Steve, and it had taken that long for this feeling of being watched to finally recede, ever so slowly, but surely. The sounds around me took on new life. It had taken me so long to stop flinching when a door slammed after we moved away from my dad … and now this new freedom.

The idea of not having to answer to someone. To freely have a drink, smoke a cigarette, and wear whatever I wanted. To make love looking into someone's deep dark eyes and see them looking at me. Me. Not thinking of me as something else or someone else. To get out of my car and pump my own gas. To not have a boyfriend who hovered over me, blocking any male from the view of my body.

Chris was the opposite of Steve in every single way. Every glorious way. He listened to me talk. He listened to my stupid ideas, my silly writings. I listened to him talk on and on about songs, books, and movies. We read in bed together, and most often I fell asleep while he lay next to me reading. He didn't talk about hot chicks and sexy lingerie. Didn't want to spend hours at the arcade and never talked about cars. We talked about our dreams … we shared our love of movies and even talked about moving to California one day together.

We went to shows, saw bands, drove around, and explored. He was serious, silly, crass, controversial, and sweet. We became a couple. A steady, secure force. I had never felt so comfortable with someone.

46 | SHAME
"Gimme Some Truth," John Lennon

Winter doesn't settle in with a cozy hug in Richmond. It kicks you in the butt hard, reminding you that you're poor if you can't afford oil for heat. To show you you're at the mercy of nature and the system, equally. Streets come to a halt when the snow comes in; there aren't enough plows to take care of the storm. A feeling of isolation and being trapped can creep over you. But after seven months with Chris, I felt at peace. I wasn't worried the cold would get to me.

Chris and I were lying side-by-side on the long blue couch watching a movie. A commercial break came on, and a Richmond advertisement started up with none other than Dave Brockie and his new band GWAR. They looked so silly all dressed up with fur rugs tied around their waists and helmets on. We laughed out loud; it was so funny.

What are they up to now? I wondered.

The phone rang. The sound of it made me jump. I worked my way out of Chris's embrace and went into the bedroom where the phone was sitting on the side table next to the bed.

The man on the phone identified himself as Detective William Goldman.

"Is this Suzanne I'm speaking to?"

"Yes ..." I sat down on the edge of the bed.

"Do you know a man by the name of Steve Greene?"

My stomach lurched when he said his name, and my elbows felt weak.

When I didn't answer he cleared his throat and continued, "Listen, I understand you dated him for a few years so this might come as a shock." I held my breath, waiting for the horrible news of a car accident, or worse. "Steve was arrested on charges involving child pornography. We had a tip on two fellows trading or possibly selling photos of minors—underage girls. Steve Greene was one of the men."

"Underage girls?" I whispered. I felt sick, and shocked by what he was saying.

"We think it's been going on for a long time. The selling and trade part of it, we aren't sure yet, but we found a lot of photos in his room at his parents' house in a locked closet. We had a search warrant, so we searched his room and his brother's."

"His brother's?" I repeated.

"What is it?" Chris said behind me. I turned and looked at him. Whatever showed in my eyes made him come over and sit down next to me and hold my hand.

He asked me if I would come up to Northern Virginia to the station so he could talk to me in person. "There's a lot of information here, but there are still a lot of questions we have that we think you can help us with. I'm pretty sure we have enough to build a case against him, but you could help seal it."

"Um, just talk?" I asked nervously.

"Yes, I just want to ask you some questions and show you some photos."

"Oh ... okay."

After I hung up, I let out my breath and turned to look into Chris's questioning eyes.

"I have to go to Northern Virginia next week and talk to this detective," I whispered, pointing at the phone like it was the detective, and then I explained everything. As much as I could, without knowing much.

Maybe it was how I treated everything that was too hard to think about. I just put it out of my mind. It was easier that way. Chris didn't question me further. I think in some way, he knew I needed to deal with this in my own way.

A week later, we headed up to Northern Virginia. We didn't stop at my mother's; instead, we went straight to see the detective. I didn't tell anyone about his call. About any of it. Just Chris.

I stepped out of the car—leaving Chris to wait for me inside—then stopped and looked at the building. I was filled with dread. But I had to do this. I had to know what happened. I had to face it.

It's so hard to think of that day, when the detective laid the evidence before me that proved all my original suspicions and fears to be true: Steve had affairs and he lied to me. He cheated on me. I never expected to find out in the way I did. To have a complete stranger show me the proof, and ask me the most personal, painful questions I would ever be asked in my whole life.

I felt cold despite the sweat dripping down the inside of my arm as I sat in his office listening to him tell me the full story.

"His brother is a very sick guy," the detective started. "The stuff we found in his room went younger than fifteen years old. And fifteen, sixteen seems to be the age that Steve was interested in. I'm surprised your relationship lasted until just this last year," he said with curiosity. "You were ... what, nineteen when you broke up? From my research I found, all his previous relationships, he stopped dating the girls when they reached seventeen."

I wasn't sure if that made me special, or just a fool.

He said they had been watching Steve and Shaun from a distance because they both fit the description of the two men seen trading pictures of minors in a local bar. The description said the two men looked alike. Like twins. Eventually, they sent in Detective Goldman undercover, posing as a man interested in purchasing these photos. It worked, and they were both arrested. Then the police received warrants to search their rooms.

The same room I had spent the last three years in.

"Yes, I know the room," I said, trying to focus on the facts. "Their parents live on the ground floor. They both live upstairs." I looked down at my hands in my lap. "They're a sweet old couple, but Steve and Shaun bully them around." I looked up at the detective, who had stopped going through his report and was staring at me. "Steve told me he had really bad acne in high school and was bullied and made fun of by the other boys. So he started to lift weights, you know ... a bodybuilder. He wanted to be able to show them he couldn't be picked on."

"Did he bully you?" he asked me quietly.

I looked away, but there was nowhere to look. The blinds were down, and the bright, fluorescent lights made me feel extra vulnerable. "He bullied everyone."

"Did you know he applied to the Fairfax County Police Academy?"

"Yes, I did."

"Do you know why he wasn't accepted?" His elbows were resting on the folder in front of him, his fingers intertwined with his chin resting on them, as if what I had to say was very important.

"He was very upset about that. But I don't remember the excuse he gave me. Around the same time, my brother and his friends had been investigated because of some neon signs they stole. He implied it was because of that ... that his connections spoiled it."

"That's not why he was rejected," he said, leaning back. "He failed his psychological test."

"What?"

"He displayed aggression and dominant behavior patterns. A loose cannon. There were a lot of concerns."

"I didn't know ..." I said in a whisper, looking at my fingers and chipped black nail polish. I quickly hid them under my legs.

"You wouldn't have. He wouldn't have told you—it would be too revealing. Too humiliating." He smiled in an attempt to make me feel at ease.

"In Shaun's room we found photos of underage children. He's a sick guy, goes for little girls ... under twelve." He cleared his throat and continued, "Most of these pictures looked like they were taken in parks and playgrounds. Voyeuristic stuff. Nothing suggesting the girls were aware of it. He didn't lure them back home, thank god."

Yeah, thank God. Now I knew why he had taken such an interest in the little girl I was babysitting, and why Steve grabbed her away from him. Steve didn't want me alone with him, didn't even want me near him. But he never told me why.

The detective looked at me kind of funny and I sensed he was embarrassed for me. "In Steve's room, we found this closet with a padlock on it."

"Yeah, I know, he wouldn't let me go into it," I said quietly. The closet. The mysterious closet with the padlock. The one he wouldn't talk about, would literally get pissed off if I asked, telling me I was being intrusive. The walls were starting to close in on me.

"Well, I can tell you why. We found lots of photos and camera equipment, a tripod setup. We suspect that Shaun might have been in the closet with the camera while Steve brought home these teenage girls."

Then he reached over to the corner of his desk, picked up a folder, and set it down between us, opening it up. "I was hoping you could help me identify some of the girls in these photos."

I felt like I was going to be sick. But not a tear or quiver in my voice. Anger is what pushed me forward. I sat up straighter and leaned forward. "Okay."

He placed photo after photo in front of me. And I started to recognize a few of the girls. I knew one that was younger than me. To my horror I realized she was the younger sister of one of his friends. And another girl I recognized as the school slut. Same age as me. But I could tell from the photo that she was seventeen at the time it was taken, and that's when the final traces of hope that this had all happened after we broke up fell away completely. I now knew for a fact he had been doing this the whole time ... from the first time we met.

All these photos were of willing girls. They were all posing for the camera. Just like I had done. But there were also some taken while he was having sex with them. It did seem like his brother was either in the closet taking the photos, or that he just had his camera set up on a tripod. I couldn't imagine either, but the latter was the easiest to swallow.

"You know, his brother might not have been in the closet. I mean, he was quite convincing ... he set up the tripod with us." I said this without thinking. And that prompted the detective to set a few other pictures in front of me. Ones of myself.

"Are these of you?" he asked gently, looking directly into my eyes.

I gasped. There I was! Naked and semi-naked. Smiling coyly at the camera. I recognized the royal blue teddy he gave me on my birthday. A sixteen-year-old doing soft porn shots for her boyfriend. Never knowing or thinking where these photos would end up. They were never meant for anyone to see but me and my boyfriend.

"Yes, they are. There's nothing wrong with it ... it was meant to be private."

"Absolutely, for two consenting adults who respect each other," he said sadly, leaving the rest of what he could say filtering through my brain. Yes, adults. I know ... I was underage, not an adult when I started dating him. And look what happened!

In a strange way, I was relieved the police had found these, because if they hadn't that would have meant they might have been traded or sold. But all the photos of me were from Polaroid pictures. Some of the ones of the other girls weren't. Mine had no negatives, which meant no prying eyes of a developer. He would never want anyone to look at me.

As the detective closed the folder, he started to ask me questions. Questions that have answers you definitely don't share with strangers, or adults. Maybe your girlfriend. Maybe. And I don't know if it was that he was handsome, or too kind, but I became even more uncomfortable in his presence.

The questions were about sex and what we did. Everything, every little detail. There was a long pause as he nervously ran his hand through his dark blond hair.

"You were a minor, and you were obviously being persuaded to do things." He cleared his throat again. "We have enough evidence here, and with your testimony we could put them both away behind bars." He looked at me with deep concern. "Are you willing to be a witness for us?"

"To go to court? To testify in front of him? With him sitting there watching me?" I felt panic rising in me, but I squashed it back down.

"Yes. It would really help our case."

I sat there silently for some time. Then slowly, I nodded my head. "Okay. Yeah, I guess."

"We have people here I can set you up with if you want to talk with them about this ... about anything. It might help. You should really think about it."

I stood up a little bit too fast. "Thank you, but I'm okay."

"Oh. Okay, yes." He stood up and reached his hand out. "Thank you very much for coming. This is my card. Please call me if you need anything. I'll call you to let you know when the trial is, and when we need you, but it probably won't be until spring."

I turned on my heels and bolted out of there as fast as I could. I let Chris drive as I sat staring straight ahead, unreachable, all the way back to Richmond.

47 | WINTER'S GLOOM

"Life Goes On," The Damned

When we returned home, I went through every photo album and found every picture I had of him, including my prom photos, and tore up every last one. Then I found the folder, the one that I had stashed the photos from my dorm wall in, and also tore those up and threw them out.

I couldn't wrap my head around it. I paced the apartment, tears streaking my face, shaking with anger and nausea. Chris found me, gently took my hand, led me to the couch, and pulled me down onto it with him. We just lay there, my head on his shoulder, his arms wrapped around me securely, and watched old movies.

I tried hard not to think about it at all after that. I didn't tell anyone about it, so it was easy to pretend it wasn't happening. I tried to concentrate on my schoolwork, my photography and art. But it was hard to escape my thoughts and all the unanswered questions I had. I couldn't shut out the image of the detective laying those photos on the desk in front of me. Or all his questions.

As the weeks passed, I studied less, losing interest in my work. Instead, I began to drink more, go out more, blow off class. Anything to drown out the mental chatter. The feeling of being ashamed. For allowing myself to fall for his lies. And mostly, for not ending it when he started with the ultimatums. Making me shut out my friends. I was so grateful that Moe never gave up on me. But what about Marybeth? Did she hate me? She slipped away too because she'd been part of the prom. And even though I saw her—she was still dating Joe—Steve had always been rude to her.

Winter's gloom spread out, matching my mood, and Chris moved out. Not because we were having problems. Actually, things were going great, but Chris didn't love living with Jamie and me at the same time. Probably too much female energy. He wanted to move back in with the guys at the Crew House. I didn't really mind, I knew we would just crash at each other's places, and it would be cheaper because I wouldn't have to pay two-thirds of the rent. I suspected that was the real reason—the rent. He wasn't making that much. At least this time he wouldn't be sleeping in the closet. He had graduated to his own room. When my lease was up at the end of the summer, I planned to move in with him.

Jamie and I rented my bedroom to Barry—a total art freak who was into the rockabilly scene, with his Buddy Holly black-rimmed glasses and bolo tie—while Jamie and I shared a room. It felt like musical bedrooms, and it was a great distraction from the horrible conversation I'd had with the detective. I hadn't heard from him in several months, so I was starting to think the trial wouldn't happen. Maybe the whole thing had been a dream.

Some nights I got so drunk I'd just get sick but never unravel. I held on to my story. When I first got back from that meeting, I didn't tell Jamie. I didn't even talk about it to Chris. He would gently ask me if I was okay, and if I wanted to, but I kept telling him I was fine. We'd talk another time.

But finally, one night, shaking yet holding it together, I told Chris everything. All of it. Everything the detective had said to me. Enough time had passed that I was able to talk without getting too upset. I could tell he was pissed. Not at me, but at Steve.

When Chris wasn't with me and Jamie was at work, in class, or doing homework, I was Barry's sidekick. He'd beg me to stay up late with him so he could finish some project, and he'd bribe me with cocaine. That was his thing, as it turned out, and he always had it.

Jamie and I couldn't figure out where he got all the money to buy drugs, rent limos for dates, and buy all the new stuff for his room. He finally shared that he was living off a trust fund from his granny. I had no reason not to believe him. And doing lines with him was a nice distraction from my own monkey mind.

And then I started to forget about it. Just bury it away. The detective wouldn't call. It would just go away.

Six months after that phone call from the detective, he finally called to tell me the trial date had been set. Two weeks from Tuesday. I was terrified about going to trial. Just seeing Steve again haunted me. I didn't know if I could do it, not after all this time. I was dating someone I loved. I had new friends, people who meant something to me. I didn't need to stir all this past up into my future. So, I didn't talk to anyone. I didn't share how I felt, how it was burning a hole in me with Chris or Jamie. I could handle it myself.

But eventually I had to tell Jamie. Chris would be leaving town that week, on Tuesday, doing deliveries for his job. He couldn't get out of it; he needed the money, and I assured him I'd be fine. I was handling it all just fine. I asked Jamie if she would drive with me, and she said she would. I needed someone, someone to keep me grounded, or I knew I would completely lose it.

The next two weeks flew by. Funny how when you don't want something to happen time flies, but when you do, it crawls.

The night before my court date, I found myself wedged on the couch in Scott's room between some of our friends watching old black-and-white horror films and chain-smoking Camel Lights. I had started smoking more lately.

The faces around me had long since gone blurry; I had lost count of how many beers I'd consumed. I hated beer, but I'd already had a few shots of tequila with Jamie before we left the apartment, so my taste buds had lost their usual discernment. My eyes were burning from the smoke, and everything around me was becoming irrelevant. I kept forgetting where I was and who the people were sitting next to me.

The shapes on the TV started to split into pairs and what seemed like an apparition of Steve seemed to materialize out of it. His haunting, ghostlike figure loomed in my mind, making my head spin. Blinking it away, I knew logically he wasn't there, and yet it felt like he was standing in the shadows watching me, ready to demand that I come with him.

My eyes drifted closed again, then they opened, and I squinted at the TV. More images came. Stuff he forced me to do with him. People he had been rude to that I cared about and then kept me from seeing. Doors locked. I was locked in. He was locking me in. And that closet. What was really in that closet?

I was already burying and forgetting. Forcing down what was too painful to look at. It made it all easier. The guilt. Dark, mysterious shadows replaced where there used to be light.

I saw Jerry's knife just lying on the table in front of me. As if in slow motion, I picked it up and began dragging the tip across my wrist where my old scars were. It seemed so long ago now, that day when I first found out Steve was cheating on me.

I wasn't trying to cut myself. I was just tickling the area ... trying to wake it up. It felt good. That little bit of pain. And I remembered why I did that to begin with. The mental pain vanished as the skin awakened to the sharp pull of the knife. The images faded.

"Hey, what are you doing?" said a voice. I didn't know who it was. A shape, a face. A body. My vision was blurry, my eyes stung. There were no tears; my eyes were so dry they felt raw. And then hands reached out to grab the knife from me. But I yanked my hand away and held it up.

"What? I'm fine," I said, my voice sounding far away but angry. "I'm fine, leave me alone."

There was a commotion, noises, voices. Someone called for Chris. *Chris? Is he here?* I thought. *I'm sure he isn't here. He's leaving tomorrow.* The pounding in my chest seemed to reach my ears, with a growing sense of panic. *I'm leaving tomorrow. I have to drive to court.*

"Come on now, give me the knife." A soft deep voice ... Chris's voice. So grounding.

"Fuck you all." I slammed the knife down on the table, got up, and ran out of the room. My boots pounded all the way down the stairs toward the front door, and I heard someone following me. I skidded to a halt at the bottom, whipping around. I was blinded with anger, with fear. But it was Chris.

"Nothing is wrong," I cried, the tears finally flowing down my cheeks.

"Fuck him. God damn it to hell," Chris yelled, his voice angry and pained. I saw his love, his anguish clearly. Then with everything he had, he punched the wall next to the door.

"Argh!" I don't know why this pissed me off. *God damn guys. Always so tough!* I turned to face the door. I wanted to do the same thing. The door was wooden but had little peekaboo windowpanes running along either side, so you could look out and see who was out there. With all my might, I punched the side of my fist into the glass. It went through clean, and instinctively I pulled it back. It didn't come back so clean.

"God damn it," Chris said again, but this time with concern. "Why the fuck did you do that?" He grabbed my hand in his.

"Well," I started, between sobs and laughter. "Because you fucking macho guys are always putting fists in walls." I didn't finish. "Ouch, it hurts." I sniffed.

He carefully led me upstairs and into the kitchen where Greta was.

I found myself in a very familiar situation with her there and me sitting in a chair next to the kitchen table. Was it just over a year ago I sat there while she took my temperature before that week in the hospital with pneumonia?

This time she wrapped a bandage around my cut and offered support in that gentle way mothers do. Greta was like the house mother to us wild and reckless kids. My head was so blurry from all the alcohol, so the words she said didn't stay with me. But I would never forget her firm but tender care and that she didn't ask me why I did what I did. I felt like she just got it.

The next morning, I sat in the passenger seat as Jamie drove us up 95 toward the dreadful appointment. My head was splitting because of a severe hangover, and I kept playing in my head over and over again the scenario of me walking into the courtroom and seeing Steve sitting there. I thought I'd never have to see him again after that day last summer. The very sound of his name filled me with fear and anxiety.

I could feel Jamie looking at me. "It'll be okay," she said. "I'll be with you. And he can't hurt you."

I had to keep concentrating. I couldn't look at her. *Focus on the road*, I told myself. Like when you're on a sailboat, and you have to focus on the land so you don't get motion sick. Too late.

We drove directly to my mom's house first because we had plenty of time to kill. I thought it would be a good idea to stop in and say hi first. I had finally called her and told her why I was coming. Not the whole story, but part of it. I didn't want her to know all of it. I knew it would really upset her.

When we pulled up to the townhouse, she was standing at the door waiting for us.

"A detective called about an hour ago," she began, sounding uncomfortable and apologetic, "and asked me to tell you that the trial has been canceled." Her eyes searched mine. "They settled out of court."

"What do you mean? Settled out of court? What does that mean?" My voice started to get louder. I felt panic. I didn't want to go to court. Far from it. I hated the idea of seeing him again, hearing his voice, getting up on the stand and testifying. Would it be justice like in the movies, where the prosecutor asks me to point to the guilty party?

No, I didn't want to go at all. But if I didn't go, it meant he didn't actually pay for what he did. It meant he got away with it. It meant I went through all this—this anxiety, fear, and dread—for nothing.

"Look, it just means they took what the prosecutors were offering. A set sentence or something. That happens a lot, people settle out of court." She tried to put her arm around me, but I shrugged away.

"That doesn't make sense. Why did I have to come all the way here if they were going to settle!" My hands were shaking.

"Why don't you call the detective?" Jamie asked, putting her arms around me.

I looked at her and suddenly I realized I didn't want any more to do with it. I just wanted to walk away from the whole thing. Let it be over. For good.

"Oh, fuck it." I wiped my eyes, still shaking. "I don't know what happened, and I don't care. I didn't want to see him anyhow, and now I don't have to see him again. Ever. It's over."

They both looked at each other with worry in their eyes. I leaned over and kissed my mother goodbye, then jumped right back in Jamie's car. Jamie climbed into the driver's seat and waved goodbye to my mom.

"Wait, don't you want to stay and have a drink and rest before you head back?"

"Honestly, Mom, I don't. I just want to go back to my life." I gave her the best smile I had in me. "I'll come back next weekend. I promise."

As we drove out of the neighborhood, I leaned over and turned on the stereo, turning it up really loud as we headed home, back to Richmond.

I sang along to the Damned, at the top of my lungs: " ... always remember, this is the happiest day of your life."

We made a two-hour trip in an hour and fifteen minutes. The whole way there I chain-smoked, wrestling away the last remaining ties to another life. I inhaled deep and stuck my head out the window, resting the side of my face on the edge, and looked up into the blue sky. With each release of my breath, I let the pain go.

Let it all go, put it all away with all the other pieces, in my pocket of pain.

EPILOGUE | SOME TIME LATER

"I Will Survive," Gloria Gaynor

On that day, I closed the door to my story. Locked it up and shoved it firmly away. When we came home and opened the door to our apartment, Jamie and I were met with a whole new set of problems. Problems that thankfully were not mine but enough to distract me from my own.

In a way, nothing seemed different as we opened that door, but there was a shift in the atmosphere. As if someone was or had been in our space. Our studio area was a mess, with open paint tubes and paper everywhere. But that was normal. A hodgepodge of tattered furniture bought at various flea markets or Goodwill. The huge blue quilted couch where we spent much of our time, avoiding our homework, and watching TV, my Siouxsie and the Banshees poster taped to the wall over the couch curling up at the bottom, the tape coming unstuck, and Barry's broken mannequin, adorned with a purple feather hat and fur collar all welcomed our return.

Everything seemed ordinary. I walked over to my drafting table and noticed a little piece of paper. It was quite official looking. A notice of some kind. I stood over it, looking down, reading it, Jamie peering over my shoulder.

She poked me. "What does it say?"

"Um, seems like Barry has been arrested."

"What?" she gasped.

"Yeah. It says, 'Barry Keisler, arrested under the suspicion of robbing five banks on Broad Street, Richmond, Virginia.'"

"What?!" Gasp again.

"Then it gives dates, times, and the different banks."

"Huh? Arrested, under suspicion? Give me that." She tore it out of my hand and with furrowed brows read the whole thing, at least three times.

"I ... I can't believe this! Barry? Simple, quiet, Barry? New wave rockabilly Barry? Barry with the jet-black hair and Buddy Holly glasses? Barry with his bolo tie and pointy patent leather shoes?" She seemed quite indignant. As if he was playing a practical joke on us.

A quick check in his room confirmed that something was definitely not right. The pink pastel homage to Pollack that was his art was still there; no one would touch that. But his room was a tornado. He was usually quite neat, unless he was in one of his super-coked-up periods. Which was happening more of late. We looked around to see if something in his room would tell us anything about what had happened. Besides bedsheets, clothes, and records littering the place, it didn't look obvious that we were living with a bank robber. It smelled pretty bad, but that was also normal.

"Geez, it stinks like patchouli in here. I wish he would realize that wearing patchouli is like wearing a sign that says, 'I don't bathe, I smell, and now I smell like patchouli and shit.'" Jamie rolled her eyes at me. "Nice."

"What is this on his shelf?" I said as I stepped over a pile of dirty clothes. "Look—it's one of those papers you find on a bankroll. You know, the kind of paper that binds a stack of bills." Well, come to think of it, Barry was always flashing hundred-dollar bills around. Things were starting to add up, sort of.

After the room inspection, we tried to track him down. Jamie called the police station, but they didn't seem to want to help her and put her on hold. Eventually they put her through to someone else who finally told her that Barry had, yes, been arrested and was being held in the county jail. The officer on the phone asked if Jamie was a relative, and when she said, "No, but I'm his roomma—" they hung up, saying information would only be given out to family. And that was that.

For now.

I wish I could wrap up my story all pretty and Hollywood. I wish I could say that I didn't make any more poor boyfriend choices and that I "recovered" overnight without burying myself in drugs or alcohol or sex. But I was in denial for some time. The good thing was that Chris was there to ground me during the worst of it. He kept me from harming myself, somehow. He reminded me that I could be loved for being myself, and that love wasn't a game, or all about sex. He kept me present, and I never looked back, at least not when I was sober.

But as far as Steve was concerned, I thought it was over. However, it would take me about three years to fully get rid of those demons. I never talked about it when I was sober. The subject was off limits to all my friends, including Chris. However, it was dangerous if I ever experimented with drugs, or got drunk—because when I did, I would open my soul and pour it all out. I would tell whoever was there the whole story. All the sordid details. It was always to somebody I'd never met before. I would focus in on this person. And every morning after, suffering from that hazy headache that follows, I would also feel sick to my stomach for revealing such personal details to somebody I didn't know. And for reliving it all over again.

Then there were the nightmares. These would haunt me almost every night for the next few years, with or without any kind of stimulants. In fact, I'm pretty sure that stopping the drugs and alcohol made it a lot easier for them to surface. The dream followed me from college to college and boyfriend to boyfriend. Yes, Chris and I eventually broke up, but we always remained friends. He never wanted anything from me, which helped me gain back my independence, and strength.

The dream goes like this:

I'm in a relationship with whoever I'm with at the time. I say goodbye to my boyfriend, and head back to my apartment. When I walk through the door, I sense that somebody is there. As I walk slowly into the living room, I see him. Steve is standing in the dark, with the light filtering in through the dusty metal shades from behind him, so all I see is his dark silhouette. In a sinister voice, he demands to know where I've been. Before I know it, I find myself back in that relationship with him. But I don't want to be. I want to break up, and get back to my other boyfriend, my real one. But I feel like I'm being restrained, and when I walk out the door, it's not me running away, but him leading me by the elbow to his car—that gold Pontiac. I finally tell him it's over, we aren't dating anymore, but he doesn't hear me. It's as if I'm there but I have no voice. As if an invisible hand is preventing me from opening my mouth. I need to find my voice. I try to scream, to struggle, to pull away from him, but I keep walking right along with him. I am trapped in his world. Then I wake up with that feeling of trying to shed him from my life again. But he is always there, lurking.

There are photos of me from every birthday up to the age of sixteen. All those special days were recorded religiously. Then, no more photos between sixteen and twenty-one. There's no record of my growing another year older. A five-year gap. Then at twenty-one, the record resumes. But whatever happened to those five years in between?

One of the consequences of burying my bad memories was that it took with it chunks of memories, whether good or bad. The recovery process has been slow and delicate. And I honestly don't remember the full story. There are plenty of demons buried for good.

The worst of it was that I looked for love buried in sex. Even with the gentle transition with Chris, as I reentered the dating world, it was hard to navigate sex and what it meant. Having sex didn't equal love. This was a lesson I would learn over and over again.

The important lesson I learned was that no one could rescue me. My fantasy of being carried off by a strong man who would protect me was exposed as just that: a fantasy. It wasn't real and it wasn't to be trusted. This way of thinking was a trap. In one way or another, you would pay dearly.

I suppose I can say this: the experience brought out the opposite in me. I am now a strong, fierce woman who takes no bullshit and will not let herself ever be pushed around or told what to do.

ACKNOWLEDGEMENTS

There are so many people to thank for their encouragement and advice when I started writing this book, and then again the next generation fifteen years later who encouraged and advised when I started writing it again. I could not have started or finished it without their support.

Dominic Preziosi, for asking me what the story was with the chaperone on the ski trip. Blair Mastbaum, for encouraging me to change the voice of the narrator to the girl in the story. Chris Stoddard, for lost memories and support. Guru Jagat, for your divine interaction and showing me it was time to keep writing. Jen Knox, for your professional and personal support. Barbara Zelsdorf, for more lost memories and being my investigator. Rania Lisas, for your detailed reviews and encouragement. Susannah Noel, for your stellar copyediting. Maurine Houser, for your P.I. skill and encouragement. To Jamie, for being there for me during a pretty upsetting time. To Graves, I wish you were still here, I have something fun to tell you.

And to all my friends who have said, "Write your story!"--thank you. There are hidden stories in all of us.

ABOUT THE AUTHOR

LadyWarfield lives in Richmond, Virgina and New York. She is a Milliner, Artist, and Audiobook Narrator. A graduate from Art Center College of Design, in Pasadena Califoria, she once appeared on the Gong Show in the late 80's, hosted GWAR in her home in Pasadena, California during their tour in the early 90's, and as noted in Pocket of Pain, she lived with a bank robber.

She has a feature article published in the International Magazine "2029 - Hamburger's, Art & Design #No10," titled: Painter Suzanne Szukaj meets Dr. Viege Traub; friend to Anäis Nin, Fritz Lang, and Rock Hudson.

Subscribe to LadyWarfield's newsletter on her author's website to stay in the loop on all her projects!

BY LADYWARFIELD

WWW.LADYWARFIELD.COM

THE PLAYLIST

Get the playlist on SPOTIFY! The subtitles represent songs I was listening to at the time, or had another, possibly deeper meaning relted to the chapter..

https://www.ladywarfield.com/playlist
or search **"Pocket of Pain Soundtrack"** on Spotify